The Workplace Within

MIT Press Series on Organization Studies
John Van Maanen, general editor

The Workplace Within
Psychodynamics of Organizational Life

Larry Hirschhorn

The MIT Press
Cambridge, Massachusetts
London, England

Sixth printing, 1995
First MIT Press paperback edition, 1990

© 1988 Massachusetts Institute of Technology

Printed and bound in the United States of America by Maple-Vail, Inc.

Library of Congress Cataloging-in-Publication Data

Hirschhorn, Larry.
   The workplace within : the psychodynamics of organizational life
Larry Hirschhorn.
      p. cm.—(MIT Press series on organization studies ; 8)
   Bibliography: p.
   Includes index.
   1. Psychology, Industrial.   2. Industrial sociology.   3. Machinery
in industry   4. Man-machine systems.   5. Work design.   I. Title.
II. Series.
HF5548.8.H493   1988
158.7—dc 19   87-20144
   ISBN 0-262-08169-5 (hardcover)   CIP
        0-262-58101-9 (paperback)

To Eric Trist

and

To the Management and Behavioral Science Center
1977–1986

A Good Place to Work

Contents

Acknowledgments

Many people have helped me write this book. Jim Krantz, my student, colleague, and teacher, introduced me to the fundamentals of a psychodynamic approach to organizations and was consistently helpful in supervising my consulting work. Tom Gilmore, my close colleague and friend for a decade, introduced me to consulting work, created a climate for learning at the center he managed for many years, and has been consistently warm, supportive, helpful, and stimulating as I tried to understand my failures and successes as a consultant. Howard Schwartz, who has written brilliantly on issues of organizational psychodynamics, has provided me with innumerable insights which emerged from his generative concept of organizational narcissism. It has been a pleasure to work with him.

Fred Block, a close friend and colleague for over fifteen years, was, as he always is, my best and most demanding critic—always available to review my work, always generous with his time, always available to help in the hard times. I deeply appreciate his contributions to my thinking.

My colleagues at the A. K. Rice Institutes in Washington, New York, Los Angeles, and Washington, D.C., provided me with invaluable learning opportunities as a participant in their scientific meetings and as a member in their many group relations conferences. Committed to understanding and improving group life, they have helped me to understand my personal struggles with authority. Marvin Geller, Nancy Adams, and Ed Schapiro have been invaluable teachers.

I would also like to thank my colleagues, Larry Gould, Don Levine, Howard Schwartz, Michael Diamond, Gidon Kunda, and Howard Baum, who, along with others and me, founded the International Society for the Psychoanalytic Study of Organizations. The society, now in its second year, has provided me with an important forum for testing my ideas and meeting scholars and practitioners from around the world.

Like all of us who inherit the world from our elders, I owe a special debt of gratitude to the founders of the Tavistock Institute who had the special genius to synthesize psychoanalysis with systems theory, concepts of management with an understanding of individual psychology, and theory with practice. In many ways this book represents a reworking of their original insights and a desire to recover these insights for the present generation.

I would also like to thank my colleagues at the Wharton Center for Applied Research who have created a supportive and enabling environment for work. Vincent Carroll, its managing director, is a warm and demanding leader who has shaped an organizational climate of trust and regard. Lynn Oppenheim and Tom Gilmore, its two associate directors, have contributed significantly to its vitality, and both have pushed me to develop as a professional.

Chris Argyris has been an invaluable critic and reviewer of my writing. His openness to new ideas combined with a demand for rigor and precision have been important to my development.

I would like to thank Nina Gunzenhauser, the quintessential editor, who shepherded my manuscript through its many stages of development, challenging my thinking and writing where it was muddy and helping me produce a document that actually says what I was thinking while helping me think through what I wanted to say.

I also thank my clients for working with me and taking the many risks entailed in addressing and solving their problems. I learned so much from them.

Finally I would like to thank my family for creating a world to live for. Marla Isaacs, my wife, and Aaron and Daniel, my two sons, bring so much pleasure to my life.

The names of people and organizations have been changed for confidentiality purposes.

The Workplace Within

Introduction: The Psychodynamics of the Workplace

As a consultant, I once spent some time at a large testing laboratory that had difficulty allocating resources for exploring new markets for its services. After interviewing the key officers, I learned that the president had asked the division heads, usually the chief scientist of a group, to list what new markets they wanted to explore. Feeling compelled to come up with at least some ideas lest they look uncreative, the division heads often submitted proposals they did not really believe in. Facing a potpourri of unrelated proposals, the president and his staff simply divided the marketing resources among the divisions according to their respective sizes and contribution to profits. The resulting set of market development activities lacked coherence and failed to help the company expand its sales.

When I worked with the senior management group at a retreat, I realized that the president was anxious about assuming the authority of his role with the scientists, some of whom had national reputations, and was abdicating leadership by hoping that the division responses might add up to a coherent strategy. Similarly, the division heads lacked the conviction of their proposals but participated in the process to avoid looking unimaginative. Thus, although the process appeared rational on the surface and seemed to fit the modern idea of "participative management," it was actually a cover for the president's flight from the work of allocating scarce investment resources among the different scientific divisions. To avoid the anxiety of facing one another, of bringing their personal feelings, likes, and dislikes to their roles and relationships, the president and the division heads projected their sense of agency and authority into a ritualistic process of dividing up the available marketing resources. This process functioned as a *social defense*.

Isabel Menzies first developed the concept of social defenses in her study of nursing practices in a British hospital.[1] She noticed that nurses woke patients up to give them drugs even when it was more beneficial for them to sleep. Finding as well that nurses rotated frequently in and out of wards, Menzies argued that such procedures were not designed to help patients but rather enabled the nurses to contain the anxiety of working with sick and sometimes dying patients. Nurses would feel calmer if they could depersonalize their relationships to their patients. By rotating through the wards, they developed only weak ties to patients and, by administering drugs regardless of need, they denied each patient's unique situation. They did not have to think about what they were doing. Indeed, Menzies suggested that even the nurses' uniforms helped to create and sustain a psychosocial drama in which the nurses, far from being individuals with ties to particular patients, were part of a faceless army of interchangeable helpers. Rituals induce thoughtlessness and, by not thinking, people avoid feeling anxious. Menzies called such rituals social defenses.

The Psychodynamics of the Social Defenses

The social defenses work through such processes as *splitting*, *projection*, and *introjection*, terms used by theorists and practitioners of the object-relations school of psychoanalysis.[2] The nurses in Menzies's hospital felt the anxiety and stress of helping sick patients who might die and often engaged in tasks that "by ordinary standards are distasteful, disgusting, and frightening."[3] Caught between compassion and disgust and unable to sustain both feelings with balance and continuity, the nurses welcomed depersonalization to relieve themselves of such contradictory feelings. By splitting off their sense of personal authority and agency from their own experience and projecting it onto the social defense—for example, the ritual of drug administration—they relieved themselves of responsibility for the patient's experience. They were just following rules and no longer needed to feel personally connected either to their physical tasks or to their patients' resulting well-being. As a ritual, a particular nursing practice became an end in itself rather than a means to the end of helping sick people. Finally, the nurses psychologically took in or "introjected" the new authority of the rituals to justify their depersonalized relationship to the patients. They woke the patients regardless of need, because as implementers of an important rule they had been ordered to do so. Thus, through the linked processes of splitting, projection, and introjection the nurses lent their individual and collective authority to a ritual, which in turn authorized them to behave in a depersonalized way. Far from responding in contextually sensitive ways to particular patients, they only followed orders. Through the processes of splitting, projection, and introjection, they allowed a practice that they once created to dominate them.

Irrational processes highlight the limits of classical organization theory. Theorists such as Simon, Thompson, and Galbraith[4] have argued that all organizations face continuing uncertainties and have suggested that organizational routines and structures, such as maintaining inventory to meet unpredictable demands for products, are mechanisms for reducing uncertainty. But because these theorists have not linked the experience of uncertainty to people's feelings of anxiety, they have posed the issue of uncertainty too narrowly and have proposed solutions that rely on such rational methods as mathematical calculation and organization design. When anxiety intrudes, rational procedures are distorted by irrational processes. For example, the managers of the manufacturing and sales departments in many companies fight chronically with one another over inventory policy, each blaming the other for the gap between market demand and company supply. Because they feel anxious, they project their sense of blame and failure outward, often scapegoating the person they must cooperate with to reduce the uncertainty they face. Bureaucratic practices, the basis for much of modern organization, are too frequently disguised forms of social defense. Parading as efficient procedures, they actually waste resources. Excessive paper helps contain the anxiety of face-to-face communication; excessive checking and monitoring reduces the anxiety of making difficult decisions by diffusing accountability.

By using the psychodynamic concepts of splitting, projection, and introjection, we can develop an interpersonal theory of organizational processes and still retain psychodynamic concepts that describe individual behavior. By recognizing the limits of classical psychoanalytic theory, which focuses primarily on the tension between an individual's instincts and defenses, and drawing on modern object-relations theory, which highlights how people use one another to stabilize their inner lives, we can understand how psychodynamic processes *within* people help shape the relationships *between* them. Family life, for example, is frequently shaped by projection and introjection. Uncomfortable with her angry feelings, a wife may provoke her husband to feel angry, so that she can then experience her own anger at a safe distance. Similarly, parents often project their unacknowledged ambitions onto their children.

Such processes shape work experience as well. Consider the following possible relationship between a manager and a subordinate. The subordinate, facing significant uncertainty in estimating the demand for his product, feels at first persecuted by prospective customers who ignore his product and then angry at competitors who steal his customers. But he is unable to tolerate such feelings inside himself for long; they paralyze him by making him feel bad and undeserving. Because he is a subordinate, he *projects* these feelings onto his manager, believing the manager to be angry. He then *introjects* or identifies with his manager's anger (which is really the subordinate's fantasy of the manager's anger) and in turn feels angry. But now the manager, not the subordinate, owns the anger, and the subordinate no longer feels endangered by it. *He has used his leader to allow himself to feel angry at his competitors.*

This sequence of psychological operations is common. It is what enables frightened or anxious people to feel and act aggressively. Moreover—and this is key—the manager or leader may willingly accept these projections. He may, for example, welcome people's presumptions that he is angry, because that prevents him from becoming more intimate with his followers. The anxiety of being intimate is greater than the anxiety of being an angry "object" to his followers. Thus distorted relationships are social constructions in which neurosis is contained in the psychological space between people. Through splitting, projection, and introjection people create shared illusions.

The Postindustrial Milieu

The new postindustrial technologies of automation and communication are less forgiving and more demanding. Creating what Perrow[5] has called tightly coupled systems that are controlled at a distance, they increase the penalties of thoughtlessness, ritualization, and irrational behavior. The nuclear power worker who ignores a leak and the pilot who ignores a warning chime can create disasters. The cost of maintaining social defenses grows.

Consider the sad drama of the space shuttle *Challenger*, which exploded seconds after launch, killing seven astronauts. In assessing the accident, one reporter suggested that "pride," "self-deception," and "hubris" led scientists and managers to ignore obvious warning signs that the shuttle's key booster seals might fail.[6] Far from acting rationally, managers and engineers refused to face facts, believing instead that their past successes protected them from future failure. As journalists investigating NASA suggested, contradictory pressures from Congress and the White House and leadership instability at NASA contributed to the shuttle's devastating accident. Instead of appropriating needed funds to secure the shuttle's viability, cheerleader members of Congress took pride in the shuttle's apparent technological sophistication; and NASA, lacking a coherent leadership cadre for two years preceding the accident, was unable to obtain those funds and set more realistic goals.

When technical and political realities pose uncommon stresses and anxieties such as these, we can either face them directly or use wishful thinking to escape them. NASA's arrogance enabled its senior managers to engage in wishful thinking and to ignore the warning signs of impending failure. As the reporter noted, "NASA was blinded by its pride in its past achievements, dazzled by its record of success."[7]

Melanie Klein, psychoanalyst and founder of the object-relations school of thought,[8] argues that pride and arrogance are frequently psychological defenses against feelings of vulnerability and dependency. Like the person who whistles in the dark to deny his fear, the arrogant person is employing what Klein calls the manic defense to deny his vulnerability. NASA personnel denied the simple laws of probability by assuming that successful launches in the past protected them from future failures. When a coin toss yields five heads in a row, the chances of a tail on the sixth toss are not reduced below 50 percent. Yet as many analysts noted, after each successful launch NASA managers unreasonably lowered their standards for the next flight. Richard Feynman, a member of the presidential commission investigating the accident, noted that NASA was engaged in "a kind of Russian roulette, or a perpetual movement heading for trouble."[9] Unprotected by leaders and facing a difficult and unforgiving technology, senior managers and engineers at NASA created a delusional system that induced thoughtlessness on a grand scale in order to deny the uncertainties they faced.

The postindustrial milieu is particularly stressful because it progressively integrates a once fragmented division of labor, forcing workers to take account of many more facts, people, and claims. It becomes harder to ritualize work and reduce it to a set of regular procedures and formulas. When I studied an information services company, I saw how once simple selling jobs were becoming more complicated and anxiety provoking. The company sales force in the past had simply sold bibliographies to librarians in organizations with large research units. But as competition grew and computers made it easier to create specialized bibliographies, the company found that it had to develop custom-made bibliographies of scholarly articles and books for particular academic disciplines and researchers. Moreover, they discovered that the researchers increasingly wanted to search for references using computer-based tools.

This shift in demand complicated the sales task. Instead of selling a fixed product, the salesperson had to work with the customers' researchers, information specialists, and librarians to design a specialized product. The sales process was broadened to include such activities as investigation, design, and negotiation as the product was increasingly coproduced with the customer. Moreover, the salesperson had to interact more intensively with the production specialists in her own company to make sure that they could provide the requested services. The old sales call was transformed into a riskier design-and-negotiation process. By entering more deeply into the customer's world, the salesperson integrated producer and consumer by knowing much more about each.

The sales manager of the service felt that her sales force was unprepared. She was not sure they had the skills to coordinate and integrate the work of the company's and customer's specialists. Standing at a more complicated boundary between producer and consumer, the salesperson could no longer simply follow proven practices for selling the company's product but had to appreciate the unique features of each new sales encounter.

As this example suggests, the postindustrial milieu poses two complementary challenges: Work becomes more situational and less routine, and people must integrate an increasingly diverse set of facts, interests, and claims. The world of work implodes. Nuclear power workers and managers work in such settings. Workers operating an automated plant intervene only when the automatic controls fail. Such failures are frequently unpredictable and highlight previously overlooked connections between diverse parts of the plant— linking, for example, an open valve in the feedwater system to a pipe that bursts in the containment itself. Workers must psychologically place themselves at the boundaries between these diverse parts of the plant and try to imagine, anticipate, and discover the connections between them. If they cannot take such a comprehensive view of the plant and remain focused instead on a narrow aspect of its functioning, they will be unable to prevent accidents.

Similarly, in operating a dangerous technology, nuclear power workers and managers must cooperate with safety inspectors who audit records to ensure that required procedures are followed. When I interviewed managers, I found that they resented the "nitpicking" safety inspectors and preferred to ignore their findings. After exploring the relationship between the safety workers on the one hand and the line workers and managers on the other, I concluded that the latter controlled their anxiety by "blaming the messenger," the safety inspectors, for the bad news, rather than paying attention to their findings. Instead of identifying closely with the inspectors' work and seeing safety issues from their point of view, workers and managers scapegoated the inspector.

Thus the postindustrial milieu challenges the social defenses. As the risks of working grow, anxiety increases as well. In their efforts to reduce anxiety, people may create social defenses that narrow their range of experience and understanding just when it should be expanding. Although the new technologies may increasingly integrate divisions, units, and roles, creating more complex relationships among them, people may compensate by seeing the work world as increasingly segmented. If they fragment an increasingly integrated technical and social domain, they will behave more irrationally at work.

Reparation

There may, however, be countervailing forces to the growing irrationality and fragmentation. Harry Levinson tells the story of a utility that mobilized its work force to repair power lines and restore electricity in the midst of a devastating storm and flood.[10] Working at great speed and under inhospitable conditions, the linemen restored power without incurring a single injury. The salience of the task itself—its singular importance and the clarity of its purpose—enabled workers to work with great speed while remaining absolutely attentive to the task at hand. The employees overcame common divisions and obstacles to effectiveness, such as infighting, scapegoating, sloppiness, and daydreaming, and worked without injuring themselves or others because they wanted to contribute to a project whose value was indisputable—restoring the conditions of life.

As this example suggests, the wish to restore the world and make it whole may overcome people's flight into narrow thinking, inattention, and ritualized behavior. Research on the psychology of work reveals the importance of completing tasks and making objects whole. For example, gestalt psychologists have shown that people are deeply motivated to complete a task they have begun and are frustrated and upset when they are blocked from filling out the implicit structure, or "gestalt," of the work.[11] Similarly, Tavistock theorists have shown that, when people work in groups responsible for relatively whole steps in the chain of production, they value the group, not because it is composed of friends but because it connects them to a more complete work gestalt.[12] The group symbolically and practically represents the wholeness of work.

Klein provides a psychodynamic foundation for understanding how the wish for wholeness may shape the work experience. Although people labor to avoid anxiety by splitting their consciousness and by projecting their bad feelings onto others, they also wish to restore their own sense of wholeness. But to do so, they must take back their projections and therefore see others as whole and real people who are both good and bad. For example, the subordinate who uses his manager to feel angry develops an image of the manager as a bad and persecuting person. To acknowledge his own anger and overcome his split consciousness, the subordinate must acknowledge that the manager does not simply persecute others but has friendly and protective feelings as well. Recognizing at just such moments that he has psychologically exploited a person he values, the subordinate wishes to make amends by giving the manager something good and important. Moreover, just as people give gifts in memory of dead relatives or friends to complete their relationship to the deceased, the subordinate may give gifts to the manager's symbolic substitutes, thus restoring or repairing the image of the manager in his mind. Indeed, in Klein's world view the images we have of others in our minds, what she calls our internal objects, are the prisms of perception that shape how we see others in the objective world.

Klein called this constellation of psychological experiences the process of *reparation*[13] and argued that throughout life we struggle with the tension of reconciling the splitting and healing of our consciousness, the images we have of others, and our relationships to them. Arguing that at critical moments throughout life we are stimulated to face how we have psychologically damaged others or our internal representations of them, Klein made her theory of reparation the cornerstone of her developmental conception of human life. Moreover, she believed that her theory of reparation helped to explain the artist's wish to create works of beauty. Facing an inner world filled with internal objects that are divided between the good and the bad, the artist tries to restore a personal sense of wholeness by restoring the outer world. The work of art, in its harmony and beauty, then helps to complete the fragmented gestalt of the inner world while enabling recipients of the art to feel complete and satisfied as well.

A psychodynamic theory of work can draw on just such a theory of reparation. Workers desire to restore their inner psychological worlds, the outer world, and the connection between the two. They are therefore motivated to understand the links between the work or service they help produce and the unmet needs of consumers and clients they serve. This is the psychodynamic foundation for workers' desire to complete a work gestalt. Facing so salient a task as restoring power lines, workers can directly apprehend how they produce value for others. But in the industrial division of labor the links between individual effort and final value are typically obscure. By reversing the industrial division of labor, the postindustrial milieu offers people the opportunity to understand the nature of the whole task they face and the ways in which they may contribute to its value. The salesperson managing the links between the researchers and the information service company enters more deeply into each world and so has a greater sense of meeting the needs of her customers. But as we have also seen, such work may promote even greater anxiety. Thus, in facing the psychodynamics of work in a postindustrial milieu, we are confronted with the regressive pull of anxiety and splitting and the developmental pull of risk taking and reparation.

Main Argument

By describing the psychodynamics of work in a postindustrial milieu, in this book I assess the regressive and developmental pulls of work, which are based on seven propositions.

1. Feelings of anxiety are the fundamental roots of distorted or alienated relationships at work. These feelings in turn are related to the primary operational and developmental tasks of the organization.

2. A work group manages its anxiety by developing and deploying a set of social defenses. By using these social defenses, people retreat from role, task, and organizational boundaries. Every social defense depersonalizes relationships at work and distorts the group's capacity to accomplish its primary task.

3. The social defenses at work frequently create a distorted relationship between the group and its wider environment, that is, its customers, clients, and competitors. These systematic distortions relieve the group of part of its anxiety. The "outside" is scapegoated or devalued in some way to preserve the "inside." A group dominated by its own social defenses retreats from the boundary it shares with its environment into its collective fantasies and delusions.

4. Group development takes place when group members stop scapegoating others, when they cease using each other or outsiders to manage their shared anxiety. In so doing, they come close to confronting their primary task. But this is a difficult and frequently limited process.

5. Although people rely on social defenses to contain their anxiety and consequently scapegoat clients, customers, or co-workers, they also desire to restore their experience of psychological wholeness and repair the real or imagined psychological damage they have done in devaluing others. This desire for reparation helps to limit the level of social irrationality in any group setting and provides a strong basis for moments of group development.

6. To assess the salience of the reparative motive, we must compare the need for reparation with the level of anxiety people feel. As the technologies and culture of a postindustrial milieu integrate once divided roles, units, divisions, and organizations, the division of labor of the industrial world is reversed. But in facing whole rather than divided tasks, people may be too anxious to acknowledge and understand the experiences of those in other roles, units, divisions, and organizations. To contain their anxiety, they may resort to even

more primitive processes of scapegoating and projection. Ironically, an imploding world may create even more pervasive and violent psychological splits.

7. People may be unable to restore psychological balance to their work lives by relying on the resources and supports of a single organization alone. To acknowledge the new, intergrated complexity of a postindustrial world, they may need to understand how the society as a whole values the goods and services it produces. Working under the cultural umbrella of a coherent set of economic values, people can tolerate the uncertainty of a more integrated world. With feelings of uncertainty contained, they can begin the psychological and practical work of reparation. Economics and culture set the conditions for each person's capacity to repair his or her relationship to the world.

Thus the psychodynamics of our work life in the coming decades will be shaped by four factors: (1) the postindustrial job structure, in which once divided roles, units, divisions, and organizations are increasingly integrated; (2) people's wish to limit the level of anxiety they feel; (3) the strength of their reparative desires; and (4) the degree to which a set of coherent economic values helps people to understand the purposes of their work and the value it creates for others.

The Organization of This Book

This book is divided into four parts. The first part, composed of four chapters, shows how work, role, and anxiety affect one another. In chapter 1 I show how organizations create "normal" psychological injuries as people face the anxiety of taking their work roles. In chapter 2 I examine the links connecting anxiety, organizational boundaries, and feelings of aggression, and in chapter 3 I explore the details of these connections by assessing how people take and violate roles. The first three chapters thus establish the basic terms and theory for a psychodynamic conception of work.

I then move from a focus on individual psychology to a focus on group behavior in chapter 4, describing three forms of social defense: the basic assumption, the covert coalition, and the organizational ritual. Each defense helps groups to contain the anxiety of working. Basic assumption behavior occurs when members of a group create short-lived *unconscious* assumptions or fantasies about their group life. They may assume, for example, that they have come together to fight an enemy or to find a savior. The covert coalition, by contrast, is embedded more permanently in long-term relationships between people. Such relationships are modeled after family ones: I call them covert because they operate beneath the surface of observable organizational roles and are often invisible to those who enact them. In producing covert coalitions, co-workers act as though they are siblings or parents and children. Finally, the organizational ritual appropriates the most rational and technical features of organizational life for irrational purposes. Like the drug administration routine that Menzies described, the ritual cloaks its psychodynamic function inside visible work rules.

After the key themes of the book are introduced in part I, in part II I examine the social defenses in greater detail through two case studies. In chapter 5 I examine the dynamics of a covert coalition in an environmental review division of a state agency. I show how the anxiety produced by environmental risks in a politically dynamic situation led a group of senior managers to undermine their director. By remaining loyal to their former director, who through ruthless management had transformed the anxiety of the work itself into his subordinates' fear of and dependency on him, the subordinates reproduced a primitive coalition system in which siblings "killed off" the hated father yet retained him by distributing his characteristics among themselves. The new director was caught in this primitive process.

In chapter 6 I examine how management training can function as an organizational ritual, helping managers contain the anxiety of using their feelings when evaluating subordinates. Through a study of a training session I conducted for executive nurses, I discuss how training limits managers' ability to understand the interpersonal dimension of managing others. In addition, I suggest that the anxiety of using one's feelings grows in settings where men and women work together as equals. The anxieties associated with sexual feelings can further distort the relationships among workers.

In part III I examine what happens when the social defenses are challenged by the postindustrial milieu. In chapter 7 I introduce the theme of the postindustrial milieu, assessing its possible impacts on the social defenses. By presenting examples from nuclear power plants, an information systems group, three plants based on the principle of self-managing teams, and a setting where managers and trainers tried to create a more participative climate, I argue that the postindustrial milieu integrates once divided roles, units, and divisions, thus increasing the complexity and the risk associated with work. Finding that inherited social defenses may no longer contain the anxiety of working, I argue that managers and workers must enact sophisticated boundaries that help people to acknowledge the claims of outside stakeholders while protecting the coherence of the work group. In failing to do so, they may retreat from role, task, and organizational boundaries and create a more illusory and irrational world than that found in an industrial milieu.

I extend and deepen this argument with three case studies that explore people's responses to the challenge of enacting and maintaining sophisticated boundaries in this milieu. In chapter 8 I examine how a bank, bureaucratically organized and facing competition and deregulation, tried to delegate authority to lower-level employees while developing more complicated relationships with its customers. By examining my experiences with managers, workers, and training staff, I show how, despite senior managers' attempts to create a nonbureaucratic culture, they create a more punishing and vindictive culture. Their bureaucratic practices had functioned as social defenses, and in their absence feelings of punishment and persecution paradoxically grew.

In chapter 9 I examine a prison in crisis and revisit the shuttle accident in greater detail. I show how the postindustrial milieu may lead managers and workers, unprotected by working social defenses, to create both excessively closed and excessively open organizational systems. In turn, such systems produce growing psychological and sometimes physical violence, as organization members, overwhelmed by anxiety, seek out scapegoats who are either inside or outside the group.

In part IV I explore the broader forces for social development that may take people beyond the social defenses and enable them to cope with anxieties of working in the postindustrial milieu. In chapter 10 I examine the dynamics of reparation, highlighting its links to feelings of shame and to the process of sublimation. In chapter 11, composed of two case studies, I describe the features of a reparative organization. By comparing the start-up of two high technology factories, I show how the leader of the first factory glorified the company's new tools and its wonderful future, forgetting that an organization is ultimately an instrument of its purpose. By contrast, the plant manager in the second factory acknowledged the pain of a start-up and focused on the plant's ultimate purposes from the beginning.

In chapter 12 I link the psychodynamics of reparation to broad social trends. I assess key themes in the history of work since the Industrial Revolution and suggest that bourgeois life tied people to work through the psychological interplay of guilt, compulsion, and triumph. In arguing that a postindustrial work world cannot be safely based on such a psychological substructure, I suggest that Klein's theory of reparation might provide an alternative practical psychology for examining and reconstructing the way we work and the work we do. This suggests that the goods and services we produce can function as reparative gifts, helping people overcome their anxiety and feelings of inner punishment and guilt.

But whatever hope we have for the power of a reparative process, we must acknowledge that the emerging postindustrial work system is a double-edged sword. On the one hand, postindustrial jobs offer significant reparative opportunities. As people work more closely with customers and supervise total systems of production, they feel closer to the product of their work. On the other hand, postindustrial jobs create more anxiety. As social defenses are challenged, people are likely to destroy as well as repair their real and symbolic relationships to others. Finally, I argue that the answer to this dilemma does not lie in the character or structure of any single work organization alone but in the society's culture of work. This culture helps people impute value to the work they do and to the goods and services they produce. But if the products and services we offer to the marketplace are to function in this way, we need to live and work in an economy that gives coherent economic value to the products we produce and consume. If, by contrast, we live in a society whose members cannot agree on what they value, where what some people regard as good and useful is to others bad and destructive, then the products of our work may not help us overcome the anxiety of working. To counter the effects of failed social defenses in that case, we need to reconstruct our political economy, the methods and institutions through which we give value to the goods and services we produce. We need to go beyond the social defenses, beyond the single organization, and develop the cultural and political space between organizations and institutions. We must move from the psychodynamic to the political terrain.

A Note on Method

In this book I use the clinical method of exposition and argument. By working with particular cases of organizational process and examining incidents, transcripts, and my own feelings, I interpret events to assess both the manifest and latent meanings of particular communications. The goal of such interpretive work is to find the common thread of meaning that unifies many apparently disparate encounters, in this way uncovering the purpose and meaning of a person's or a group's particular action and experience.

Like all field methods, interpretations do not produce irrefutable explanations. Instead, the writer and the reader assess an interpretation on the basis of its economy, its ability to account for many phenomena, including the writer's own experience and feelings, and its capacity to yield further, often unexpected meanings. In developing the cases in this book, I give the reader my own interpretations and the data I have used for inference, and of course I may be wrong. I have two purposes here: to link my consulting experiences to a theory of work in a postindustrial society and to develop a psychodynamic conception of work life. To achieve the latter, the reader need not agree with all my explanations. Rather, accepting for the moment that unconscious process and unstated feelings play a critical role in shaping work life, the reader can also take up the interpretive method, proposing alternative explanations where mine seem incorrect or incomplete. The appendix presents a more complete description of consulting as a method of research.

I

The Social Defenses

The Normal Psychological Injuries of Work

I had just completed a taxing two days of consulting. The work was fulfilling, if at times difficult. At the end of my meetings with the fifteen managers, each of them reflected on what he or she had learned, and several thanked me for my contributions. And yet there I was, an hour later, having dinner alone in a strange city. One of the managers had even said, as we were packing up to leave the conference room, "Hey, shouldn't we be taking him out to dinner?" But the only response from Louise, who was rushing off to a business meeting, had been a look that was both quizzical and embarrassed. Her face seemed to say both "I don't understand" and "Perhaps something is out of joint here." I felt neglected and hurt.

An Anhedonic Culture

Louise and the fifteen managers ran a public legal services program. The program was functioning in a hostile setting. Conservatives in the county were objecting to services it gave the poor, and funding for its activities was insecure. Louise therefore felt that the program could no longer afford to be simply combative and adversarial. Instead, she was trying to develop close ties to the bar association of the city, to senior partners of law firms, and to sympathetic business managers. In addition, she had decided that the program should cooperate with the county, state, and federal funders, who were demanding that it provide continuing evidence that its lawyers were serving the poor without violating program guidelines (for example, that they were not helping anyone whose income exceeded the eligibility ceiling and that they were not helping illegal immigrants).

Louise was also committed to the program's mission of social change. She had joined the program in the 1970s, when its social activism was at its height and its lawyers were winning important court cases defending the rights of poor people. Louise thus faced a difficult balancing act—keeping enemies at bay by cooperating with them while supporting the program's adversarial stance and activist mission.

Louise's preoccupation with county and national politics was having its costs. The legal staff was challenging her authority. They did not know what she did, felt that she was unavailable, and wondered if she were not wasting her time. They resented what they considered her excessive demands for paperwork, which she had imposed to protect the program against hostile audits. They felt she was invisible yet burdensome. They questioned her competence. Could she lead them?

Louise's lack of authority made it difficult for program members to maintain the program's social change mission. In order to mount and sustain complex litigation in the state and federal courts, the senior lawyers in the program needed to develop and manage an effective system for producing and sustaining litigation strategies, husband the program's scarce legal talent, and develop younger lawyers with litigation abilities. But Louise was not providing the leadership that could enable them to work together as a group. Consequently many senior lawyers felt isolated and burdened with too many court cases, whereas the younger lawyers felt excluded from litigation work. Louise's lack of authority thus blocked the program from deploying its resources strategically. Louise asked if I could help them develop an organization design and process that would enable them to use their scarce legal talent more effectively.

I worked with the group in an intensive two-day retreat. We examined cultural and structural obstacles to the development of line authority in their program and sketched an organization design through which they could invest litigation authority in certain key roles. The group worked hard and well, and for me the expected sequel would have been for at least some of us to unwind together over a drink or dinner to celebrate the two days' accomplishments. It is possible of course that, when this did not happen, I could not tolerate the loss of the connections and the good feelings I had experienced during the day. I felt neglected. But, because one of the managers had indicated that she too experienced something disjointed and incomplete in the program's relationship to me, let us assume that my feelings reflected some aspect of the total emotional situation at the moment.

Much reflection in the succeeding months led me to the following hypothesis. Louise's quizzical and embarrassed look as she left reflected her "anhedonic" stance, her belief that she should not take pleasure in her work. She had to experience it first and foremost as a burden. If she took pleasure in her relationship to me, by celebrating her subordinates' good work, she would be taking unwarranted pleasure in her own experience as an executive. Therefore I could have no pleasure because she could have none. Indeed, she had scheduled her business meeting for that evening long in advance, ensuring that she would be unable to relax after the retreat.

Clearly, insofar as Louise was a workaholic, she was struggling with how she personally experienced work. Yet I think that the anhedonic impulse I sensed in her reflected the wider culture of the program as well. After all, no one else went out with me, not even John, whom I had met previously. The most brilliant lawyer in the program, John appeared extremely serious and sober. To many in the program he appeared as the distant hero whose life was completely wrapped up in the program's litigation activity. I felt close to John nonetheless. He had recommended me highly to Louise and had been my key informant when I interviewed program personnel. Yet he too had run off after the meeting!

Louise's Transference

Recall that Louise had to contend with much hostility to the program; yet in doing so, she felt isolated and alone. Indeed many program managers did not understand her role and resented the control systems she had developed. It struck me that my experience with her mirrored her experience with her subordinates. Just as I felt unacknowledged after the conference, Louise too must have felt systematically unacknowledged and unappreciated by her subordinates.

One vignette is striking in this context. Shortly before the conference broke up, the group was trying to set up a series of follow-up meetings to work on issues they had explored during the conference. All took out their calendars. Louise ferociously turned the pages of her calendar and vetoed many proposed dates for a key executive-level meeting because of previous commitments. Helen, an active and committed manager, expressed surprise at the extent of Louise's prior obligations. Louise replied with pride, "You see, I told you how busy I was." This was a moment of real pleasure for her, but it was a complex one. It reflected the pleasure of her burdens, of her sacrifices, and most important, of her momentary triumph. It was as though she were saying to Helen and the others, "Now you see how right I have been all along. I'm very busy, and you didn't know it! I win and you lose."

Klein notes that triumphant feelings frequently function as defenses against feelings of dependence, anxiety, and vulnerability.[1] By feeling victorious over others, we deny the ways in which we depend on them and are vulnerable to their actions and intentions. Just as we behave with bravado to mask fear, we express triumph to mask vulnerability. Louise's comments thus had a double meaning. She was victorious at that moment—she had proven how busy she was—but she was also acknowledging her vulnerability and dependence. In her business, in her preoccupation with the hostile political forces surrounding the program, she felt isolated and alone. Her managers were not behind her.

I believe that my feelings of isolation at the end of meeting did indeed mirror Louise's. As frequently happens in consulting (and in therapy), Louise transferred the quality of the relationship between herself and her subordinates to our relationship. I became the projective screen for her entangled but unexamined feelings toward her subordinates. Just as she could not affirm her desire to be more connected to her subordinates, so she could not affirm her emotional connection to me and her appreciation for me. She could push me away by taking an anhedonic posture in relationship to her work. By taking no pleasure in our collaboration and in the authentic work her subordinates had accomplished in those two days, she could distance herself from me. Paradoxically, in taking a triumphant stand to deny her dependence, she in fact denied herself the pleasures of her real victories.

The Vicious Circle

Louise was undermining herself, but her subordinates were undermining her as well. Her subordinates were skeptical of the value of Louise's activities and strikingly ignorant about them. They felt that she "persecuted" them by asking them to fill out unnecessary forms, even though she frequently said that such forms would help her defend the program against hostile audits by government overseers. Her subordinates' ignorance thus appeared willful. The program was in jeopardy, and a responsible executive had to spend the bulk of her time protecting it. Apparently Louise's subordinates knew the situation was dangerous but preferred not to face it. Like the Greeks who killed the bearer of bad news, the subordinates avoided acknowledging the danger by devaluing Louise. Paradoxically Louise came to symbolize the hostile political actors she was trying to fend off.

The extent to which the group devalued Louise and her contribution was made clear during the two-day retreat. Group members spent the bulk of their time examining their litigation system (this was their "presenting complaint"). To help them, I asked the program managers to fill out a responsibility chart that mapped their implicit theory of how responsibility for litigation was and should be organized. I was struck by the fact that Louise's name rarely appeared on these charts. Although she was the program's director and in fact had to ratify all decisions to bring a legal action, the program managers saw little role for her under the present system or in any future one.

Yet it also became apparent that Louise helped her subordinates make her invisible. Throughout much of the two-day discussion Louise was silent until the group set about determining the dates for the next series of meetings. At that point she became animated and assertive. Many dates were suggested, and some were agreed on. Bertha, another program manager, asked, "How will we remember all these dates and meetings?" Louise, who had been actively recording all the suggestions, looked up and said with visible energy, "Don't worry, I will put together a memo." I was struck then by the contrast in Louise's behavior. When the group was doing difficult substantive work on their relationships, she was largely silent. When the group finished its work and was establishing the logistics for the next set of discussions, however, she stepped to the fore. It seemed as though Louise could be aggressive only when the issues were administrative in nature. Thus, just as the group denied the contributions she made to the welfare of the program, she colluded to sustain her status as an invisible leader. She became visible only when she could be helpful in keeping track of dates and organizing meetings, as though she were a staff assistant to the program managers.

This vignette suggests why Louise cooperated in her own psychological assassination. People come alive when they feel safe. It is threat and anxiety that inhibit and deaden them. Louise felt psychologically safe and secure when she could take up the role of staff assistant to the program managers. Louise, of course, was no coward.

She had done an extraordinary job in managing the conservative political forces that threatened the program. But her behavior suggested that she preferred to think of herself as being of service to the program, rather than leading it. It was as though her subordinates had hired her to protect them, and she was successfully complying.

But why should Louise psychologically take up the staff role? I suggest that in this role she felt less anxiety in facing the hostile political groups who threatened the program. If Louise was in fact working for the program managers, then they were the ultimate bosses who had relegated her role to the boundary of the program. Louise was the hired security guard. As the real bosses, the program managers could ultimately protect her when and if she failed.

We thus arrive at a peculiar vicious circle. The subordinates were sufficiently threatened by the external environment to deny its reality. They imagined that Louise was simply engaged in busywork. Louise accepted their denial because it allowed her to deny her leadership role and take up the role as staff to the program managers. As a result both Louise and the staff felt safer, but at the cost of psychologically injuring each other. Louise felt discounted and burdened, hence her anhedonic stance. Her subordinates felt persecuted and ignored, hence their hostility to her.

This analysis suggests why the program had difficulty organizing the litigation system. As in many consultation cases, the stated or presenting problem was a refracted expression of underlying dynamics. The vicious circle undermined line authority in the program as a whole. If neither Louise nor her subordinates could acknowledge her leadership, the authority that came with her role, neither she nor they could vest her with the authority to integrate and coordinate the program's litigation efforts. That is why ultimately the program managers left Louise off the responsibility charts.

A Parallel Process

Hurtful relationships in the executive office itself mirrored this vicious circle. Louise worked closely with Bob and Tom, although Bob was clearly her closest and most favored colleague and adviser. Bob functioned as both a litigation specialist and a policy adviser, but Tom was the official director of litigation. During my interviews Tom complained frequently about his work overload. He felt that Louise, busy as she was, delegated too many administrative tasks to him, and consequently he had little time to supervise the program's litigation effort.

But an incident on the afternoon on the second day of the retreat exposed a deeper and more chronic source of his irritation and hurt. The group talked about setting up a subcommittee to help implement the changes they had been discussing. All agreed that Louise should be on the subcommittee. Bob then volunteered to join it as well, although he did so with a sigh, as if to signify his overload. Jim, a managing attorney, objected, noting that Bob and Louise were too close: "They see too eye to eye." To ensure that diverse views were represented, he suggested that another senior attorney join the committee instead.

Tom agreed that Bob should not join the committee. He then noted, with surprising bitterness, that "Bob is free to do what he wants. He likes his job," pointing out that he himself had little freedom to take on the work he wanted to do. I turned to Bob and Louise and asked if they believed this to be true. They appeared puzzled and unsure. I suggested that perhaps their close working relationship (they had worked together for many years even before Louise's ascendancy to the position of executive director) made it difficult for them to accept a third partner, such as Tom.

This subject clearly provoked anxiety in the group, for they quickly fled from it. Margaret, a program manager, asked, "If the relationship [between Louise and Bob] is good, why play with it?" Tom noted, "You have to be careful with everything." And Kathy, an office manager, complained in a manner seemingly unconnected to the conversation about her administrative burdens as an office manager. This led Dennis, a senior attorney, to reflect on the growing strength of the right wing in the state and the danger this posed for the program.

When a conversation shifts so quickly from the concrete to the abstract, it is a sign that it has provoked much anxiety. Indeed, Tom's puzzling comment, "You have to be careful with everything," may be interpreted as a comment about the conversation at that moment. Realizing that he had stepped into dangerous terrain—after all, Margaret does not want to change the relationship between Louise and Bob—he retreats. Kathy then supports Tom's retreat by shifting the conversation from his burdens to hers, and Dennis supports Kathy's gesture by depersonalizing the entire encounter.

What was so threatening here? Bob was court adviser to Louise, helping her assess policy options and informally managing her relationships with her subordinates. Louise trusted and relied on him. She gave him the freedom to pick and choose his work. As a result Tom got stuck with the bureaucratic work and felt that Louise treated him badly. But this system of relationships was embedded in the broader relationship between Louise and her subordinates. Her distant and strained relationship with them was balanced by her close and relaxed relationship with Bob. Her relationship with Bob protected her from the injuries of her relationship with the program managers. Her subordinates, I suggest, implicitly recognized this. They knew that, if Tom upset the apple cart in the executive office by refusing to do the bureaucratic work, Louise might succumb to the psychological pressures they themselves imposed on her by discounting her contributions to the program and not accepting her authority. She might, for example, resign. Tom had to let Bob function as the relief valve. Thus the set of interpersonal relationships within the program was organized by the architecture of a "parallel process."[2] Relationships within the executive office paralleled and balanced relationships between the executive office and the program managers. But this parallel process injured Tom.

The System of Normal Psychological Injuries

I have described an interpersonal process through which people felt discounted and injured. Yet it should be kept in mind that this was a well-functioning organization with a dedicated staff and a proactive director. The program was able to carry out its mission despite the hostile forces it faced.

The program as a paradigm represents the structure and functioning of what I call *normal psychological injuries*. These are the normal, expectable hurts that people experience as they try to collaborate with others in implementing an organization's primary tasks within an uncertain environment. The case described here suggests that (1) an organization's environment shapes the key contingencies that people within it face, (2) people experience these contingencies as threatening and anxiety provoking, and (3) this anxiety it is in turn *bound* or organized by a particular set of relationships within the organization.

The political hostility that the program faced made its members anxious. To cope with their anxiety, the program managers dumped the "work of worry" onto Louise and then acted as though she were worrying needlessly and doing work they did not understand. Louise, to cope with her anxiety, took up the role of staff to the program managers, thus creating the fantasy that ultimately they could protect the program if she failed. Finally, to help Louise function and to protect the staff, Tom accepted the role of the injured victim in the executive office. Louise could then rely freely on Bob. This interpersonal process represented a method for binding primary anxiety, the anxiety that stems from the work and purposes of the organization itself.

These interpersonal processes reduce the organization members' sense of threat by erecting symbolic representations of this threat in the form of particular people. We cannot fully know or predict the world beyond the organization, but we can know and may even hope to predict the behavior of our co-workers. Indeed, insofar as we can shape their behavior, we can entertain the unconscious fantasy that we can control the outside world. In the legal services program Louise became the outer environment, Tom became the bureaucratic burdens it imposed, and Bob perhaps represented the fantasy that the program could be freewheeling.

Thus the unknown environment becomes known symbolically as particular people represent its different dimensions. Consequently the experience of threat is reduced, but the experience of injury grows. Interpersonal injuries psychologically substitute for environmental threats. Because most organizations face unknown threats and opportunities, injuries are thus always normal and expectable.

Finally, by deploying organization members as psychological representatives of the environment, this process brings the environment in, *across* the boundary. But the boundary signifies the limits of the organization itself, its vulnerability as well as its coherence. Psychodynamically the boundary is a psychospatial representation of what Freud called the reality principle. When organization members collude to reduce primary anxiety, they are violating the reality principle. They are constructing a collective fantasy in which the organization's limits and therefore environmental threats are denied. In this way an organization's tendency to produce normal injuries parallels an individual's tendency to become neurotic. In each case fantasy substitutes for reality as the boundary between inner and outer reality is violated.

The Injured Staff Group: Confusing Role and Person

Such psychodynamics are not limited to organizations, such as the legal services program, that face a particularly hostile environment and operate within nonauthoritarian cultures. A group of staff planners for a large multidivisional electronics company encountered a similar construct. The company had five major plants in the Northeast and a headquarters staff in a major metropolitan area. It had 6,000 employees and sales of a quarter of a billion dollars. Historically, it had been decentralized, but headquarters staff was responsible for financial management and long-range planning. The new chief executive officer felt that more centralized decision making was necessary to cope with a changing market. In recent years, therefore, various ad hoc multidivisional committees had been established to work on company-wide issues. Corporate headquarters employees were assigned to staff these committees.

The planning committee was charged with projecting likely changes in service center requirements as customers bought increasingly computer-based products that required continued servicing over the life of the product. The company had several centers dispersed throughout the Northeast, but the president believed that a primary center attached to one manufacturing plant might prove necessary. The committee was asked to look into (1) the prospective growth of particular products, (2) unexpected final uses that might emerge for these products, (3) likely product design and technology trends that might shape their scheduled and unscheduled maintenance requirements, (4) customer education requirements, and (5) the best location for a primary company service center. The committee was initially given six months to submit its recommendations to the corporate policy committee.

A predictable problem was that committee members from at least some of the plants would not willingly confront the fifth and final charge. The plant that got the service center would risk being classified as a service unit and thus might lose its research facility— and its prestige in the corporation.

The strategy of the corporate headquarters planning staff was initially to emphasize the first four charges of the committee, in the hope that before committee members confronted the fifth and most difficult issue they might shed what staff termed their "parochial" and plant-specific interests for a more corporate perspective. The staff also prepared a rather extensive position paper on the first four issues in order to give the committee some direction, a boost in getting started, and a better opportunity for initial success. The report included background data, data analysis, alternative proposals, and in some cases recommendations.

At an early meeting of the committee the staff gave a supplementary oral presentation of the written report. One of the committee's most influential members in terms of position and persuasiveness and the one who had the most to be concerned with regarding the final charge quickly dismissed the planning staff report and recommendations and proposed instead that a subcommittee be established to look at other alternatives. That member was appointed chair of this subcommittee. The subcommittee met on several occasions and then recommended to the committee that a three- to six-month study be conducted on the first two charges. As a result the subcommittee was still studying the first two of the five charges six months after the subcommittee had first met.

The planning staff was frustrated. The subcommittee did not meet its scheduled objectives, and the subcommittee took on a life of its own. Some committee members became cynical about the strategic planning process. The staff planners felt that the company's strategic planning program had lost credibility. The company lost potential supporters of a new approach to strategic planning and the development of a corporate identity.

Analysis

Like the legal services case, this example highlights how threat, anxiety, and normal injuries are connected. The planning staff was clearly anxious about its competence, about its ability to convince the line that it was important to develop a new approach to strategic planning. Three processes stand out. First, in its anxiety the headquarters staff labeled plant representatives as "parochial." Second, to control line discussion, the staff co-opted much of the line's work by preparing an extensive study of the key issues. Third, the staff fantasized that it could shape the morale and spirit of the group by postponing the discussion of the core political issues.

Clearly the staff was anxious and tried to manipulate the line managers on the committee. Under the guise of protecting them from their own disputes, they actually deauthorized them. The staff could not collaborate with the line managers. But the psychological mechanisms underlying the process of deauthorization are revealing. They match the experiences of Louise and her managers.

The staff called the line managers "parochial," a term for people who think narrowly, who for idiosyncratic and psychological reasons refuse to see the larger picture. The line managers, however, were not representing themselves on the committee; they were representing the interests of their plant. In their *roles*, as opposed to their *persons*, they had to take the interests of their own manufacturing sites to heart. Clearly the committee had been constructed to elicit and therefore resolve differences of interest among the plants. But the staff found this inherently unpredictable political process anxiety provoking. To control their anxiety, they imagined that the committee members did not represent particular interests but were simply parochial people. They confused role and person. In so doing, they could entertain the fantasy of manipulating or controlling *people* and so avoid the more difficult task of helping to coordinate diverse political *interests*.

The staff group's dilemma mirrors that of Louise and her managers in three ways. First, the legal services managers took in the threatening environment by electing different members to represent its parts. In this way unpredictable forces were made familiar and thus controllable. In the company case the staff turned *interests* into *persons*; in the legal services case managers turned *persons* into *interests*. In each case the boundary between inner and outer reality was violated.

Second, in each case role reversals exposed a dysfunctional group process. Louise acted as though she were a staff assistant to her subordinates; in the company case the staff acted as though they could control and were thus superior to the line managers. In each case line and staff roles were reversed. These role reversals signify that the role occupants could not bear the anxiety associated with the role. To escape, they enacted roles that worked against the grain of the task itself. The task in turn was linked to the outer reality. Thus, in escaping from their roles, Louise and the company staff limited their competence and effectiveness.

Third, the process created normal injuries. In each case everyone involved felt discounted. Louise felt unappreciated, her program managers felt persecuted, the company staff felt frustrated, and the company line managers felt manipulated.

2

Boundaries

Both of the cases described in the last chapter highlight how people set up psychological boundaries to contain anxiety. The staff of the legal services organization created an imaginary boundary between themselves and Louise, transforming outside threats into threats from insiders. Similarly, the planning staff of the manufacturing organization replaced the real boundary that separates staff from line personnel with an imaginary boundary that placed the two inside a single unit. The staff could then enact the fantasy of controlling line managers.

Organizational theories have long emphasized the significance of the boundary that separates the organization from its environment, one division from another, and people from the roles they play. In classical systems theory the organization imports resources and information across its boundary, transforms them into useful products or services, and then exports them across the boundary to customers and client.[1] The boundary separates the outer world of opportunities and challenges from the inner world of work and transformation.

Similarly, in the last two decades theorists such as Simon, Thompson, and Galbraith have defined the organization's boundary as the point where uncertainty is converted into information and decisions.[2] By assessing and interpreting challenges and opportunities outside the organization, senior managers organize the flow of internal resources to meet them. Without such a boundary each unit would respond in its own way to the environment, so that the relationships within the organization would be as unpredictable as the marketplace as a whole. By "standing at the boundary," senior managers create a more controllable world in which activities within the boundary are relatively predictable and organized and can therefore be coordinated to respond to an uncertain outer world. The boundary separates managers' psychological region of certainty from a broader region of uncertainty.

Organization design theorists such as Galbraith, Miller, and Rice[3] further argue that, when boundaries are poorly designed and managed, they can cause considerable stress and anxiety. For example, the worker who cannot influence the stockroom attendant controlling the toolroom, the salesperson with a weak relationship to the plant manager who produces the goods to be sold, the quality inspector unable to identify who made a faulty part and why—all face work boundaries that limit their competence. Unable to influence the people on whom they depend, they cannot reduce the uncertainty they face when doing their work. Managers often face the difficult task of finding just the right boundary to mark off a work group. If the boundary encompasses too many roles, it may prove unmanageable, as different role holders pursue different goals and use different tools and resources. But if it includes too few roles, people inside the boundary may feel unable to influence other role holders on whom they depend.

The Subjective Boundary

Such a rational conception of a boundary, although important, fails to account for its subjective properties. As we saw in the case of the legal services organization, although the official boundary may sensibly correspond to the organization's task, budget, or location, people create and sustain psychological boundaries that become as powerful and real as pragmatic boundaries based on task, money, or location.

Theorists such as Trist, Jaques, Menzies, Rice, and Miller,[4] all from the Tavistock Institute, an applied research organization in London, made ground-breaking contributions in the 1950s and 1960s to our understanding of these subjective boundaries. They argue that, when people face uncertainty and feel at risk, they set up psychological boundaries that violate pragmatic boundaries based on tasks simply to reduce anxiety. For example, by experiencing Louise as the enemy, the staff of the legal services organization created a boundary that brought hostile forces outside the organization inside it, where in fantasy they could control them. Although this imaginary boundary limited their ability to help Louise defend the organization, it nonetheless helped them contain their anxiety.

Aggression

Feelings associated with acting aggressively and exercising power play a special role in shaping the anxiety of working. Work entails risks, and risks are experienced psychologically as threats that must be aggressively met, contained, and ultimately transformed into challenges and opportunities. Seemingly mundane and trivial tasks, such as selling a bank product or pricing a job, as well as such apparently complex tasks as implementing a strategic plan or designing a machine produce psychological dilemmas associated with exercising power—rejecting someone's advice, pushing one's own idea, preventing some people from influencing a decision. In retreating from a task boundary and creating an imaginary world, people are frequently retreating from the imagined consequences of either injuring another or being injured in turn.

An example clarifies how this happens. A national bank, hoping to increase the profitability of its branch operations, wanted its clerks on the platform to sell bank services and loans rather than simply respond to customer requests. I interviewed the clerks and found that they experienced considerable anxiety in selling bank services because they now had to be more aggressive in their relationship to the customers. In the past they had simply called out "Next, please" to the line of waiting customers and then responded as completely as they could to a customer's request for help, such as reviewing an account for errors and omissions or supplying a loan application. They exercised no control over the length of the line and were guided by a philosophy of total service; they faced no decisions and few risks. They were frustrated only when the waiting line became too long and the bank manager did not get extra help to reduce the customers' waiting time.

But when faced with the task of selling to customers, their job became more complicated and risky. They could no longer simply meet a customer's need but now had to direct the customer's attention to a particular bank service and take the risk of violating the customer's conception of the purposes of the encounter. As one clerk told me in describing her experiences as a salesperson: "It does more damage to push a service when the customers only want one thing. They get aggravated, and I'm afraid they're going to think, 'Forget this person and forget this bank.' " Moreover, as many told me, they could no longer spend as much time with a customer as the customer might like but instead had to cut off the transaction when it seemed complete, lest they lose the opportunity to sell the bank's services to another customer. Many were afraid to be so aggressive, fearing that, if they took the risk of controlling the encounter as well as ending it, they might face angry or rejecting customers. Comfortable with their past dependency on a waiting line and customer-initiated encounters, many were unable to mobilize the aggression required to exercise some control over the encounter while more directly influencing the length of time customers waited on line.

In facing real risks, as the clerks did, people are naturally anxious and must mobilize aggression to contend with the challenge of the task. But I have also found that they often feel anxious because they fear the consequences of their own aggression, imagining that, if they take a position or make a claim, others will respond angrily and aggressively in turn. They frequently exaggerate the consequences of acting aggressively, saying no, or establishing a limit.

For example, while consulting for an accounting firm, I interviewed the senior partners, assessing how they billed their clients and priced their services. My interviews highlighted a pattern of cutting bills or discounting prices because partners felt that the bill was too high or that a junior associate had worked inefficiently on the project.

I was puzzled by these feelings because the firm had an excellent reputation in the city for high-quality service. The partners seemed to lack nerve and confidence in managing their relationship to the marketplace. Further study and consulting suggested that the firm had no organized marketing effort and that the partners were quite reluctant to market their services, believing that good performance would sell itself. Yet, although ostensibly believing that the demonstrated value of their service would protect them from losing business, they acknowledged feeling vulnerable and adrift. For example, they valued highly the collegial and democratic culture of the firm, which they regarded as unique in the industry, but they had almost agreed to merge with a much larger company that would have certainly undermined their collegial system of relationships. When I asked one partner about the reasons for the merger, he said, "If we had merged, it would have been a noble experiment that failed, and what was so bad about that?" Lacking conviction about the firm's future, he suggested that the firm was "seeking out a big brother to supply our clients and take care of our needs."

When I worked with the partners at a retreat, it became apparent that the senior partners were reluctant to take the risks of claiming their entitlements in the marketplace, of pricing their services at full value and risking either rejection or anger from their clients. As one partner told me: "I did a piece of work. I told the client it would be hard to estimate how much it would cost, and when it was finished, he was incredibly pleased. But when I sent him the bill for $30,000, I felt terrible. I was sure he would go through the roof." Rather than risk aggression and rejection, many of the partners wished to escape from the boundary between the firm and the market by finding a larger firm to protect them and supply them with clients.

To be sure, in setting high prices, they faced the genuine risks of losing customers but, had they been behaving rationally, they would have simply tested the market to see the impact of a particular pricing structure on total firm revenues. In helping them to cope with their marketplace dilemmas, I understood how they behaved irrationally, exaggerating the potentially destructive consequences of a pricing policy that simply promised to give them fair compensation.

Their collegial and democratic culture, based in part on their latent and unacknowledged rivalries, was central here. Afraid of behaving aggressively with one another—for example, holding one another accountable for standards of productivity—they projected this fear onto the boundary between the firm and the marketplace, imagining that, just as their firm would be shattered if power were exercised, so would their clients destroy them if they demanded fair compensation. Moreover, because they were afraid of facing potentially angry clients, they needed a collegial culture in which partners did not assess one another's contributions to the firm's profits. Consequently, although they created an atmosphere free of the pettiness of office politics, some partners increasingly resented the fact that their large contributions to firm profits were not acknowledged. A climate of good feeling masked growing discontent.

The firm's relationships to the marketplace and the partners' relationships among themselves reinforced one another. Both were organized so that the partners could avoid the imagined consequences of behaving aggressively and exercising power when working with customers or with one another. They were failing at two boundaries: in their own internal role relationships and in their transactions with customers. Although the partners enjoyed the undoubted benefits of collegiality and openness, they paid a price for them. Unable to sustain power and leadership, they allowed silent resentment to build while they drifted and made themselves vulnerable to a takeover offer.

Power and Its Dysfunctions

People fear exercising power when they do not have a sufficiently good internal image of their character, when they feel they are fundamentally bad. If they believe that they are partly bad and mean, they are reluctant to wield power, fearing that they will be unable to contain their anger and will therefore hurt others and be hurt in turn. Aggression and power conjure up an imagined world where people persecute one another. In psychodynamic terms we can say that such people have too punishing or too harsh a superego, a conscience that is too strict and constantly reprimands them for the smallest misdeeds or for simply bad or forbidden thoughts.

Indeed, when the burdens of anxiety become too great, people frequently abdicate the work of being aggressive to the narcissistic leader who, fearing that failure and defeat will destroy his self-image as a beautiful and wonderful person, is compelled to destroy others first. Paradoxically, because organization members want to protect others and themselves, they create a leader who may destroy them and others.

The links connecting anxiety, boundaries, and aggression highlight the paradoxical roots of the normal psychological injuries of working. People psychologically injure one another because they are unable to mobilize aggression at the boundary of the role, task, or organization. By retreating from the boundary and enacting a psychological fantasy, they wind up chronically discounting and hurting one another. They replace the focused and task-appropriate mobilization of aggression with the diffuse and displaced expression of hostility and discontent. For example, by denying the reality of power, the partners of the accounting firm created an overt climate of good feeling while chronically discounting and hurting partners who believed that their contributions were unacknowledged.

This analysis demonstrates the psychodynamic importance of roles and skills. People who fear risk and their own aggression retreat from the work boundary. But when people believe that their roles and skills help them create value for others, they feel more secure in acting aggressively to accomplish their work. Because roles and skills help people to feel that they are good, they become confident that they can contain and direct their aggression. This is why the design of task-appropriate roles is so important.

Summary

A boundary can create anxiety in three ways. First, when inappropriately drawn, it creates destabilizing dependencies so that people are unable to accomplish their tasks. Second, when appropriately drawn, the boundary may highlight the risks people face in trying to accomplish their tasks. Thus Louise and her staff faced the realistic risk of protecting the legal services program from hostile political forces. Third, when appropriately drawn, the boundary may stimulate the feared consequences of one's own aggression or aggression from others.

In each case there is a strong impulse to retreat from the boundary and deny its reality. In the first case, workers who are unable to affect critical interdependencies at the workplace may narrow the psychological scope of their jobs. Because they feel that they lack material support, they become alienated. In the second case, people may retreat from the boundary by creating an unconscious fantasy in which roles on the two sides of the boundary are reversed; what is inside appears to be outside, and what is outside appears to be inside. As we saw in Louise's case, people blamed those inside the boundary for the problems that lay outside it; as we saw in the case of the electronics firm, planners imagined that line managers outside the staff organization were controllable employees inside it. In the third case, in facing a realistic boundary, workers may prove unable to mobilize the aggression required to transact their business across the boundary. Fearing the consequences of their own aggression, uncertain about their entitlements, and worried about the anger and aggression of others, they may, as we saw in the case of the accounting firm, retreat from the boundary, look for protectors who will meet their needs, and chronically discount some members.

In all three cases risk and uncertainty are the common denominators. In each case people who cannot control the outcome of an encounter or situation retreat from a boundary and create a fantasy world in which they are either in control or protected from risk by benevolent caretakers. Alienated workers deny risk by giving up responsibility and by exercising control over their limited workplace and their accompanying daydreams. The legal service lawyers denied risk by imagining that, by controlling Louise, they could control the outer world of hostile political forces. Similarly, the accounting firm partners denied risk by undervaluing the price of their services and looking for merger partners who would protect them from the marketplace.

This extended argument highlights the following analytic model, which will guide my arguments in the coming chapters.

1. Organizations can function only when its managers draw and maintain appropriate boundaries between the organization and its environment and between its different divisions and units. These boundaries determine where particular responsibilities and authorizations begin and end. They represent a particular articulation of the organization's division of labor.

2. A boundary creates anxiety by signifying where the risk of working and deciding is located and where aggression must be mobilized.

3. In responding to anxiety, people retreat from the boundary. The root of this anxiety is typically a compound of an estimate of the genuine risks being faced, the links connecting these risks and the inner fantasies of being rejected or destroyed, and a fear of mobilizing aggression lest it destroy others.

4. Much of an organization's process is directed toward managing the anxiety of working by systematically organizing the retreat from the boundary.

5. When people retreat from boundaries, they psychologically injure their co-workers.

6. By occupying task-appropriate roles and mastering task-appropriate skills, people may be able to stay at the boundary because the inherent value of the work they do contains their fear of hurting others or being hurt in turn.

When people retreat from a task boundary and replace it with a more appealing psychological fiction, they lose sight of the boundary itself and are no longer aware of their retreat. As we saw in the case of the legal services organization, the retreat is self-reinforcing. Nonetheless, when people enter into new relationships, face new tasks, or establish new settings, they are more aware of the choices they face and are more in tune with the dynamics of their own feelings of anxiety and aggression than when they are reproducing old relationships. Consultants face such *choice points* frequently. When encountering new clients, consultants must consciously define their relationships to them and so come in touch with the feelings and thoughts that shape the way they take up or violate the consultant role. In the next chapter I use two of my own consulting experiences to explore how anxiety and boundaries shaped my choices when developing relationships to the people I was helping. Such an extended study will help us to develop a deeper understanding of the links connecting anxiety, aggression, and boundaries.

3

The Psychodynamics of Taking a Role

The county office of a state welfare department had to develop new criteria for determining elderly people's eligibility for home health services. These criteria would be used to channel a sizable increase in service money to various providers throughout the county. My colleagues, Jane and Henry, contacted Robert, the deputy director of the office, and offered their consulting services. They argued that the office faced a complex political and policy problem. What planning process could the office use so that the resulting criteria would be both technically and politically credible to hospital administrators, mental health centers, and interest groups that represented the elderly?

The deputy director was frustrating do deal with. At first he said he was interested in our center's service, but he failed to return our phone calls or answer our letters. After a month of silence he contacted Jane and Henry, and the two met with him to discuss the possible scope of the work. The conversation was a difficult one. Robert was aggressive and indirectly demeaning. How could the consultants really be of help to him? What could they do that social workers couldn't? What was their distinctive competence? Unspecified "others" believed that they had none. He then told Jane and Henry of his plans. He was going to establish two committees, one technical and one policy, to draw up the new criteria. He would set up the technical committee first because the policy committee would have to deal with the more complex issues of interorganizational and interest group politics. Could the consultants really help here? If they were simply good at "process" and "planning," what contributions could they make to the technical committee?

My colleagues returned from the meeting uncertain of what to do next and asked me to consult with them. As they described their meeting, I was struck by their depression. They had been hurt by Robert's attack and felt vulnerable, anxious, and demeaned.

I suggested that Robert's plan was inadequate. He was dividing the work between two committees, but could the two be clearly differentiated? First, if technical committee members came from organizations that served the aging, would they represent just themselves or their home agencies? How would this be clarified? Wouldn't Robert first have to consult the directors of these organizations so that the tasks of technical experts on the committee could be clarified? And selecting members for a technical committee is a political process. Second, could the work of the two committees be differentiated in their substance? Robert imagined that the technical committee might create sample eligibility forms containing an array of medical and social service information. But the asked and unasked questions had policy and therefore political implications. For example, if the questionnaire emphasized medical status and downplayed relationships to relatives and neighbors, the resulting service and funding patterns might favor hospitals over social work services. I argued that perhaps Robert himself was quite anxious about the process and had created a fictitious division between policy and technical matters as a way of avoiding the difficult political tasks he faced.

Jane and Henry took my comments uneasily. I seemed to be depressing them more. Jane protested that the technical committee could be constructed without regard to political considerations; perhaps I did not appreciate that the field of aging services was a "mushy" one in which people frequently changed roles. I replied that, if this were true, people would then be even more confused about their roles, mandate, and delegation on the technical committee.

Jane asked what they should do. I advised them to write Robert a letter reflecting on his plan to create two committees. The letter could highlight the risks that Robert faced in separating the two without first negotiating with key stakeholders in the field of services to the aging. Such a letter, if thoughtful and supportive, would show Robert how Jane and Henry could deploy their skills to help him. The letter would end with a sketch of a work plan and an estimate of the contract cost.

Jane remained anxious. She worried that Robert would ignore that letter just as he had the previous ones. They had to make an appointment and carry the letter to him by hand. I advised them not to trap

Robert. They were outsiders and could not scheme against him as if they were insiders. Because the process of entering and contracting with an organization so centrally shapes the consultation itself, it was important for them to negotiate with Robert in a direct manner. If they got a contract, they would get it with terms and conditions that would facilitate good work.

Jane and Henry appeared even more depressed. They seemed resigned to my advice in particular and my authority in general. My emerging authority had undermined theirs. More important, their depression stimulated feelings of victory in me, as though I had conquered them by revealing their flaws. These feelings were further stimulated when Jane, noting that Henry had to leave for another appointment, suggested that the two of us wrap up the meeting. I demurred, feeling that Jane was somehow aligning with me against Henry. This was after all Henry's project, not mine. But in protecting Henry, I again felt victorious, as though I had once again exposed Jane's weaknesses.

We ended the meeting and, as I left Henry's office, my feelings of competence and mastery soured. I felt guilty and concerned. Had I paradoxically hurt my colleagues by helping them? I turned to Jane and asked her if she had read the draft report for a different project we were working on together. She looked at me quizzically and asked, "Which report?" I described it to her. "Oh, yes," she replied tepidly. I felt punished. She "obviously" did not like my report.

The Anxiety Chain

This vignette highlights several interconnected processes. First, anxiety about work can lead people to step out of their work roles. In this way they turn away from work realities and create a surreal world in which challenges can be met with fantasies of omnipotence, dependence, or defensive denial. Second, when people depend on one another to do effective work, when they must collaborate, one person's anxiety may trigger an *anxiety chain* through which people deploy collective fantasies to deny risks. Third, these fantasies are filled with violence, as people both punish themselves for their own failings and imagine that others are their persecutors. Fourth, as people step out of role, they also step away from one another. They experience real others as though the others embodied the characteristics of fantasy figures, particularly fragmented or caricatured figures who are either all good and beautiful or all bad and evil. Such images, stimulated by fresh experiences of anxiety, draw on both infantile experiences of parents and siblings and juvenile memories of fairy tales and fantasies. Thus paradoxically we are not alienated from one another because roles separate us. Rather, we lose touch with one another when we violate the roles that might help us collaborate. Let us examine these propositions in greater detail.

I did not meet and experience Robert directly, but surely his behavior toward Jane and Henry was peculiar. They were potential resources for him, yet he terrorized them. Jane and Henry's obvious anxiety and sense of incompetence was surely some measure of Robert's aggression against them. Why did he act in this way? Let me propose the following hypotheses about his behavior.

Robert faced a difficult political problem—how to create an eligibility system that met the test of technical and political credibility. He faced real risks, for in constructing a policy, he would have to manage many interest groups so that they produced a consensus that did not undermine his own's agency position and credibility. His behavior suggests that he could not directly face those risks and take the role of a convener and manager of a political process. Instead, he created a fiction of two separate processes, one called technical and one called policy, hoping that the technical committee might limit his risks when he faced the policy one. This fiction, I suggest, enabled him to create an unconscious fantasy of control. He could control a corps of free-floating technicians (who might be manipulatable in a "mushy" social service field) and so deny his actual dependence on unpredictable political processes. In fact, his control over the technicians would be limited as well. As he stepped away from reality and out of role, as he failed to supply leadership, the technicians themselves would be thoroughly confused about their roles on the committee. This confusion would quickly reintroduce the interest group politics he sought to avoid.

Klein speaks of the "manic defense" as a psychological system for avoiding feelings of dependence on others.[1] People repress such feelings of dependence if they evoke memories of earlier dependence on punishing and often hated parents. The manic defense cloaks these memories of injury and violence in the fantasy of control and omnipotence. However, the renewed experience of early punishment does not simply disappear. Rather, as in all defense systems, the feeling is transposed, and anxious and in fact overly dependent people try to punish other people, in the process feeling triumphant over them and therefore secure in their own once threatening and risky environment.

Klein's description of the manic defense may explain Robert's behavior toward Henry and Jane. I hypothesized that he was anxious when facing his work and that his two-committee strategy in fantasy limited his dependence on potentially hostile others. In trying to sell their consulting services, Henry and Jane were in turn dependent on him. They consequently became ready targets for his fantasies of omnipotence and feelings of punishment. He terrorized them because he was feeling punished by the real risks he faced.

Now consider the ways in which Jane and I interacted. When I entered Henry's office, Jane seemed anxious and, as I advised the two, she seemed increasingly depressed. Her depression suggested that I was punishing her by advising her. At the same time her punished look stimulated feelings of victory and contempt in me. What was going on?

Klein talks of the process of *projective identification*,[2] a psychological interaction in which one person deposits unwanted feelings into another person's feeling system. The first person, wishing to get rid of an unwanted feeling, treats the other as if that person were experiencing the feeling state. For example, someone burdened with intolerable sorrow may imagine that it is others who are sorrowful and treat them as people to be pitied. By pitying others, the first person may deny her own feelings of misery. The others may respond in two ways. They may experience the projection consciously, feel uncomfortable at having been given a part in the person's internal drama, and resist being pitied, or they may respond unconsciously to the projection, taking the exported feeling as if it were their own, thus confirming the sorrowful person's projection. The latter possibility is most likely when the others have a natural inclination for the projected feeling state. Those who value being pitied may welcome the projections of those who cannot face their own sorrow.

Jane and I were engaged in just such a psychological dance. Jane was feeling punished. She had internalized Robert's attack on her personal competence. It stimulated her own superego voices, those voices within all of us that evoke the early reprimands of our parents who upbraided us for our failings, for "being bad." Such voices are frightening because they reside within us. They can spy on us and hold us accountable for failings we hide from everyone else. These are the voices that shame us in front of ourselves alone. Jane projected these punishing voices onto me to diminish their power within her. The voice embodied in a real other, particularly one who is a friend, becomes less terrifying even if more real. I therefore became her persecutory agent, the source of her misery. That is why I began to feel unaccountably victorious and triumphant over Henry and her. As a persecutory agent, I had the job of catching others in their failings.

But I also had a natural inclination for this role, for such feelings of triumph. I believe that, when I first entered Henry's office, the pain and discomfort of my colleagues made me uncomfortable. Their pain evoked in me all-too-painful feelings of past professional failures. Like Robert, I consequently deployed a manic defense, a defense against feelings of vulnerability, by accepting Jane's projection. By feeling triumphant, I could deny past and current feelings of pain and injury.

My behavior after the meeting, asking Jane to evaluate my report, is telling here. As I left the meeting, I once again became aware of Jane's pain and felt guilty and ashamed for having triumphed over her. I then asked her to judge my work, just as I had judged hers, but clearly I was less interested in her opinion and more interested in simply submitting to her. After all, I only inferred from her tepid response that she thought little of my work. I did not engage her in conversation. By submitting to her, by offering myself up to her for evaluation, I hoped to relieve my guilt. I would sacrifice myself. It is possible, of course, that my wish to submit stimulated a symmetric wish in Jane to punish. She could take back her punishing voice, for now it could punish me for my failings rather than her for her felt limitations. In such a case her tepid response *was* meant to punish, but clearly I had asked for it.

The sequelae of this incident are revealing. I returned to my office to begin work on another project. Another colleague and I had contracted to work with a legal firm composed of six partners, numerous associates, and a large staff. One partner had just had a heart attack, and the others complained that the work was difficult and demanding and that it frequently gave no pleasure. We were to begin by interviewing the six partners. I sat down to write a letter to them explaining the interview format. Peculiarly, I stumbled on the problem of confidentiality. Although I had interviewed clients in preparation for work on many other projects, the problem of confidentiality suddenly loomed large. What would the rules be? What should they tell us or not tell us? Would they hamstring us by revealing secrets in private that we could not use at the retreat itself? I composed a letter. It was written starkly, as if I were pronouncing a set of logical propositions or laws of behavior. I reproduce the relevant part of the draft here.

Our ground rules for confidentiality are based on the following assumptions:

To be effective as consultants to the group, we need to understand the processes, choices, preferences, and values that are affecting your development;

To be effective, we need to share our learnings and data with the group;

Therefore, individual partners should share that information with us that they feel the group of partners should know and understand.

The letter is bizarre. In content it is strikingly noncollaborative, asking clients whom I barely know to take on the full burden of revealing and concealing information. I would provide no assistance, nor could I be trusted—this despite the fact that in most other consulting activities I find it relatively easy to take organizational secrets and present them back so that no single person can be identified as the source. Moreover, as my colleague pointed out, what was the point of private interviews if not to get information that was not readily revealed in public? He wondered if I was being too uncollaborative and had failed to think carefully about the problems of entry into the organization.

The tone of the letter is even more suggestive. It is strikingly unemotional, lacking in affect. Its format—a set of logical propositions—is a sign that it emanates from an overly rational or rationalized mind, as if affect and feeling were too dangerous. The expression "merciless logic" comes to mind, because no mercy or consideration was shown for the burden I was placing on the partners. Yet, as I composed the letter, I felt strikingly strong, even proud, that I was so clearly defining *my* role and now they had to define *theirs*.

The manic defenses are once again evident. The pain of my last interaction with Jane spilled over into my other work. I retrieved my triumphant feelings, this time by demanding that my potential clients submit to my logical rules for conducting interviews. A chain of punishment and guilt extended from Robert's initial anxiety to my hapless letter to the lawyers. Fortunately I did not send the letter.

Themes from the Case

Let me examine five key themes that emerge from this case. First, real uncertainty and risk underlie this entire dynamic. The vicissitudes of work are ultimately grounded in the fact that people have to undertake tasks that present risks and pose challenges. People's anxiety is not simply rooted in their internal voices or private preoccupations but reflects real threats to professional identity. Robert faced a real challenge to himself and the interests of his organization in trying to coordinate a diverse set of political interests. Jane and Henry faced real uncertainties in trying to collaborate with a difficult client who might refuse to give them a contract. Finally, I faced real uncertainties in my role as an adviser and teacher. If I could not help Jane and Henry to understand their situation, I would fail as their consultant.

Second, if the anxiety grounded in work is too great, too difficult to bear, people will escape by stepping out of role. The role shapes their vision so that they see the work reality for what it is. But if they cannot bear the work reality, they need to step out of role so that they can step away from reality. Jane confused her role as a consultant who stands outside the organizational boundary with that of an employee or member who stands within it. This was why she could scheme against Robert and plan to trap him. The fantasy of entrapment enabled her to turn away from the real uncertainty she faced—that as an outsider Robert had no commitments to her and might not give her a contract. Her fantasy enabled her to deny her essential dependence on the unpredictable behavior of others.

Similarly, in response to Jane and Henry's pain, I stepped out of role twice. Jane and Henry engaged me as a consultant and teacher, but instead of focusing my efforts on helping them, I used my skill to undermine them. My skill became my cleverness, the counterpoint voice to their failings. Thus the more I helped them, the more I weakened them. I exploited their vulnerability as people asking for help. I again stepped out of role when Jane and I left the room and I gave her an opportunity to triumph over me, even though I was her adviser at the moment, simply to relieve my guilt.

Robert too stepped out of role. His capacity to operate in the social field surrounding his organization depended ultimately on his negotiating and political skills. Yet he imagined that he had the authority to convene and direct a committee composed of people from other organizations without negotiating with their supervisors and directors. He stepped out of his political role.

Note that in each case stepping out of role means violating a boundary in the social or interpersonal field. Thus Robert violated the organizational boundaries in the field of aging services, Jane violated the consultant-client boundary, and I violated the teacher-student boundary. The boundary expresses the limiting conditions of reality itself, the constraints of operating and taking risks within it. When people find reality too frightening, they construct a counterworld in fantasy in which such boundaries disappear.

Third, anxiety is transmitted along a chain of interaction through the psychological process of projection and introjection. Robert began the process of punishing my colleagues; I ended it by punishing the lawyers. The anxiety chain emerges through time and over space. Like magical and wishful thinking, it admits to the constraint of neither. In each case people's unconscious and near-instantaneous reaction to the projections of others creates a protected channel for the transmission of anxiety.

Fourth, psychological violence frequently forges the links in the anxiety chain as a result of the interplay between anxiety created by real uncertainty and anxiety created by threatening voices within. The superego voices are mobilized when the real uncertainty evokes memories of having been "bad" children, of having failed in the eyes of our parents. Unconsciously we link the threat from without with a feeling of our worthlessness, as though "good" people would or should never face such a threat. These parental voices are punishing ones, and paradoxically we can feel bad even before we have failed in reality.

To be sure, some people can use these inner voices as prods for action. The verdict "You are bad" is translated into the injunction "You must become ———." We then act to satisfy our parents, so that they will stop punishing us. But frequently, if the threat is severe enough or if the superego is strong enough, we project these punishing feelings onto others. Robert punished Jane, and I almost punished the lawyers to escape self-punishment. Thus the anxiety chain leads people to violate boundaries *and* persons. Indeed, each

violation implies the other. Each springs from the same source—
the real challenge.

Fifth and finally, when anxiety mobilizes our behavior, we experience other people not as they are but as we *need* them to be, so that
they can play roles in our internal drama. When I triumphed over
Jane and Henry, I did not see them as whole people who periodically
suffer and make mistakes, who are both "good" and "bad," but
rather as weak enemies unworthy of my support because of their
inadequacies. In Klein's terms I saw them as "part-objects" rather
than "whole-objects."[3] They became extensions of my internal psychological drama, a drama shaped by my need to deny the existence
of pain and suffering in others. Thus paradoxically we depersonalize
others when we step out of role. By implication we personalize our
relationships when we take our role.

Taking a Role: An Incident

Thus far I have analyzed the dynamics of stepping out of role. Let me
now explore the dynamics of taking it. I was working with an
architecture and engineering company, which I will call AE Inc. The
firm built and serviced nuclear power plants, and they helped
utilities to set up monitoring and control systems (called quality
assurance systems) that ensure that workers follow safety procedures when maintaining, inspecting, and operating the power plant.
It became apparent after the Three Mile Island nuclear accident that
behavioral or psychological processes limit the impact of such systems. Managers and supervisors resent doing the paperwork required to demonstrate compliance with required procedures, and
many workers and supervisors feel that quality assurance monitors
are busybodies, nitpicking bureaucrats who do not understand the
technical dynamics of a power plant.

A senior manager at AE Inc. asked me if I would work with them
to develop training and intervention modules based on a behavioral
approach to quality assurance. I was assigned to work with John and
his subordinate, Jim. Not surprisingly, the concept of a behavioral
approach was a strange one to most of the engineers at AE Inc. (My
senior manager contact was an exception.) In speaking with them, I
found that many believed psychology to be primarily a science for
influencing others, a subspecialty of marketing and advertising. John
in particular seemed cautious and concerned. He decided that, after I

became familiar with the issues through interviews with senior engineers at AE Inc. and their utility customers, I should make three presentations: first to the internal Quality Assurance Group, then to a broader cross section of mid-level managers, and finally to the divisional vice-presidents and the president. If the presentation was accepted by each audience in succession, he would feel comfortable developing a training and consulting package to be marketed to utilities.

The first two presentations went extremely well. "Behavior" as a frame of reference was acceptable, even stimulating. But John became nervous when the time came for the vice-presidents' meeting. He had a difficult time scheduling the meeting but finally set a date. I met with Jim two weeks before the meeting to discuss the content of the presentation.

Jim told me that John was concerned that I "not be too theoretical," that I give the vice-presidents "some behavioral tools" so that they could "walk away with something." I became anxious. I told Jim that my success in the first two meetings was proof that an overview of key behavioral issues, based on theory as well as on data, had worked. I felt that I had spoken to the audience's reality and that they felt I understood them. Jim countered that the vice-presidents were particularly busy and had to feel that their time was used productively.

An anxiety chain was in the making. John's anxiety in presenting novel material to people with little time had been transmitted to me. The phrase "too theoretical" had particular personal meanings for me. It conveyed not only that I was not in touch with facts but more significantly that I appeared as an absentminded professor, as a person with little contact with reality and who is passive in relations to others. Despite two experiences of success, the phrase evoked old but still operating self-concepts that made me feel weak and bad.

We continued to talk, and Jim, perhaps out of his own anxiety at making a decision and actually directing me, suggested that I "do a little bit of both," that I give them both a "diagnosis" and some "behavioral tools." I felt tempted to compromise but then remembered that such compromises frequently served neither diagnosis nor training well. In retrospect, the phrase "a little bit" was telling and may have put me in touch with my anxiety. To do "a little bit" of anything is to do not much of anything. If I agreed with Jim, I would be colluding with him in not taking a risk. But I knew as a professional consultant that I had to take just such risks. The process of establishing a collaborative relationship with a client is always uncertain.

When I recognized that Jim and I might be avoiding rather than taking risks, I was able to step back into my professional persona, my role. I told Jim that I thought my primary task (and I used this professional term with him) was to establish a working alliance with the vice-presidents, that as a result of the presentation they had to trust me as one who could understand their reality. "Training" them would not only divert me from this task but in all likelihood communicate that I was not a collaborator. If I were to train them, I would then be acting as the expert who understood their reality without exploring it, without learning *from* them. Surprisingly Jim agreed. He thought that I could not do both and should therefore use my experience in the first two successful talks to shape my presentation to the vice-presidents. We agreed to take the risk. My presentation was successful.

An Analysis of the Case

The engineering culture at AE Inc. did not support attention to "behavioral factors" at work. I had the feeling that the engineers there believed that psychologists actually read minds. Early on I had asked Jim and his colleagues if I might attend and observe a quality assurance division meeting in which auditing and monitoring issues were discussed. They were uncomfortable with the prospect of a stranger observing their colleagues. Wouldn't the attendees feel that I was scrutinizing and judging them? I dropped the request. I concluded provisionally that theirs was a culture in which people rarely disclosed difficult thoughts and feelings. (This hypothesis was confirmed many times over in my later work with the company.) To them, a behavioral scientist or psychologist became a projective screen for the guilt they felt when they did not say what they meant or mean what they said. The psychologist would "smoke them out," would uncover the crime of nondisclosure. I suspect that John, as a member of this culture, shared these same fears. The discussion of behavioral issues at the vice-presidents' meeting may have come to represent the danger of disclosure in general. If disclosure was a taboo and I represented disclosure, then John would be bringing a taboo person and subject to the central law-making body of the company, the body that sanctioned taboos. John would be guilty by association for violating the taboo.

But what happened between Jim and me to limit the reach of the anxiety chain? Two affective moments stand out for me. First, when I took hold of my professional persona, when I took my role, I felt aggressive and commanding. Second, when Jim agreed with me, I felt warm toward him. I appreciated him. These two moments of aggression and warmth hold the key to the psychodynamics of taking a role.

Consider the aggression. Where did it come from? Why did I feel commanding in making my claim to Jim? I suggest that the aggression had two sources: one that we can call biopsychological and one that was strictly psychological. Clearly I faced a real challenge. Jim's request made me aware, or at least more consciously aware, of the stakes of the upcoming meeting. If I failed, the contract was over. Such real threats mobilize flight-fight reactions, fundamentally a desire to *move* physically and to do so aggressively. The biopsychological roots of aggression are thus based on an appreciation of reality, on the dangers and challenges "out there."

But my ambivalence, my hesitation, and my anxiety, all of which suggest that I was for the moment paralyzed, point to a psychological source of aggression, one *not* focused on reality. In his essay on anxiety Freud argued that anxiety feelings can function as signals of *impending* threats.[4] Such threats emerge when a person has forbidden fantasies of sex or aggression. The sequence is as follows: One has the fantasy, one feels anxious for having the fantasy, one punishes oneself for having the fantasy (by berating oneself, for example) and so relieves the anxiety. Under these conditions the anxiety is the signal of the upcoming self-punishment.

I suggest that my vulnerability to the anxiety chain was triggered by my sense of *impending* failure. I believed unconsciously that I would fail because the phrase "too theoretical" triggered feelings of worthlessness. These feelings in turn were amplified by the voice of self-punishment, by superego voices that punished me for failing to live up to the requirements of strength and success. Thus feelings of aggression were rooted in my experience of aggressing against myself.

This analysis suggests that aggression at the moment of taking or not taking a role is shaped by two processes that pull in opposite directions, one toward reality and the external challenge and one away from it, toward the threats rooted in one's infantile past. The question is, How will this admixture of aggression be directed? In psychodynamic terms, will it be placed in the service of the ego, as a ground for acting on reality, or will it be placed in the service of the superego, as a vehicle for escaping from reality? I was at a branch point. To escape my punishing voices, I could turn away from reality and collude with Jim, ignoring the real risks and real challenges we faced. We might, for example, have formed a "victims" group and gained emotional sympathy from one another for being at the mercy of such a rigid boss as John. This victims group could have provided enough immediate gratification to stave off the experience of both real and superego threats. We could have redirected the anger we deployed against ourselves onto our horrible boss.

The Role and the Observing Ego

The concept of my role, however, provided me with an "observing ego" for reviewing the meaning of my anxiety. I could step back from my immediate emotional setting because I could step into a role. It is telling that, at the moment I stepped into role and disagreed with Jim, I used the professional consulting term "primary task."[5] It was as though I was talking out loud to myself, to create within myself a countervoice to my superego voice. The resulting deployment of aggression was then shaped by the relative strength of the two voices. My professional voice, represented concretely by my skills, enabled me to stay in contact with reality. My ego could escape significant punishment and deploy both the biopsychological and psychological roots of aggression in the service of taking a risk and meeting a challenge. By deploying my professional skills, I could contain the destructive or bad parts of my aggressive feelings by using them to perform a worthwhile service. Looking at it psychodynamically, we can say that the role enabled me to sublimate my aggression. It was no longer used to punish me or others (the boss, for example) but was used to master an objective reality.

Clearly Jim's behavior, his willingness to follow my advice, was also important. He was thoughtful, not apprehensive, when he told me of John's objections. He was not reacting to John's anxiety. He struck me as a professional who understood his limits. Although he initially seemed to be self-deprecating and unambitious, I gradually saw him as someone who had come to terms with ambition. He was not driven by professional restlessness and fantasies of omnipotence. Perhaps this is why he could take the role of an advisee, as someone who could listen seriously to consultants without fighting or competing with them. He was a good follower. He could take risks because he was not pressed by feelings of ambition produced by the superego's injunction "You must become." If he failed, he would not feel as if he were intrinsically unworthy.

The Role and Love

But why the sense of warmth, of appreciation for Jim? As we have seen, when we form relationships through an anxiety chain, we use others as part-objects. People become depersonalized vehicles for the management of our own anger and pain. I devalued Henry and Jane to deny my own pain, Robert devalued Jane and Henry to deny his own anxiety, and Jane turned me into a punishing agent to limit the strength of her punishing voices. We hated one another.

Jim and I, however, stepped out of the anxiety chain. This suggests that, when we take a role, face reality, and step out of the anxiety chain, we see each other as whole-objects, as real people. This is why I felt warm toward Jim. I appreciated him; indeed, I felt a certain sweetness toward him because he became real to me and I could collaborate with him.

People who share a near-disaster are familiar with this process. In the moment of an acute and pervasive threat, they overcome their neurotic uses of one another and experience each other intensely, as they really are. That is why people have reunions to "celebrate" the near-disaster. The risks of work are modified or sublimated versions of such disasters. They are less life-threatening and more chronic. For that reason it is more difficult for people to personalize their relationships to one another at work. When we take our roles, however, we appreciate others because, rather than using them, we are sharing a common and problematic reality with them. Through our roles we have faced a shared and risky world. Thus in taking a role, we libidinize our relationships to our co-workers. By sublimating sexual feelings, we can love abstractions and, by sublimating aggression, we can appreciate specific, concrete others. This complementary sublimation of sex and aggression creates a more secure and stable world of relationships.

The Task and the Role

There are two ways to enact a role. We can take it by facing the real work it represents, or we can violate it by escaping the risks such work poses. When we violate it, we help create and sustain an anxiety chain through which we hurt our co-workers. At each point along the chain a person violates a role by crossing a boundary. These boundaries have a twofold character: They represent a real difference between people and situations, and they represent the fundamental difference between reality and fantasy. Thus boundary violations represent people's wish to live in an illusory world where risk is absent.

By contrast, when we take a role, we limit the consequences of our own fear. We accept the boundary it represents. As a result, the aggression in response to risk is turned not inward but rather outward toward the work itself. We are then free to appreciate our co-workers as collaborators and see them as people who can contribute to our welfare.

But to take our role, we must of course understand our task. As we have seen, in working with Jim, I was able to retrieve my understanding of the consulting task. I deployed it as an alter ego to limit my anxiety. But when tasks are not clear, we lack a context for taking our roles.

Here we face a paradox. We struggle to enact our roles in group settings. However, as we saw in the case of the legal services program, groups can create stable relationships that support chronic role and boundary violations. But the more we live inside such systems of relating, the less we can experience our real work, our real tasks. As we violate our roles, we can no longer understand what the world outside our group demands of us. Our ignorance in turn supports the ways in which we violate our roles. We enter into a vicious circle in which role violation and ignorance reinforce each other. Thus groups can collectively sustain and reproduce an irrational system of roles.

These links that connect roles, tasks, and ignorance highlight the limit of the now familiar critique of bureaucracy as a system based on alienating roles. Roles are not alienating or imprisoning in themselves; rather, they become so when they are distorted by a systematic and socially supported system of role violations. We are not alienated because we inhabit confining roles but because we take roles that are only weakly linked to the purposes of our work. Similarly, we cannot overcome our alienation by stepping beyond or outside of a role. Rather, we must take a role, with its specific boundary and limit, that links us directly to a purpose on the one side and to our co-workers on the other.

Several decades of experience and observation suggest that groups develop specific mechanisms to support and institutionalize a consistent pattern of role violations. Menzies called these mechanisms the social defenses. They relieve individuals of the burden of managing their escape into illusion, of turning away from reality, by creating social systems that support systematic role violations. The social defenses *externalize* individual defenses. Thus, to understand how groups prevent individuals from taking roles and how individuals in turn sustain group irrationality, we must examine the social defenses.

4

The Social Defenses

The work of Bion and Menzies and my own analysis suggest that there are three modes of social defense: *basic assumption*, *covert coalition*, and *organizational ritual*. All these defenses help groups to avoid their tasks, but they differ in their stability and continuity. The basic assumption defense is the most ephemeral, the ritualized activity is the most institutionalized, and the covert coalition lies in between. Let us examine each in turn.

The Basic Assumption

Wilfred Bion, a student of Melanie Klein, founded the psychoanalytic study of group life. The concept of a group's basic assumption was fundamental to his thinking.[1] The basic assumption is represented by a particular pattern of group behavior. The group acts as though it believes or assumes that a cohesive group mind exists and can be sustained *without* work or development. People experience the group as a magical entity. It has a purpose and a life independent of the conscious and collaborative efforts of its individual members. Basic assumption behavior thus expresses people's primitive wish that they can create a benign environment without work. When the group's tasks promote anxiety, the basic assumption experience enables members to limit their feelings of isolation and depersonalization.

Bion argued that there are three basic assumptions that groups typically make. They assume that the group has been brought together (1) to either *fight* an enemy or *flee* from it, (2) to be *dependent* on a powerful leader, or (3) to oversee the marriage of a *pair* who will produce a powerful savior or messiah. These assumptions are called the *fight/flight*, *dependency*, and *pairing* assumptions. The central feature of basic assumption behavior is the rapidity and ease with which groups take up and display these assumptions. They do not go through a process of group development; rather, the group magically creates a group culture or climate. The ease of producing this behavior, Bion argues, means that members have unconscious feelings and can reinforce each other's sentiments without being aware of them. These feelings are in turn centrally related to feelings of anxiety.

The Dependency Assumption

Consider the following example of a basic assumption dependency group. I have often consulted for small teams that to me felt lumpish and dead. I have noticed that at such "dead" moments many members of the group will look at the flip chart in the room and then resume conversation. Indeed, an implicit rule seems to be at work. Silence is to be met by stares at the flip chart before conversation can begin again. The group behaves as though it has an unconscious agreement to punctuate its silences in a particular way. But where did the agreement come from?

Further reflection suggests that the group is lumpish because it feels helpless in pursuing its task. Members fear revealing their hidden agendas and are therefore reluctant to authorize any individual to take leadership. The flip chart, particularly when the consultant is the one who writes on it, becomes the surrogate leader. The group makes the basic assumption that in fact it has a leader, represented in the flip chart, and that its members are permitted to break silences only when they stare at the leader.

Such an unconscious agreement most often emerges through nonverbal behaviors. The group confronts its own silence, anxiety grows, and someone looks at the chart, is comforted (it displays the consultant's wise words), and speaks. Others then feel less anxious because someone has spoken.

A rule of conversation is quickly established. The group has created a leader, the flip chart, without consciously confronting its leadership problem. Thus it achieves group unity magically, without real work.

Of course, the flip chart does not really solve the leadership problem. The group does not really develop by confronting members' agendas. Rather, by displaying basic assumption behavior, the group minimizes anxiety, enabling its members at least to stick together despite the fact that they cannot work together. Thus, as Bion suggests, the individual members' desire to be in a group per se, irrespective of its capacity to work, predominates. Basic assumption behavior makes groups unproductive because group members are living in a dream.

The Fight/Flight Assumption

Similarly, I once worked with a group of supervisors in a government agency. They were delegated by the director to assess why their organization was not functioning. I was hired to help the group develop and to conduct a survey of all members of the organization. I met with the group in the morning, and not surprisingly they were anxious. But their anxiety took the form of a fight with me on the one side and a flight from the task on the other. For example, some group members insisted that they knew all the problems, that a survey was redundant, that they were in touch with their staffs, and that they could write the recommendations for change right now. One member of the group said this quite combatively to me, suggesting that in fact I had imposed the task on them. It became clear to me that the group had quickly coalesced around a program to fight me as a "bad" person who burdened them with unnecessary work.

Again, behaviors below awareness were key here. The supervisors were feeling anxious. Consequently they allowed one of those who dealt with anxiety by fighting to take the floor and hold it. By unconsciously authorizing a fighter to take leadership, they also could use him as a projective screen. They projected onto him their own feelings of anger (for having to do "senseless" work) and thus reinforced their unconscious commitment to his authority. I responded by not fighting, acknowledging that indeed the group might know all the answers. The group therefore lost its enemy and so once again had to confront its anxiety. Shortly afterward, the same person who had led the fight became active in trying to assess the scope and purposes of a written survey.

This example suggests again that basic assumption behavior emerges without development, without work. Fight/flight leaders do not consciously nominate themselves but rather respond to anxiety in a particularly personal way. If their responses resonate with the feelings of others, they will be supported through nonverbal communication—silence by others, eye contact with others, visual space created for the new leader, and so on. Thus they are pushed into leadership roles as much as they choose them. It is because conscious choice and rational thought are absent that the basic assumption group can emerge so quickly.

These examples also suggest that basic assumption behavior is volatile. It fluctuates within and through group life, much as daydreams flit in and out of conscious thought. Indeed, Bion suggests that a group moves between basic assumption behavior and actual work with great frequency. No group is free of the irrationalities of basic assumption behavior. Rather it is the ratio of the two kinds of group life that determines the ultimate effectiveness of the group.

The Pairing Assumption

An extended example is useful here. It begins with a basic assumption dependency. My colleague and I consulted for a group of pediatric residents who were interested in assessing their first year of work and study. We helped them to design a retreat and took the role of facilitators. Our work was both easy and difficult: easy because group members spoke readily about their experiences in the program and the hospital and difficult because both my colleague and I found it difficult to be helpful.

It was not that we were ignored. On the contrary, the group considered everything we said, but our comments were taken in too quickly, almost swallowed up by the group. We felt unacknowledged, as though our thoughts and our persons could be disconnected. For example, I suggested that, although they seemed to feel special in attending such a reputable residency program, perhaps many of them feared looking stupid in the company of such obviously capable peers. One member acknowledged the feeling, another amplified it, and quickly my interpretation became lost in their intense and inward-turning group process. Paradoxically, although I was listened to, I felt denied, annihilated. The group, it seemed, had no threshold across which one could carry out a conversation. You were either deeply in it or totally outside it.

Over the course of the two-day retreat it became apparent to me that the group functioned as a protective womb for its members, who felt dependent. Indeed, I remember returning to the retreat house the first night and finding the entire group of about fifteen huddled like children in one corner of a palatial room. It was as though the room's size threatened to dissolve or overwhelm them. Like the small child who pushes up against the wall on going to sleep, the group members needed to feel protected by a wall, a physical boundary, to secure their psychological equilibrium. They felt vulnerable.

But why? During the retreat it became clear that the residents felt abused in the hospital. They felt stupid, incompetent in front of their teachers, belittled by the hospital staff, and taken for granted by their patients. Despite their obvious capabilities, they were going through a strenuous hazing process. Moreover, most of the residents feared taking their problems home. They did not want to take out their frustrations on their spouses for fear of alienating them. Consequently the group was all they had, yet it was vulnerable. I began to understand why my colleague and I could not collaborate with the group. Because group members felt needy and swallowed up or "ate" any interpretation we offered them, there was no transaction or exchange at the group's boundary. And because they were hungry for support and explanation, they could not acknowledge us as persons for fear of disturbing their links to each other. If they took us along with our words, they might disrupt their group life. Some might prefer to have us, others might not. The group might have to authorize a work leader to manage our integration. It might have to *develop*. Thus, if they acknowledged us, they risked losing the precious equilibrium they had established to protect themselves. The group was in a basic assumption dependency state.

But this was a contradictory situation. In particular, the residents were desperate to learn how to be competent doctors, and they needed each other for guidance and feedback. Yet rarely was one member willing to critique another's practice. I conducted a role play in which I asked one resident, Gail, to replay an encounter she had had with Marie at the hospital. The two worked together on the emergency ward. One evening Gail had made an error under stress and asked Marie, who was also on the ward that night, what she would have done in the situation. Marie assured her that she would have done the same and that it was all right to make mistakes. At the retreat Gail noted that she felt disturbed by Marie's assurance, and Marie acknowledged that she had not really said what she felt. I asked Marie to say now what in fact she really felt like saying. Only with the greatest difficulty did Marie say what she really felt that night on the ward: that Gail had practiced careless medicine.

The group members therefore could not learn from each other. They believed that, if they actually helped one another become better doctors, they might destroy their protected and cohesive group life. They were in a bind. They desperately wanted to learn, to escape from the feelings of incompetence, but they could not take the risks of learning from each other. They were trapped.

The residents symbolically escaped from this trap by creating another graphic basic assumption. Over the course of two days, it became apparent that sexuality and sexual tension in the group were severely inhibited. People treated one another as siblings. From a psychological point of view this made sense, for sexual tension creates pairs that threaten to destroy group life as the couple differentiates itself out of the group.

This inhibition was costly to the group members, however. The women dressed down. They seemed to take little joy in their appearance. Those who were single joked about a prospective life of singlehood. The men seemed similarly withdrawn and neutered. They felt that they had to protect the women from the assaults of the hospital and that they were incapable of doing so.

The poignancy of this situation became apparent when, at the end of the two-day retreat, the group got together to pose for class pictures. In a moment of considerable humor, the men and women split apart. The men struck poses as weight lifters and muscle men, and the women experimented with various sexy poses and then settled on a chorus line. Humor, of course, is one road to the unconscious, the fun providing the safety to entertain unconscious wishes. In this instance both the men and the women were expressing the wish that they could be sexual in their group. But group life prevented them from experiencing their sexuality.

Yet they could not give up their sexuality entirely, and here basic assumption behavior played a critical role. During the course of the two days, one resident, Howard, played a vocal and frequently disruptive role in the group. He did not disrupt by showing anger but rather by joking about himself in a manner that evoked a cross between Woody Allen and a gossipy neighbor. I felt him to be passive and uncontrolled. There was something distinctively "feminine" in his manner, yet he often sat next to Paula, the sexiest woman in the group (or so I felt), and openly made eyes at her, leading others to laugh and titter. At one point, Paula, who was married to an airplane pilot, both joked and complained about her husband being unavailable in bed when he piloted a night flight back from the coast. Howard jokingly replied, "Well, are you available?" and the group laughed. Later, when one group member gently teased Howard about his apparent crush on a nurse, Howard, who was married, commented that his wife knew he could never get a date before they were married so she certainly wasn't going to worry now!

I puzzled over the paradox of a gossip in a sexual role in the group until I understood its symbolic meaning. The group was expressing its contradictory sentiments. Members wanted to feel more differentiated in relationship to the dependency group they had constructed. They wanted to be real, to feel sexual, to take the risk of learning from one another. But they were also afraid of being all these things. As a compromise, they constructed and reproduced a symbolic process, in the form of a basic-assumption pairing, in which the least sexual man was given the most sexual role to play. They could then create a pseudosexual life inside the group without actually disrupting their womb.

This was a classic basic assumption process. The group behaved as though it had been brought together to allow its members to differentiate from one another without facing the tasks of thinking, collaborating, and developing as a group.

The group was of course not always in this mode. Over the course of the two days Howard grew more silent as group members confronted their resistance to learning from one another. The pairing and dependency basic assumptions fluctuated in intensity, dancing in and out of group life. But as basic assumptions, they functioned as stabilizing symptoms, what Freud called compromise formations. They expressed wishes and desires while inhibiting the thinking and working required to make the wishes come true. Like dreams, basic assumptions are created effortlessly, expressing people's wishes to have a collective life without working for it. The basic assumption, which emerges from the matrix of nonverbal communication and unconscious projections, holds the group together while helping its members contain the anxiety of facing one another directly.

The Covert Coalition

Covert coalitions control anxiety through a more durable and sustained set of relationships. Most frequently these relationships echo the character of family life, but they do not do so arbitrarily or just in accordance with people's own family histories. Rather, people's propensities to take up family roles at work match the group's need to control task-induced anxieties. Two examples are helpful.

The Culture of Design

I once worked with an architecture firm that was dominated by the founder, Joe, who had been a mentor to some of the other partners. He was hard-working, demanding, and tough, and he took few pleasures outside his work. His attitude colored the firm's culture. For example, firm partners took little pleasure in the many awards they won. Certificates and plaques were not placed on the wall but were stashed away by the firm's administrator in an unused desk.

At a two-day retreat the eight partners of the firm were reflecting on their own commitments to the profession and to the firm. One partner, Will, suggested that at some point he might need to take an extended vacation, that he was overworked. But there seemed to be a covert threat in his statement. It was as though he were saying that he might abandon the firm when and if it became too stressful for him. Joe responded by reflecting on his commitment to hard work and "the dangers we take when we begin to pleasure ourselves."

Will responded with sudden anger, "Joe, are you asking me to resign?

"No, I'm not, Will."

"Well, I was about to."

"Well, fuck you," shouted Joe. "Go ahead and resign."

Will walked out. The outburst was shocking. The work until that point had been serious, and the group seemed both sober and committed to the retreat discussion. I later realized that the good work itself had paved the way for the outburst. The relative safety of the retreat helped Will to feel secure enough to reveal the anger he felt at Joe's puritanical ways.

At one level we might see this as simply the drama of a father-son relationship played out at work—the father demanding hard work, the son wanting fun. But of course Will is not a son. As an adult professional, he willingly participated and reproduced the puritanical and self-denying culture of the firm. This family drama was situated in and reinforced by a particular culture of work.

As I thought about it, it struck me that there was something functional about the culture. The firm was successful, in fact, world famous. Its success rested in part on the perfectionism of its partners. A good design covers all the bases. It succeeds when it anticipates the key contingencies and provides a blueprint that can be implemented without problems. Drafting and sketching often provide the psychological opportunity for being perfect. I have observed architecture students spend long but loving hours working over a draft until it is perfect. Their loving relationship to the draft reflects their fantasy that in fact they can create a perfect world.

The puritan culture functions in part as a psychosocial arrangement for controlling the fear of making mistakes, of not being perfect. This fear explains why, for example, the group could not display its awards. In a perfectionist culture people work to anticipate potential errors but, in anticipating them, they feel that they have already committed them. They displace the anxiety of making a mistake by the anxiety of anticipating one. In Freud's terms they replace real with signal anxiety. Indeed, this is the hallmark of the neurotic process. We feel guilty for our imagined deeds, not our real ones. Thus, in producing a perfect piece, perfectionists already feel sullied by their imagined errors and can take no pleasure in their accomplishments. (This is the same process that leads successful people to feel that they are frauds.)

I suggest that Joe and Will's father-son relationship was sustained and reinforced by the firm's culture of perfectionism. Joe's puritanism and Will's resistance symbolically represented the tensions of a perfectionist culture. The other partners managed their conflicts with perfectionism by projecting them into the struggle between Will and Joe. Just as we often find emotional relief in watching a play or a movie, the other partners could find relief by identifying with and watching the conflict between Will and Joe.

Looked at in this way, the covert coalition functions as a more organized and durable form of basic assumption behavior. It channels work-induced anxiety through relationships that are most often organized by the paradigms of family life. The durability and universality of the latter create a welcome framework for containing the anxiety. The father-son relationship enabled the partners to come together under the assumption that they could indeed be perfect without at the same time considering the costs and benefits of perfectionism. Instead of rationally assessing the costs of perfectionism and distributing its burden in some sensible way, they produced perfectionism through an unconsciously organized covert coalition. Will and Joe each had a personal valence for the role they played in this coalition, but they did not "cause" the coalition. The group created a space for such a coalition that Will and Joe could easily fill. The coalition in turn helped the partners avoid thinking and learning about its core task of design. In the end Will did not quit the firm.

A Consulting Firm

Similarly, I once worked with a consulting firm that reproduced a sibling family pattern to avoid key task-related problems. The firm was started by a vital and creative thinker and practitioner who gave it a resolutely interdisciplinary character. It was well known for its ability to approach clients from a technical, social, and psychological perspective. The founder then retired, leaving the firm to seven partners who sustained his work but were unable to give the company a new strategic direction. There was a sense that they were living off past ideas and methods.

In my interviews with the group I found that the partners took great pride in their interdisciplinary character. They all noted that each partner took up a particular specialty but coordinated his or her interests with the others.

The team character of their work was indeed an accomplishment, but it was matched, I felt, by an underdeveloped authority system. They had a loosely organized management committee system that was collegial in spirit but frequently incapable of tackling difficult problems. For example, the management committee could not define clear roles for the junior members of the firm, could not support the firm's investments in new research or service development strategies, and even had trouble tracking firm finances.

It became increasingly apparent to me that the interdisciplinary conceit of the firm was in fact a cover for repressed sibling conflicts among the partners. No one could inherit the mantle of the retired founder. This meant that no one could actually take the authority to give the firm strategic direction, to choose from its interdisciplinary talents and focus them for the purpose of developing new ideas.

Again, the character of the work played a critical role in shaping the underlying psychodynamic process. Interdisciplinary work must strike a balance between choosing a focus and deploying a multidimensional framework. Too much focus robs the work of its complexity; too little makes it diffuse and without direction. This is the core anxiety in shaping an interdisciplinary project system and its associated culture. But, unable to confront this problem, the firm's partners colluded to avoid it. This unconscious collusion was represented in a sibling relationship system in which the seven children of a powerful father agreed not to fight for the right to succeed him. By letting everyone be equal, the firm avoided the problem of consciously choosing or not choosing a new focus for the firm's work. By unconsciously controlling their central work anxiety through the mechanisms of a covert coalition, the partners faced the danger of becoming stale and uncreative.

The Organizational Ritual

The organizational ritual is the most durable and most externalized form of defense against work-related anxiety. I use the term "ritual" to express the idea of a procedure or practice that takes on a life of its own and is seemingly unconnected to a rational understanding of experience. Recall that Isabel Menzies analyzed nursing practices in a British hospital using this concept. (Menzies actually uses the term "social defense" to describe what I am calling the organizational ritual. I have appropriated her term "social defense" to describe the gamut of defenses against anxiety and have substituted the term "organizational ritual" to describe one particular form of defense.) She suggested that such procedures and routines as wearing uniforms and rotating nurses among patients were practiced primarily to control the anxiety of nursing.

The organizational ritual, in contrast to the basic assumption and the covert coalition, is impersonal in character. The defensive process is entirely externalized onto a set of mandated actions and does not depend on the emotional propensities of particular people. It helps all group members depersonalize their relationship to their work.

Depersonalization, however, is the foundation of neurotic behavior. We act out and we stay out of touch with reality by discounting the reality of other people and of ourselves. Thus the organized ritual reproduces the fundamental characteristic of neurotic behavior at the social level. People no longer participate differently in the defense. Indeed, as the nursing example suggests, the defensive routines seem absolutely natural.

The Concurrence Chain

I have come across a similar defense in government agencies and highly politicized companies. Employees who work in these settings use *concurrence chains* to organize the approval process. It works in the following way.

A director or manager writes a document that has policy significance and then circulates it to all the directors on the chain. If they agree with the document, they sign it; if not, they effectively veto it by refusing to sign. The document writer must then negotiate with each person who did not sign until everyone on the chain approves. When people on the chain feel politically exposed, they are careful in what they sign. On the other hand, feeling burdened and exposed, they will not read anything unless it is being put through the concurrence chain. This means that a manager who wants attention for *any* idea must put it through the chain. Most of management's thinking and communication is organized by the chain. Managers begin to think like lawyers. They scrutinize documents and pay undue attention to wording, fearing that if they sign they may be liable for some mistake later.

The resulting culture is one in which all members feel at risk, yet no single person feels authorized to make a decision. Delegation does not exist. Again, the nature of the task plays a critical role. In political settings the problem of interest group coordination supersedes the dictates of technical rationality. The manager cannot invoke technical criteria alone in making critical budgetary and programmatic decisions. But such political decisions promote more anxiety than technical ones. There exists no superordinate system of technical reality that can constrain interest group demands. The concurrence chain helps managers deny the primary anxiety of making political decisions by distributing decision making and accountability over the entire agency. Like the members of a firing squad, everyone shoots but no one knows whose bullet kills the victim. The concurrence chain depersonalizes the entire decision process, ultimately degrading the quality of decisions and quashing all leadership. The organized ritual completely externalizes the individual's defense against anxiety by organizing such defenses within sanctioned routines and practice. Indeed, in many government agencies managers believe that the chain supports work and decision making. It appears to fit smoothly and naturally into people's manner of working. "It favors consensus building," some managers have told me.

The Social Defenses as a Whole

We are now in a position to examine the three defenses together. They can be seen along two complementary continua: their durability and their visibility. As we have seen, the basic assumption is the least durable, whereas the organizational ritual is the most durable. Similarly, the basic assumption is the least visible; it externalizes the group's dream process and is rarely observed by its members. The organizational ritual is the most visible and therefore the most available for study. But paradoxically, as a defense becomes more visible and durable, its relationship to primary anxiety becomes harder to see and understand. People can experience a social defense simply, believing that the organizational ritual helps people to do their work and that the behaviors exemplified by the covert coalition are simply based on people's personalities, for example, "He is so bossy" or "She acts just like a child."

As a group's methods for escaping from anxiety become more durable and visible, the defenses themselves become more opaque in their meaning by appropriating an increasingly large terrain of group life. The covert coalition as a defense against anxiety appropriates people's personal valences for engaging in certain family alliances; the organizational ritual appropriates the symbols and language of the meaningful and rational, the manifest culture of the work group.

Thus the defenses against anxiety cannibalize group life. As they sink more deeply into work group practice and experience, they invade progressively larger domains of affective and cognitive experience. They appropriate dreams, then relationships, and finally actual work group practices. In the process they turn the irrational into the seemingly rational. This is why it is so hard to change the character and methods of a work group.

In order to understand the social defenses more deeply, in part II I present two case studies of their functioning. The first, a study of a covert coalition, demonstrates the origins and stability of a social defense and shows how it became less rigid through a consultation process. The case is of a disorganized leadership system in a state agency and demonstrates the links connecting uncertainty, leadership, and anxiety. By studying the consulting process I engaged in, we see how agency members reduced the power of a social defense by overcoming their dysfunctional projections and introjections.

The second study shows what happens when a social defense is attacked. The encounter is with executive nurses in a management training program. I show how my unintended and unthoughtful attack on the training program exposed its defensive and ritualized functions. The consultation occurred at a time when hospitals and other organizations were promoting women to positions of top management. My experience with the training program demonstrates the difficulties men and women face in working together. Moreover, by promoting women and enabling them to take jobs once reserved for men, organizations are stereotyping women less and consequently creating a more complicated and many-sided social milieu. This case study thus also begins to highlight some of the emerging tensions between social defenses and postindustrial settings. This latter theme is then taken up directly in part III.

II

The Social Defenses: Two Case Studies

5

A Modern Organization and the Sibling Horde: A Study of a Covert Coalition

When organizations get into trouble, the common response is to blame their leaders. Indeed, behaviorists and psychologists have developed an extensive literature on the characteristics of good leaders, emphasizing such factors as their maturity and their willingness to take risks, to learn, to delegate, and to trust. Although none of these characterizations are wrong, they are too simple, perhaps too true to be good. Missing is a theory of how a group chooses, shapes, and conditions its leaders. Common sense suggests that groups frequently get the leaders they deserve. But this wisdom poses deeper questions. How are leaders in fact produced by their settings? How do prior political and interpersonal relationships embed them in systems they haven't created?

The psychoanalyst Otto Kernberg argues that followers frequently blame their leaders to avoid facing how they themselves have contributed to the organization's actual or incipient failure.[1] Moreover, when groups face stress, they may induce behaviors in their leaders that stimulate failure rather than success. For example, followers wishing to avoid difficult and uncertain work may elevate an old or new leader to the position of a messiah. They feel protected in such a dependency role, believing that they no longer need to face the hostile environment that made them anxious in the first place. If the leader fails, as most false messiahs must, followers who trusted the leader and took no personal risks can then blame their leader rather than themselves. Here the immature group and the immature leader *together* produce organizational failure.

The Covert Coalition

The concept of the covert coalition as a social defense is helpful here. The relationship between leader and followers is patterned in part after people's experiences of authority in family life. We typically transfer feelings we have for our parents onto leaders, and leaders may imagine that their followers are in some way like children. Thus, in coming together, leaders and followers frequently follow an unconscious script in which available roles are integrally related through parent-child dyads. People enact such a system of roles if, by doing so, they can contain the anxiety of working. Such roles frequently promote conflict, but at least people are deeply familiar with them, and they can use them to fight for and defend themselves. They are on home terrain.

In this chapter I describe an organization in which a group of followers took on a role system in which the members were siblings to each other. These followers in turn were psychologically tied to a charismatic leader who had left the organization. This leader had managed to contain the anxiety and uncertainty of doing the organization's work by being tough and ruthless. The followers were afraid of him, but they felt that he could protect them from the broader risks and uncertainties they faced. They needed him. When a new leader took his place, the followers did not accept his authority. As a result, the new leader was unable to assert his authority and instead became one of the sibling group. The resulting covert coalition reproduced the primitive process described by Freud in *Totem and Taboo*,[2] in which a sibling horde struggles to possess and appropriate the person and body of the dead and powerful father. In the process some siblings form an alliance to "kill" other contenders for the father's body. Describing a covert coalition in such primitive terms seems bizarre, but the accuracy of the description testifies to the impact that covert coalitions as social defenses can have on work organizations.

The Problems of the Environmental Review Division

The Environmental Review Division (ERD) was a large independent division in the Department of the Interior of a state executive branch. Its seventy-five employees reviewed the environmental impacts of state-sponsored development projects or state-mandated plans and programs. The governor believed that the division was potentially instrumental in helping him to shape environmental policy, and he actively sought the division's advice and review. The division also reviewed the planning documents of private and public contractors engaged on state-funded environmental work.

The problem of toxic waste disposal preoccupied the division's leadership. The legislature had just funded a significant program for removing chemical wastes from poorly managed dumps and placing them in state-sponsored and state-managed dumping sites. Another division of the Department of the Interior, Parks and Waterfront (P&W), was commissioned to prepare the sites. ERD was asked to review and comment on P&W's plans, and the legislature had established an administrative hearing procedure to review both P&W's choices and ERD's comments.

The division's leadership had to cope with technical and political problems. The technical work was difficult. Hydrologists, geologists, and biologists on the ERD staff could not rely on proven models of chemical-waste leakage or ecosystem dynamics. It was difficult, for example, to know precisely how groundwater movement might interact with rock mechanics to create chemical seepage into rivers and lakes. Yet the ERD staff had to make such judgments continually when reviewing and evaluating P&W's work.

They also faced substantial political problems. For example, when a project team monitoring a waste site visited P&W personnel at the site, the members faced the delicate political question of whether community representatives should be invited to attend. On the one hand, they needed an informal meeting with P&W to thrash out difficult technical issues. On the other hand, communities might later claim that the division was colluding with P&W, striking deals and making compromises in private that would hurt communities and neighborhoods.

The division's leaders did not manage these problems well. Instead, the line engineers frequently felt that they made technical and political decisions with little guidance and support from top management. In one instance a project team reviewing a P&W document about a waste site near a river faced difficult policy questions: How broad or narrow should the review be? Should the staff informally consult with the P&W team? Should they advise P&W on the best way to model a particular process, or should they simply ask them to consider other approaches? The engineering staff complained with considerable bitterness that they had little help from the division's leaders in answering these questions. They felt set up to fail because the policy assumptions they made were sure to be contested later.

To cope, the staff engineers and scientists held back documents until everyone interested in their contents was satisfied with the arguments and conclusions. This procedure led to lengthy delays in

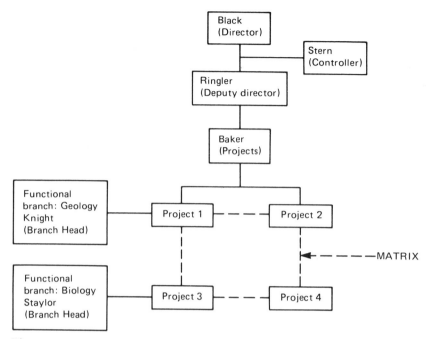

Figure 5.1
Official organization of ERD.

completing work and to conclusions that were ambiguous precisely because they represented forced compromises. In other words, because of the felt lack of leadership, the staff members did not feel authorized to take a technical position, to exercise their professional judgment. Many felt personally at risk for any technical initiative they did take. When our consultants interviewed the staff, they were struck by their anxiety and anger. The staff felt uncertain about the meaning, impact, and relevance of their work. Some even feared talking with us, thinking that they might be punished.

Some Organizational Dysfunctions

ERD's organizational design suggests why its leaders were ineffective. ERD was formally organized as a matrix. Engineers and scientists belonged both to a functional branch, such as biology or geology, and to a project, usually organized around a toxic waste problem at a specific site. Each engineer thus officially had two bosses, a project manager and a functional supervisor. But in the face of unresolved conflicts and long-term tensions, people felt that their

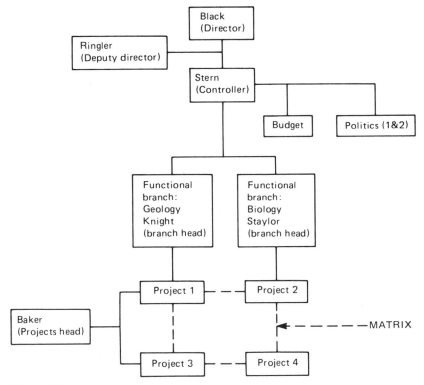

Figure 5.2
Actual organization of ERD.

official job descriptions did not fully match their existing power and role relationships. The manifest or official organization is depicted in figure 5.1, the actual organization in figure 5.2.

Three dysfunctions are evident from these two figures. As figure 5.1 shows, Ringler was the official deputy director to Black, yet Ringler actually functioned as a staff assistant to him. (Therefore in figure 5.2 he is drawn to the side of Black rather than below him, as in figure 5.1.) My consultants and I analyzed a set of decision charts that the leadership group constructed, and it was clear that no one ever experienced Ringler as having Black's executive authority. Black could not delegate his executive power to Ringler, so, when conflicts emerged—for example, between Baker and Knight or between Stern and Baker—Black was pulled in to resolve them. He could not rely on Ringler to keep him out of the daily fray.

Second, as the head of the different projects, Baker had to perform the critical task of technical integration. He had to integrate the work of the biologists, hydrologists, and geologists so that the division could produce technically sound policy recommendations. He was responsible for the division's final product. Thus in figure 5.1 he is placed in the chain of command, whereas Knight and Staylor are drawn in as support staff to the projects. Yet as figure 5.2 shows, the matrix was actually titled in favor of the functional branches. Baker did not have the authority and resources to meet his obligations as project head. Knight and Staylor had independent line authority. This was not rational. Organization design theory suggests that functional branches, such as biology and geology, should dominate only when research and invention are their primary tasks. If functional staff members primarily *support* project work, then they should be in a staff role, subsumed into the projects.

Third, Stern had control over a line activity that was integrally related to project work. Yet he and Baker fought constantly and could not coordinate their work. The division, as we have seen, had two political tasks: to manage its relationships to the legislature and other governing bodies and to involve communities and neighborhoods in its planning. The latter task in particular was central to Baker's work. Whenever Baker had meetings with P&W, he had to weigh the costs and benefits of inviting community representatives to these meetings. Similarly, communities frequently hired their own experts to review ERD's work and wanted access to certain technical documents. Baker frequently faced the dilemma of simply giving them the relevant documents or forcing them to go through a quasi-legal procedure of demanding access through a state ombudsman.

Yet Stern, though officially the controller, ultimately regulated the relationships between the projects and the communities because he could override Baker's decisions. Historical accident was significant here. In ERD's earliest years Stern had been acting director and, when he was appointed (actually demoted) to the controller's position, he retained the connections and controls over community relationships he had developed during his short reign.

This arrangement had two deleterious consequences. As the controller, Stern did not directly work with project personnel. Therefore, to regulate ERD-community relationships, he worked to formulate rules and policies governing project members' interactions with community groups. For example, he argued that informal meetings with P&W were politically dangerous and insisted that the division develop a procedure for calling and staffing such meetings. Project staff believed that such rules and policies limited their flexibility. They argued that formal policies did not match the unpredictable character of their monitoring work. Moreover, even though they ultimately had to review P&W work, they needed the chance to develop informal relationships with P&W staff.

Second, Stern and Baker did not get along. They fought over control of the projects, Baker arguing that Stern wanted rules where flexibility was required and Stern arguing that Baker's search for flexibility was jeopardizing ERD. Of course, differences in position between divisions are not uncommon. Such differences require that division heads negotiate with one another and separate roles from personalities. The conflict between Stern and Baker, however, was personalized. Neither liked the other, and they could not work out their conflicts.

Stern first contacted me several months before I began to work with ERD. He said that the senior managers were having difficulty working within a matrix organization. He asked if my team and I could train ERD executives to successfully manage a matrix organization. I suggested that a training program alone was insufficient. If ERD managers were to function more effectively, it was important for them to understand what difficulties they faced and why. Stern agreed and hired my team and me to work with ERD. Over the next half-year I periodically met with Black alone, with ERD staff members, and with the executive team.

Four meetings were particularly important. I first met ERD's executive team and their assistants when a different consulting group gave ERD managers a course on matrix management. Stern's assistant, Cameron, asked that I speak briefly to the managers at the end of the training program explaining how I would help them implement their matrix. Second, shortly after, my team and I interviewed the key ERD managers (the managers appearing on the organizational charts of figures 5.1 and 5.2) as well as some of the technical staff. I then wrote a working note to the executive team highlighting our findings and sent it to Black. Black distributed it to the executive team, and we then worked with the team for a full day to feed back our findings and assess the note's meaning. Third, as a result of this feedback meeting, the team asked us to assess more carefully how they had divided their roles and responsibilities. We then reinterviewed the executive team, using a decision-charting technique to map the division's structure of roles and responsibilities. We examined which managers had what kind of responsibilities for which set of decisions and met with the team again to review our findings. Finally, as a result of this meeting, the executive team and a colleague and I met for a two-day retreat to review the critical management issues.

Black As a Leader

When I first became acquainted with Black and the division, I guessed that Black's leadership abilities were central to the problems within ERD. Clearly his staff felt little support and leadership from the top. I learned it was Stern, not Black, who had taken the initiative in developing the matrix system itself and was in charge of bringing in consultants to help implement it. At the first meeting on matrix management, conducted by a consultant from another company, Black seemed to be playing a retiring role and participated as though he were just another staff member. Black seemed to be a kind of "shadow" leader.

A small but symptomatic incident early on was evidence of his passivity and carelessness. Before the feedback meeting we conducted with the leadership, I prepared a draft working note; I sent it to Black, got his agreement, and then sent down a final version. But Black distributed the *draft* to his team and, when I arrived, he jokingly wondered which copy he had indeed circulated. I felt undermined by his carelessness. He could not protect the conditions necessary for me to work effectively.

Another event before the feedback meeting helped me to understand how Black in fact undermined himself. I met with him before writing the working note, and we discussed what cover memo he would write to transmit the note to the leadership group. I said that in the cover memo he need not agree with the contents of the note—in fact, he might very well disagree with much of it—but that he should support the level of disclosure and frank discussion implicit in the note. He agreed but did so without affect, as though the stakes were negligible and he didn't care. His response made me anxious, and I became more aggressive. I told him that I would like to see the cover memo before he sent it off—perhaps he could read it to me on the phone. My response seemed to irritate him, and he suggested, as though out of pique, that I could write the memo myself. I felt the impulse to accept his offer but then pulled back and said no, he should write it. But I expressed my concern that what he wrote would shape my effectiveness as a consultant to the team. (In the end he wrote the memo and did not show it to me first.)

It is common to find the key dysfunctional relationships in an organization reproduced in the relationships between the consultant and the organization's leaders. This phenomenon is the analogue of the transference in the psychotherapeutic relationship, through which clients relate to their therapist the same way that they relate to other significant people in their lives. I believe that I was being inducted into a pattern of relating that mirrored Black's relationships to his subordinates. As I was doing, they would come to him with decisions and tasks. He would appear to be without feeling; they would become anxious and, to protect their effectiveness, they would undermine his leadership (as I almost did in the matter of writing his memo). Black in turn would withdraw further, confirming to his subordinates that in fact he could not lead and support them. I suspect that his affectless posture was a defense, a signal that he was anxious when expected to lead. If my experiences mirrored those of Black's subordinates, he and his subordinates created a "force field" of anxiety in which his anxiety as leader and their anxiety as followers undermined the relationships between them. Because the problem was not just within Black but in a field of relationships, it appeared that, if this force field could be changed, if new behaviors could unbalance the repetitive and stalemated dance of Black's withdrawal and his followers' retreat, Black's behavior could itself change.

The Feedback Meeting

Up until the feedback meeting I felt that Black was weak, indecisive, and overwhelmed by the conflicts and uncertainty around him. Black's behavior at the meeting was surprising. He was direct, sometimes blunt, and open about the dilemmas he had created for others. The day-long meeting included Black, his executive team (Ringler, Baker, Stern, Knight and Staylor) and Stern's assistant, Cameron. Some excerpts from the transcript of the meeting are illuminating.

1. [*After a long pause after the group members had finished giving their comments on the consultant team's working note.*]
BLACK: I'd like to touch on political versus technical. We should keep political issues on the top and not push them down on the staff.

Comment   "Political versus technical" is a way of talking about Stern versus Baker. Black is going to the heart of the issue after the first round of discussion and testing is over.

2. [*Stern has just finished talking about some of the dilemmas of his own role.*]

STERN: What is the identity of my branch, technical or political?

HIRSCHHORN: Can you develop guidelines for linking political with technical issues?

BLACK: Often Stern appears like the bad guy. Maybe we need a body for decision making?

HIRSCHHORN: Why is Stern taking the flack? Why don't staff see that the buck stops with you, Black?

BLACK: I'm hiding behind Stern.

Comment   Black confronts his own behavior in public, acknowledges the burden he is placing on Stern, and affirms his prior inability to lead.

3. [*There is further discussion of the difficulty of extracting technical from political issues and of knowing in general when technical issues pose implicit policy dilemmas.*]

BLACK: Let's take a case. Knight, what about case X?

KNIGHT: Case Y is better.

STERN: That case was straight technical, not policy.

HIRSCHHORN: Is this a problem, distinguishing between the two?

[*Discussion of the case follows, with confusion about its implications.*]

BLACK: How do you recognize whether it has policy implications or not? I'm not sure if I can do it. I depend on Stern to do it. This frustrates the hell out of you, Stern.

Comment   Again, Black empathizes with Stern and acknowledges that he must support Stern and participate more effectively in the formulation of policy.

4. [*They have been discussing some of the difficult problems entailed in inviting community representatives to meetings between ERD and P&W. If you invite them, it takes inordinately long to set up a meeting, and the meeting itself takes on a more formal and legal tone. But if you do not invite them, you risk having your decision reversed by the governor or the administrative court. Black acknowledges that they must develop clear guidelines here, but he believes that ERD cannot stop its work with P&W while the guidelines are being developed.*]

STERN: If you move too fast, the communities will get you later.

HIRSCHHORN: At any given moment there will be risks to take.

BLACK: I told Baker and he won't listen [won't hold the next informal meeting in the absence of guidelines].

BAKER: There is a perception that we are not sensitive to the communities. We need to figure out the real cost of due process.

BLACK: You are telling me that you're going to show me that it won't work.

HIRSCHHORN: Black is taking the risk, not you, Baker.

BAKER: This last issue [deciding if one can go ahead without inviting the communities] was a one to one with Stern. I have to coordinate better with Stern. There is a danger if you go too fast with these meetings.

STERN: I agree

HIRSCHHORN: This is a leadership issue.

[*I am supporting Black. It is up to him, not Baker or Stern, to decide whether ERD will go ahead with such meetings before contacting the community.*]

BLACK [to Baker]: Go have the meeting. I told you to go!

BAKER: I need to change the way I come to you.

BLACK: It's not the process.

[*Black is now insisting on his leadership prerogatives: "Listen to me, don't argue."*]

STAYLOR: I'd be happy with a procedure for having these meetings.

BAKER: The procedure is being worked on.

HIRSCHHORN [to Baker]: Who is speaking for the division? Do you believe Black is?

BLACK: Evidently not.

[*Black has confronted Baker, telling Baker that he is engaged in a "have it your way" tactic, bringing the discussion to bear on Baker's reluctance to follow him.*]

These samples are not extraordinary in their character. They reflect Black's general posture. He attacks issues directly, reflects on his own failings and limitations, acknowledges the ways in which he may be burdening his subordinates, asserts his leadership, and indeed confronts Baker about the latter's followership. This is not a passive or cowardly leader.

A Working Alliance

It is possible of course that, contrary to my original impressions and to the feelings of the staff, Black was indeed strong. But, if this were the case, it would be hard to account for the vacuum of authority felt among the technicians and scientists as well as the irrationalities of the organization design itself. I suggest that something more complex was happening: that I had formed a strong working alliance with Black. In the field of forces that had selected or highlighted his tendency for passive behavior, my alliance changed the balance of forces and allowed him to advance beyond his regressed and anxiety-ridden emotional position. Two vignettes are striking here. Recall the moment when Black asked me to write the memo to the group and I deferred. As I left the room, he asked me what I had heard about the quality of his leadership. I told him that people did not yet experience him to be a leader, that he had not yet put the stamp of his leadership on the division. He was silent, and then he thanked me, shook my hand, and then thanked me again.

What had happened? Consider the sequence. I described how he should write the memo, and he suggested that I write it. I declined and he then asked me for feedback about his leadership behavior. When I told him the truth, he thanked me. As I have argued, I had almost been inducted into a field of behavior through which Black typically invited his followers to undermine him. But rather than accepting his offer to write his memo, I was able to contain my anxiety. By withdrawing from this dance, I deflected my own countertransferential behavior and showed that I would not be like those who undermined him. *I passed a test.*[3] He could trust me to behave in a different way. Consequently he became more active and directive. He took the risk of asking me for difficult-to-hear information, heard the bad news, and thanked me twice for it. By sidestepping the behavioral field through which he typically colluded to undermine his own leadership, I helped Black get in touch with his ability to lead. Our working relationship deepened.

I passed a similar test at the beginning of the feedback meeting. At the opening of the meeting each department head briefly assessed the working note I had prepared. They liked the report and felt that it touched the key issues, although each person disagreed with some particular point or section. When each had spoken, a silence ensued. Black looked at me quizzically for about fifteen seconds, as if to ask, "What next? Where do I go from here?" I myself felt anxious. I felt that his silence and his quizzical look conveyed a question about our relationship in the room. Was I the leader of the group? Would I tell them and thus Black what to discuss next? I remained silent. It was only then that Black asserted himself by saying, "I'd like to touch on political versus technical."

Again, I believe that I had passed a test. Black looked to me for leadership, I demurred, and he could therefore assert his own authority. I had done my work as his consultant, as his collaborator, and I did not step beyond the bounds of my role to lead him. He could therefore take the authority of his role as a director. Our relationship provided a new model of relating that Black could use to develop his own leadership abilities.

The quality of our collaborative relationship, the way in which it helped to create a new field of forces surrounding Black and his role, can be understood by examining how it failed as well. Some time after the feedback meeting we met with the leadership group for a two-day retreat. They hoped to resolve key issues in their roles and relationships and to clarify the functioning of their matrix system. I came to the meeting with some anxiety. Recall that my team had met with the group earlier to review and chart the architecture of the key decisions they typically made. This decision-charting meeting had not gone well. The group could not agree on how they should organize the decision process for even one decision. I could feel their desperation. I hoped that I could help them contain their despair by providing them with a framework for discussion during the retreat and so sent them a memo on their organizational design options.

I met Black for breakfast the morning of the retreat, and he seemed confused. We discussed options for the retreat: how he might open it and whether the group might break up into dyads or triads to discuss particular issues. He noted that all issues were up for discussion except that "there would be no organizational changes." I was puzzled by his comment.

Black's confusion persisted into the meeting. He opened by noting that he had not been able to prepare a statement that "laid down assumptions" for the meeting. He then referred to a memo that Staylor had written but mistakenly called it Knight's memo. The meeting then deteriorated quickly to an overdetailed discussion of the memo, with Baker and Knight pulling out their own memos in a seemingly frantic fashion. I remained silent but felt trapped. I sensed the panic about me, but I could not act. I did not know what was happening. My colleague sent me a note saying, "The staff is undermining Black. Let's go out and talk." I demurred, fearing that to leave the room would further undermine Black. But, feeling empowered by my colleague's intervention, I told the group that it had yet to define its priorities for the meeting, that it was going too fast by jumping into detailed discussions of particular themes and options.

My comment authorized Black to take charge. He began to outline his objectives for the retreat. He noted that there was pressure from the staff, that he wanted Stern's and Ringler's roles better defined, and that the projects and functional branches must understand their relationships. He commented that ultimately he had to be satisfied about how the matrix would work, but then he repeated the injunction he had told me at breakfast: "I don't want to change the organization." The group then settled into a more orderly and less flurried and haphazard discussion. Black asked Staylor to take the floor and explain his memo.

What had happened here? Clearly both the group and I had responded to the failure of the prior decision-charting meeting with much anxiety. People had prepared memos, not simply to contribute to the discussion at the retreat but to ensure that they were heard. The memos protected individuals against the group's desperation, allowing them at least to establish their bottom lines. As Black visibly weakened, they pulled out these defensive memos. The consequent frantic and disorderly discussion was a sign that the last meeting had indeed made the group feel desperate.

I too felt desperate, and consequently I was paralyzed. I could not take my role as a consultant. Black's twice repeated comment that organizational change was not to be considered suggests how and why I became paralyzed at the opening of the retreat. Because I too felt anxious about the group's failure at the decision-charting meeting, because their failure became mine, I had written a report outlining their key organizational options. The report had a technical or technocratic air. It simply listed the key options (such as matrix, nonmatrix, staff-line organization, and so on) by recombining key elements in new ways. It represented itself as an exercise in combinatorial thinking. I was proud of it, for I felt I had presented them with an exhaustive list of their options.

But I suggest that the group members experienced this report as uncaring and unreflective, as if I could simply combine and recombine their relationships without regard to feelings, fears, and historical practice. Indeed, my pride in the note was colored by feelings of triumph, a sign that I was out of touch with my own feelings.

Before the meeting began, Staylor threw his own memo to me across the table. A copy of my memo was attached to the back of his. His gesture seemed aggressive and angry, as if to suggest that his memo could undo or obliterate mine. As the meeting got underway, my organizational options memo was ignored. It was neither discussed nor mentioned. Clearly it carried no authority. When Black finally took charge and asked Staylor to review his memo, Staylor went to the board and reviewed his model of a matrix using two organizational charts he had designed. I felt at that point that his memo was in fact substituting for mine, providing intellectual and professional guidance because I had failed to do so.

The memo and the feelings that led me to write it clarify why Black could not take charge at the opening of the retreat, why I felt paralyzed, and how in fact our feelings and behaviors were connected. I suggest that he experienced my memo as an attack on him and on ERD. Its uncaring and technocratic tone, itself a sign of my defensiveness and unwillingness to acknowledge my anxiety, communicated that I was not an ally. Black and his staff were under stress, and I was proposing to bend him and them out of shape with major reorganizations. By acting in a noncollaborative manner, I reorganized the field of forces that shaped Black's capacity to lead. He once again began acting indecisively and carelessly. Because I was out of touch with my own feelings I could not help him. As I regressed, he regressed.

Nonetheless, Black remained tied to me. When (with the help of my colleague) I recovered my role as a collaborator, Black also recovered. An incident at our breakfast meeting before the opening of the retreat highlighted our continuing interdependence. As the meeting broke up and Black left, I looked desperately for my clipboard. It was gone, and I was convinced that my anxiety had triggered a latent absentmindedness. I was not in good shape, or so I believed. I discovered on entering the group meeting room, however, that Black had accidentally taken the clipboard. In retrospect, I think that this small slip represented Black's unconscious need for me, his belief that he had lost me, and his fusion with me. Insofar as we could not collaborate as real or whole persons, he reconstructed our alliance in the plane of fantasy by taking part of me with him into the room.

This fantasy was a signpost of his continuing wish to work with me. Other people in other settings could have responded angrily to my uncaring memo, much as Staylor did. But Black's continuing tie to me enabled him to respond quickly when I transcended my anxiety and functioned once again as a collaborator. Thus, when my colleague prodded me (he later told me that it had looked as though Black and I were "sinking together"), I supported Black by highlighting the group's overly rapid rush to work, and Black then stepped in to outline his goals for the meeting. Once again, the lability of his behavior suggested that the problem of his leadership was not contained inside him but was shaped by a dynamic and fluid field of forces surrounding him.

A Covert Coalition

What behaviors shaped this field of forces? As I have already noted, Stern and Baker fought constantly. Their roles created conflicts, and they frequently had to fight to do their work. Many organizations are designed so that one division head must both fight and negotiate with another. For example, the sales division wants manufacturing to produce as quickly as it can to meet orders, but the plant manager wants to keep overtime costs to a minimum. In such a case the resulting conflict creates an optimal result; for example, sales levels are high but not as high as the sales unit wants them to be, and production levels are lower but not as low as the plant manager wants them to be. With Stern and Baker, however, there was a stalemated and uncollaborative quality to their fighting. The conflict was not functional.

An incident during the feedback meeting was quite suggestive. After the group discussed its problems and its frustrations with meetings, Baker turned to Stern and asked him to state the difference between policy and technical issues. Stern replied that policy is following division guidelines and criteria when doing reviews. Baker then stated, "Ninety-five percent of what we do is policy." The stage was set for an extended argument. Baker had challenged Stern to define the distinction between their roles and divisions. Stern had done so, and Baker had responded that in fact there was no distinction, that he, like Stern, was also engaged in policy work. But as the debate unfolded it got nowhere.

My experience was quite vivid. After awhile I could not understand what either was saying, what they really were arguing about. I found myself tuning out. More striking, everyone else was silent as well. The debate had converted the group into an audience. Feeling frustrated but also aware that something important was happening, I turned to the group and asked them if the discussion was clear to them all. Several answered no.

Baker and Stern then discussed their relationships to P&W again with no resolution. Feeling more empowered, I turned to the group and said, "There is a profound policy ambiguity here. I am shocked." Ringler tried to settle the argument or at least to create a compromise by arguing that the two agreed on key policies but disagreed on how to implement them. Stern, however, did not allow Ringler to make peace. He countered by saying that ERD did not have enough rules, that it did not give sufficient guidance to P&W, implying that Baker, who reviewed P&W's work, was not doing his job effectively. Again, after further talk dominated by Stern and Baker, I noted that the discussion had the quality of a "squeaky wheel." (Actually, I was using the term incorrectly. I meant "game without end.") Later I turned to the group and said "this squeaky wheel is stopping you from your work." Black then joined me and asked the others in an aggressive and assertive way what they thought about this whole drama. They agreed that it had blocked them.

The Enactment

What was going on here? Clearly Stern and Baker were enacting a social process within the boundary of the meeting.[4] Their stalemated and apparently meaningless debate reproduced the quality of their relationship at work and the impact of that relationship on the rest of the division. The conflict was without end and seemed unreasonable by reference to rational argument and facts. Clearly it was serving a different function. It not only paralyzed others, preventing them from thinking and talking, but it also crowded out Black. He entered into the discussion only on my coattails, when my two interruptions pushed him to interrupt the debate as well.

I had been somewhat prepared for this conflict. Our interviews before the meeting showed that people were quite preoccupied with the Stern-Baker debate. We had written in our feedback report that "the division can start to develop its organizational competence and solve its chronic problems if its leaders can better integrate their efforts . . . . Mr. Black, Mr. Stern, and Mr. Baker are key here. We suspect that the conflict between Baker and Stern crowds out Mr. Black. It is as if their struggle over resources provides little space for Mr. Black to develop his leadership." But this enactment during the meeting gave me a deeper and more empathetic understanding of this process.

The theory that Stern and Baker were simply struggling for power and resources would be inadequate. The two seemed more invested in the struggle than in its outcome. This is why the fight seemed like a ritual, like a game without end. The "crowding out" hypothesis suggests something more complex, though. Stern and Baker were arguing as a way of undermining Black's leadership. They were unconsciously colluding to "destroy" Black, using each other as vehicles. They had formed a covert coalition, modeled, as we will see, on the relationship between siblings.

Let us go back to the excerpt from the transcript of the feedback meeting in which Black confronted Baker with his refusal to go ahead and hold the community meetings. Black told Baker that he was not following orders. Baker argued first that Black did not understand the risks and, when Black did not back down, Baker suggested that Stern and he had to coordinate their work more effectively, because "there is a danger if you go too fast with these meetings." Then Stern, *for the first time since the beginning of their enacted debate,* agreed with Baker. The sequence is suggestive. When Black tried to take authority, the two antagonists became allies in stopping Black. Baker's statement that he and Stern must coordinate their efforts more effectively can be interpreted as a statement about their relationship at the moment. The two had to work together to limit Black's authority.

The Absent Leader

We have seen that a person's capacity to lead is shaped by a force field of other people's actions and reactions. Black's capacity to lead was labile, fluctuating with the dynamics of the forces around him and with the quality of his working alliance with me. The analysis thus far suggests that Stern and Baker were the key players in the leadership force field surrounding Black. What explains their behavior? Is it in their personalities to resist authority? Are they both simply jealous and competitive? To argue this would be simply to replace a personality theory of the leader with a personality theory of people in the leadership force field. We would achieve nothing.

The data point to a more systemic hypothesis, to the operation of a covert coalition. Baker, Stern, and Black were enacting a sibling system that was organized to preserve the memory and impact of an absent "father." After Baker resisted Black's authority, Knight entered the discussion, addressing Black with a strange and puzzling comment. "Well, you wanted us to be candid, so I can be candid here. I worked for a man who never made mistakes. When something was wrong, it was your fault. Black is different, and I want to protect him." At the time I found the comment puzzling and confusing, as if it came from left field. But in retrospect Knight's comment was deep and penetrating. It opened up a depth of knowing and feeling, and it came, I believe, straight from Knight's unconscious. (This is why it appeared so strange at first.)

Knight's comment highlights three psychological realities, at least as he experienced them. First, he is about to talk about something that requires candor. Second, the previous director, Harnwell, punished his subordinates and, third, a process of *reparation* is in order. Somehow the sins of Harnwell must be made up by treating Black differently. Let us explore these three realities.

People feel the burdens of candor when they have difficulty disclosing feelings, usually negative or hateful ones. They fear that, in speaking with candor, they will aggress against someone. Knight's belief that candor was required in talking about Harnwell suggests that he was or might be expressing negative feelings, feelings that could hurt someone or cause pain. But why?

People had told me about Harnwell when I conducted the initial interviews in the division. He had been experienced as a strong but frequently brutal leader, a man who would "dress down" others for their mistakes and who insisted that he never be "blind sided" by events. Grant, a subordinate of Stern, felt that Harnwell had hurt Stern. Stern had briefly been the acting director of ERD. When Harnwell arrived, he eliminated many of Stern's management systems and controls, and Grant felt that Stern never quite recovered from the murder of his legacy to the division.

At the end of the feedback meeting I directly experienced the difficulties surrounding talk about Harnwell. I noted that the division was in transition from one leader to the next, that "the previous leader had been very strong," and that he had been a mentor for some of those present. My comment met first with silence and then with some titter. Knight noted, "Well, he was mentor to *some* of us." I felt quite anxious, not, I think, because of the silence but because the group members were themselves visibly anxious. I had spoken with candor and so brought difficult feelings with their attendant anxiety to the surface.

Freud noted that people's relationships to their leaders, particularly to strong and demanding leaders, frequently reproduce the feelings we have about our parents, and in particular our fathers. Such feelings are marked by ambivalence. We want to have what our leaders have. We admire their power. But we also hate them for the burdens they impose. This conflict is frequently repressed by identifying with the leaders; we become them in our minds. We take on their characteristics and internalize the demands they place on us. We still feel ambivalence, but these feelings have now been forced into the interior of our minds. We experience them, for example, as conflicts between the demands of duty and the impulses to resist or between a grandiose image of our capabilities and periodic feelings of worthlessness. By taking in the leader, by introjecting him, we tie ourselves to the leader by restructuring our inner life. In the process both ambivalence and our identification are hidden from view.

People's experience of Harnwell, however psychologically brutal he appeared to them, was certainly marked by ambivalence. A discussion at the retreat was quite revealing. Group members noted that Black frequently seemed harried, hard to reach, and overinvolved in detail. Knight said that Black should do more "scheming and plotting" and noted with some humor that Black "should do something about his conference table" (which was always piled high with reports and memos). I noted that the conference table symbolized a role overload. Black was doing too much and did not seem to be able to delegate work to Ringler.

Knight then went to the core of his experience of Black. He said that Black was not tough enough on his subordinates, including Knight himself. "I think that one thing that Black may want to do is become more of a son of a bitch. I appreciate that you pick up an understanding of division work by reading all documents, but perhaps you need to develop a different model of supervising. You could say to someone, 'Look, I've got ten minutes. It's two o'clock. I want people to explain how this report fits into our work by ten after two!' You can jerk in the appropriate individual and you can then probe and punch as you want. That gets him in line. It forces me and my staff to worry about that kind of investigation. That is one of the things we had to do with Harnwell, and we made better products lying awake worrying about the questions we were going to get."

Knight was expressing ambivalence about Harnwell. Although Harnwell appeared to be psychologically brutal—Knight stayed awake nights worrying about an upcoming inquisition—he demanded good products. He held people accountable. He created a shop with professionalism. Note the strong military-cum-police metaphors that Knight uses: "punch and probe," "investigation," "jerk in an individual." Indeed, earlier in the meeting Stern too had used a military analogy. Reflecting on Black's sloppy desk, he noted, "At Black's level at State Police headquarters, there would be a sergeant sitting outside his door acting as an executive assistant. Nothing would get inside that the executive didn't think warranted his attention." In confronting Black's apparent disorganization and his inability to command subordinates, Knight and Stern *missed Harnwell*.

Why did Knight preface his comments about Harnwell at the feedback meeting with the supposition that he must now speak with candor? I suggest that he was struggling with his ambivalence toward Harnwell. A person's struggle for candor is linked to feelings of ambivalence and loss. As I have noted, we repress our ambivalence by identifying with the leader, transforming our ambivalent feelings into a conflict *within* our minds. But when we lose this leader, we become more in touch with our feelings and consequently with our original ambivalence. It is here that the problem of candor emerges, for in feeling our ambivalence, we become aware of our hateful feelings toward the leader, of the "damage" we have done to the leader in our fantasy life. Indeed, our anger has grown precisely because the leader has left us and made us vulnerable to the "outside" world. We worry about talking about the leader because we unconsciously imagine that, in so doing, we will do even further damage. Moreover, insofar as the leader still lives on within us, we imagine that, by talking ill of the leader, we may incite the leader to damage us. (This is the basis for the common superstition that one should not talk ill of the dead.)

Knight's preface about candor now becomes clear. The leadership struggle between Black and Baker stimulated Knight's feeling about his own personal struggle with Harnwell. But in coming into touch with these feelings, he came into touch with his hatred for Harnwell.

This is what he found so hard to talk about, what he found so painful, and what he imagined might cause pain in others. This process of coming into touch with his feelings explains Knight's peculiar comment about "protecting" Black. *He wanted to make up for this hatred.* Because Black was different from Harnwell, he wanted to treat Black differently. He wanted to have a less hateful relationship to Black.

Ambivalence, Loss, and Schisms

The question now becomes, How does this complex of loss and ambivalence explain the leadership problems at ERD? We have seen that Black was embedded in a force field shaped by his, Stern's, and Baker's behaviors. Stern and Baker colluded with each other to fight so that Black's authority was undermined. I have also suggested that the division's leaders had ambivalent feelings about Harnwell, their old leader, that they both hated and missed him. It appears that the leadership struggle, the dynamic triangle shaping Black, Stern, and Baker's relationship was embedded in the group's unresolved relationship to Harnwell.

How could this be? Consider the familiar phenomenon of a schism. When a powerful intellectual or religious leader dies, the followers frequently split into two groups, each representing a particular part or side of the dead leader. For example, the history of psychoanalytic thought might be read as a continuing reproduction of Freud's own conflicts between his scientific and his artistic impulses. Many of his students have introjected his scientific impulse, using or constructing a special language (ego, superego, cathexis) to objectify phenomena of the mind and spirit. Others have insisted that Freud's work must be interpreted humanistically, as a study of anxiety, the existential dilemma, the search for meaning, and the denial of death. They have emphasized the moral and religious character of Freud's thought. Each side is highlighting a particular dimension of Freud's work. Together they reproduce and externalize his internal conflict.

I suggest that *schisms are vehicles for denying the leader's death.* To see this, consider what would happen if there was no schism. Either the group would fall apart or a new leader would emerge by developing the old leader's thoughts. (The phenomenon of inheriting leadership through blood ties, common in family businesses, kingdoms, and certain religious sects, short-circuits this dilemma by preserving the old leader's blood in the body of a child or other relative. It too represents a vehicle for denying the leader's death.) The first possibility is not of interest here, but the second highlights the difficulties embedded in leadership transitions. The new leader, by taking or claiming leadership, is asking the followers to accept the death of the old leader together with the death of the leader's particular conflicts.

But as we have seen, the old leader's death brings us closer to our original ambivalent feelings toward him. Indeed, they intensify these feelings because we feel abandoned, all the more aware of our dependence on the old leader. Followers face a branch point. If they accept the new leader, they must come to terms with their hostility and their love, their resistance to the new and their dependency on the old. They must bring these feelings to the surface. If it is too painful to do so, they may instead keep the old leader alive in a manner that resonates with Freud's myth of the "primal horde": The brothers or followers psychologically kill the father or leader, who is then split into two parts and resurrected by being "eaten" (introjected) by the followers, among whom the leader's different "parts" (ideas, or tendencies in thought) are distributed. In this context, then, the struggle between Stern and Baker functioned as a schism to help them and the rest of the group to maintain their continuing relationship to Harnwell while denying their unresolved and hateful feelings toward him. This is why the debate went nowhere, why the group tolerated it in dumb silence, and why it prevented Black from taking the authority of his role.

Indeed, there was a striking complementarity in the postures or roles that Stern and Baker took in their endless fights. Stern represented the role that rules and controls played in organizational life, and Baker represented the requirements for flexibility. In part, these roles reflected the different organizational roles they occupied. Stern's job was to control budgets and plan systems; Baker's was to manage a highly unpredictable flow of review and assessment work. Stern needed the talents of a controller, Baker the talents of an entrepreneur.

But these complementary stances, produced in part by their complementary roles, reflected and reinforced a deeper psychodynamic complementarity. In a number of incidents over the course of my work with the group, I experienced Baker as deploying the defenses of grandiosity and Stern as deploying the defenses of depression and withdrawal.

Vignettes for each are striking. As the head of the toxic waste project, Baker clearly felt that his work was central to the division's success. At the retreat Baker insisted on his right to feel responsible for everything that affected the strategic direction of the division's projects. Knight appropriately responded that in such cases "I might as well be working for you [Baker], not Black," At the end of the first feedback meeting Baker said that, after reading our diagnostic report, he was upset and angry for the rest of the day. "We know these are our problems and have been working on them." In other words he saw the report as criticism and did not experience its authors as potential collaborators who might help. In addition, he took the criticism personally. The failures of the division were his. He *was* the division.

Yet another example of Baker's grandiosity is seen when, in preparation for the decision-charting meeting, we asked the leadership group to fill out a chart mapping how decisions were currently made and how they should ideally be made. Baker was the only member of the group to give *identical* answers for the current and the ideal procedures for each decision, as though there was no distinction between the current situation and a potentially improved one. Clearly he could not have believed that improvements were impossible; I interpreted his action as a communication to me that he did not want or need my help. He was self-sufficient. Insofar as he was acting in the transference (that is, he was transferring his way of relating to people in the division to his relationship with me)—and his bizarre behavior suggests that he was—he was also communicating that he felt self-sufficient within the division. He did not need my help, and he did not need the help of his colleagues. This was the defense of grandiosity that he brought to his role.

There was equal evidence for Stern's depression and withdrawal. After the first feedback meeting, I interviewed the leaders individually to ask them what they thought of the meeting. Stern sounded depressed. He noted that the "other antagonist" was continuing to fight and that he himself might soon give up. At the organizational diagnosis meeting the decision charts suggested that the others in the leadership group believed that Stern should not play a key controlling role in the division, that in particular he should not shape project policy. He was withdrawn throughout much of the meeting but said petulantly at one point that he did not deserve his high title and salary if his role was simply to consult on the decisions of others. When people then tried to draw him out further, he refused to talk. He seemed to be sulking.

Then at the retreat meeting Stern noted that in light of the discussion it seemed as though the toxic waste project should take on the key planning role, that his division should support but not ultimately be responsible for developing the yearly plan. He added sulkily and angrily, "If you [Baker] are supposed to initiate the planning process, then my expert, Tom, should be with you. Take him, goddamn. Don't give me a planning capability and make me into a body shop. I am perfectly willing to give my staff to you." Again, he combined anger and submission as if to say, "I've lost. I surrender. I'm worthless."

In other words, when Stern's conflicts with Baker taxed him or when he felt he might lose support from others, he withdrew and acted sulky and depressed. Despite his role as antagonist in a ritual fight, he also deployed the defense of being a victim, a dependent, who was weak and sad.

These vignettes suggest that Stern's and Baker's postures were not simply rooted in their roles but also reflected in how they managed their anxieties and deployed their defenses within their roles. Baker in his role had to emphasize the need for flexibility, for minimal constraint. But in his interpretation of his role this demand for flexibility merged with the claim of self-sufficiency, the claim that he should not experience limits or boundaries. Similarly, Stern in his role had to emphasize the centrality of controls and rules. But in his interpretation of that role the demand for controls was merged with feelings of being controlled, limited, and of little value. The schism was thus expressed by two levels of complementary behavior: the complementarity of the two roles and the complementarity of the defenses that each brought to his role.

This psychodynamic complementarity is in fact rooted in the psychodynamics of identification itself. Freud argued that, when one identifies with a leader, one can have one of two relationships to the resulting introject, or what Freud called the ego-ideal.[5] One can take this image of the leader into one's mind and then submit to it. In this case the ego-ideal becomes harsh and demanding, and one consequently feels worthless and depressed. Or one can combine or fuse one's own ego with the internalized representation of the leader or ego-ideal. In such a case one feels as powerful as the powerful leader or as grandiose. We thus arrive at the conclusion that the schism between Stern and Baker was ultimately rooted in the two alternative ways of taking in, retaining, and representing Harnwell: Harnwell as the punitive agent versus Harnwell as the omnipotent leader who brought greatness to the division.

Indeed, I suspect that Harnwell contained and displayed a parallel duality when he managed and commanded his subordinates. I never met him, but I suspect that he developed a contradictory image of the division in his own mind. I hypothesize that he imagined the division to be one that was important, engaged in great work, and central to the state's welfare, but at the same time he experienced it as vulnerable, weak, and subject to political controls. If this is true, his subordinates experienced him as alternately making them feel important and making them feel weak. In splitting him up, Stern and Baker represented these two parts of him to the rest of the division.

We thus arrive at the crux of our dilemma. Black appeared weak but not because he was weak in character. If we assume that Black has a weak character, we cannot explain his rapid gains in strength and capacity during the consultation. Rather, he was stressed by a field of forces, concretely represented in a covert coalition, in the three-way relationship among himself, Stern, and Baker. He consequently regressed to behaviors that made him weak and inadequate. But Baker and Stern's behavior cannot be explained by their personalities either. Rather, they were two parts of a schism that helped the whole group deny ambivalent and intense relationships to their lost leader. Just as Black was embedded in a force field shaped by Stern and Baker, so were Stern and Baker embedded in a force field shaped by the rest of the leadership group. Black's problem of leadership was thus shaped by a group process through which group members psychologically refused to relinquish their powerful but now absent leader.

A Change in Leadership

During the course of my intervention, Black's behavior was clearly changing. As we have seen, he was confrontational at the feedback meeting and continued to take more authority through a succession of meetings and other encounters. The quality of his change and the change in the leadership group was most evident at an all-staff meeting held several weeks after the leadership retreat. At the meeting Black and all the department heads explained how the division would work, how the matrix was to be implemented, and what philosophy would sustain its day-to-day operations. According to the reports of three people, the meeting was successful. (I did not attend.) In particular, a skeptical staff assistant to Stern reported that Black looked leaderlike at the meeting. She commented that he was active and articulate, that he answered questions effectively, and that he drew on the other department leaders to speak to particular issues. The leadership group looked like a team. In contrast, the earlier all-staff meeting on matrix management, conducted by an outside training consultant, had produced a set of angry and bitter comments from the staff. The climate of the division had clearly changed.

I believe that the two-day retreat was central to this change in climate. It crystallized and integrated the multiple learnings that were emerging over the course of the consultation. And I believe that the success of the retreat was based on the spontaneous, unplanned emergence of talk about Harnwell. The talk began with a discussion of Ringler's role, moved to a discussion of Black's aggression, and ended with expressions of ambivalent feelings toward Harnwell. Its underlying structure was organized around the relationship between Black and Harnwell.

The discussion began when the group reviewed Ringler's role. In analyzing the group's decision-making charts, we had found that most of the group believed that Ringler functioned as a staff assistant to Black. He had no independent line authority. Ringler confirmed this. He noted that he simply "bird-dogged" tasks for Black. Stern then suggested that Ringler needed to carve out his own distinctive area of work and leadership. Ringler suggested that his relationship to Black mirrored Black's previous relationship to Harnwell. (Black had been Harnwell's deputy just before Harnwell's retirement.) "Look at the way in which Harnwell and Black worked. Harnwell gave Black the low-priority waste issues, like garbage and smokestacks, and he took the chemical toxics. So when Harnwell was away and something came up, Black was in the dark." Stern, to laughter, noted that Harnwell *purposefully* kept Black in the dark. Black suggested that he thought he was treating Ringler differently, but Ringler again insisted that he simply "bird-dogged things for Black." In other words, Harnwell had emasculated Black, and Black hoped that he was repairing the damage symbolically by treating Ringler differently. Yet Black's lack of authority meant that Ringler could only bird-dog tasks, no matter how nicely Black treated him. Stern and Baker had continued Harnwell's work of emasculation.

Stern then signaled the deepening importance of the discussion by telling Ringler, "I am going to be candid. I don't mean to hurt your feelings, but I think the role you've played is more like a regular department head than a deputy director." In effect, Stern was suggesting that Ringler simply carried his previous authority as a department chief into his deputy role and consequently had developed no added authority from being deputy to the director. I noted that there was not much space for Ringler: "In a funny way you have a lot of powerful deputies in this room right here. I can count at least three."

Shortly afterward, the discussion turned to Black's role. Knight noted that Black's desk was sloppy and added, to much laughter, that his resignation would be in the mail Monday morning (presumably for insulting Black). There followed the exchanges already described in detail in which Stern suggested that there should be a sergeant at Black's door and Knight suggested that Black should be as Harnwell was—a "son of a bitch." Black agreed that he should be tougher but said that he preferred an atmosphere of learning to one of yelling and screaming. "We have people who are smart enough," he said, adding to much laughter. "They don't need the reinforcement of a son of a bitch." Then referring to his relationship with Harnwell, he concluded, "*I didn't like it.*"

At the end of the discussion Knight said that Black should be meaner, Black joked that perhaps he should dismiss people when they come to him unprepared, and Stern added somewhat plaintively, "I'm the bad guy on decisions that the staff doesn't like. On the matrix—even when you [Black] made the decision, I'm the one who was seen as the bad guy." Finally, after further discussion of the quality of their meetings, Knight noted that "in a democracy we fight each other; before we could just hate Harnwell."

This was a rich and provoking discussion. Three of its dimensions should be highlighted. First, despite the many references to Harnwell, the discussion was relaxed and frequently funny. The anxiety created in talking about Harnwell was gone. Second, it was the discussion of Ringler's role that triggered the talk of Harnwell. Indeed, Stern underlined the difficulty in discussing Ringler's lack of authority by prefacing his comments with his stated wish to be "candid." Third, through the discussion Black and Stern began to reshape their relationship by *exchanging identities or introjects*. This signified that their relationship would be less mediated by the emotional presence of the absent Harnwell and more by their current tasks. Let us explore each of these dimensions in more detail.

First, the relaxed conversation suggests that the group, and particularly the three principals, had already experienced each other in new ways. In particular, I suggest that Stern and Baker had begun to experience Black as a leader. His ability to take authority in the opening moments of the retreat and his capacity to confront Baker at the feedback meeting began to reorganize the relationship among the three.

But insofar as Black became more leaderlike, *the group had less to fear in facing their prior relationship to Harnwell*. In the past, if they had psychologically come face to face with Harnwell, two things might have happened. They might have had to acknowledge his loss fully and relinquish the relationships they produced among themselves to retain him psychologically. But doing so would have left them feeling exposed and leaderless in a hostile and uncertain environment. Or they would have had to face their hatred of Harnwell and the damage they had done to him (in their fantasies), despite the fact that he had been so "good" to them by protecting them. But to do that, to acknowledge Harnwell's goodness and his badness, would mean that they would have to come to terms with Harnwell as a real person rather than as a fantasy figure or transference object whom they internalized. In both cases they would have to give up Harnwell.

But with Black's assumption of leadership they could do both. In looking backward to Harnwell, they would no longer fear that they were without a leader. In acknowledging their hatred, they could relinquish their identifications, because Black was creating a new leader-follower system. Knight could acknowledge both the good and the bad that Harnwell brought to the division.

Second, Ringler's role triggered the Harnwell talk because it functioned as a projective medium for discussing Black's authority. Ringler was very much the "identified patient" of the dysfunctional leadership system. As I said at the retreat, there was no space for Ringler because two other pretenders to the deputy throne—Stern and Baker—were pushing him out. But Stern and Baker exercised such authority because Black could not deputize Ringler. Thus

Ringler's weakness reflected Black's lack of power. I believe that this is why Stern prefaced his comments with his wish to be candid and his fear that he might be hurting Ringler. But Ringler was quite candid about his role and persisted in acknowledging his weakness. It was Black who was uncomfortable with the discussion and tried to convince Ringler that he did more than bird-dog tasks. Stern's apparent fear of hurting Ringler displaced his deeper fear of hurting Black. Finally, insofar as the division was facing a leadership transition, Stern's fear of hurting Black was most likely nourished by the anxiety he felt in hating Harnwell. Thus, by examining Ringler's role, the group created a space within which Harnwell's emotional presence could be confronted.

Third, as the group elaborated its unconscious relationship to Harnwell, *Stern and Black could exchange identities.* A slip of the tongue was quite suggestive here. When Black was describing Harnwell, he mistakenly said, "I don't want to scream and yell at them the way Stern used to." No one but Cameron, Stern's assistant, caught the slip. She whispered, "No, Harnwell." Black had fused Stern and Harnwell in his mind. He identified the punishment he once experienced at Harnwell's hands with Stern's punishing presence; that is, he experienced Stern as blocking his functioning. This is perhaps why he insisted that, unlike Harnwell, he could not be tough. There is room for only one tough boss. Yet later he acknowledged jokingly that perhaps he should be tough. ("You mean I should dismiss people?") This joke freed Stern up to discuss his burden, and he complained that he does not always want to appear as the bad guy.

This was a complex interchange. It suggests that one reason many staff people complained about Stern was that, as controller, Stern had inherited Harnwell's psychological role. Black's slip of the tongue suggests that he too felt this way. But Stern resented this role and felt free to say so when Black in turn acknowledged that he too might be a bad guy when necessary. Black could of course acknowledge the need to be mean as the group acknowledged his leadership. Thus the two began to exchange identities. Stern relinquished his role as a part-representative of Harnwell (Baker was of course the other representative), allowing Black to succeed Harnwell psychologically. Stern released his introject, and Black took it on, transforming it to fit his particular role.

Black's behaviors and limitations, his passivity, his ineffectiveness, did not simply belong *to* him, did not reside *in* him. Rather, they were produced by a dynamic play of forces in an interpersonal field. Under these conditions change happens when the sum and direction of different forces change and individuals are not as constrained or hemmed in as before. I helped Black not by directly interpreting the core problem (indeed, I hardly understood it at the time) but by entering this force field and forming a working alliance with him. I entered it both in reality and through the transference. As a consultant to him and the group, I brought behaviors and resources that could help group members change their behavior (for example, I provided diagnoses and made interpretations). But Black also used me as a transference object. I became a representation of his conception, his internal picture, of how he related to others. By passing the tests he posed, by using my feelings as a measure of his experience, I changed the field of forces *for him.* He could then in turn change his behavior.

The Covert Coalition at ERD

Let us return to the theme of the covert coalition. Work groups construct social defenses to contain the anxiety of working. As we have seen, ERD faced significant political and technical uncertainty in doing its work. Because Harnwell was tough and brutal, he helped ERD members contain their anxiety. ERD members wanted Harnwell to push them, punish them, command them. By identifying with his power and authority over them, they felt calmer and better able to cope with their work. They traded the anxiety of doing the work for the anxiety of working for Harnwell. Consequently they could not tolerate Harnwell's absence. They missed him.

To contain their anxiety, they evolved a complex covert coalition through which Baker and Stern continued to represent Harnwell in ERD. Such a coalition, however, created much conflict. Neither Baker nor Stern could succeed Harnwell, for if either did, the group as a whole would have had to acknowledge Harnwell's absence. For the same reason the group could not allow Black to be the leader of the division. The result was a standoff in which Baker and Stern fought chronically, Black was consequently crowded out, and the remaining senior managers tolerated the battle. By enacting such a social defense, the three had retreated from the boundary of their leadership role and created a policy vacuum in the division as a whole.

I suggest that this resulting covert coalition reproduced a primitive family dynamic in which siblings fight each other for the parent's mantle. Unable to resolve their conflicts by banding behind one sibling, they ultimately divide the parent up so that no one can claim the parent's "throne." This scenario may at first sound farfetched, but as I have argued, it characterizes schismatic processes in many social and intellectual movements.

In *Totem and Taboo* Freud argues that this same process characterizes the underlying dynamic of much of family life and highlights why the incest taboo is so crucial and nearly universal. Freud spun the fantastic tale of a primal horde of brothers ruled by the brutal father who monopolizes the women. The brothers kill the father to get his women, but then, feeling guilty for murdering someone they loved as well as hated, they forswear any relationship to the women—the sisters—of the tribe. The incest taboo thus emerges to prevent a son from displacing his father in the family of origin. Freud presents the story as a plausible history of cultural development, but we can also view it as a primal myth, as a way of understanding the fundamentals of family life. The myth highlights three processes: Sons love and hate their father; the father is privileged because he alone among the sons can have sex inside the home; and sons compete with the father and among themselves for the attention of their mother and sisters. The incest taboo regulates these conflicts, ultimately preserving the family. Sons identify with the father rather than kill him; fathers protect their sons by keeping their sexual life private and out of view (and threaten them when the sons intrude); and brothers find sexual satisfaction outside the family.

Yet as Freud emphasized, the conflicts that family life promotes are not simply resolved; rather, they are internalized. In the same way that followers identify with leaders, a son identifies with the father through a complicated development process in which the son takes in the father as both an admired and a hated figure. The presence of a punishing father as an image or internal object in the son's imagination sustains the earlier external conflict and competition between the two. This uneasy internal equilibrium means that men in particular are likely to project this internal conflict outward once again, to experience it outside of themselves rather than inside themselves, when anxiety or stress promotes feelings of dependency and vulnerability. By projecting it outward, they hope to rid themselves of the psychological burden it creates while giving themselves a second chance to resolve it, perhaps this time in their favor.

Men are thus likely to create schismatic coalitions when the anxiety of working becomes too great. They project this shared family dynamic onto their relationships with their colleagues and so reproduce the original conflicts they felt in their struggle for authority, power, and prestige inside the family. The covert coalition at ERD functioned as a powerful social defense. By projecting out a shared image of family life onto the terrain of the organization, the senior managers of ERD could sustain the unconscious hope that their powerful father was still present, that he was not dead, that he would still protect them from the difficult technical and political dangers they faced. In this way they could contain the anxiety of working, though at the cost of chronic conflict.

6

Management Training As a Social Defense

As we have seen, the social defenses range in visibility and social depth. The basic assumption is the least visible, but it lacks depth. It moves in and out of group life without shaping the more permanent features of work and organization. By contrast, the organized ritual is more visible, taking the form of rational action and decision making. Yet at the same time it sinks deep roots into work life, creating permanent and structural mechanisms for containing and channeling anxiety. Because it is masked by rational and manifest procedures and policies, its latent function and impact are hidden from view.

In this chapter I examine management training as such a ritual, an organized system of behavior whose manifest and covert functions contradict each other.[1] By examining the links between a training program for executive nurses and the ritualized character of training events, I also highlight the impact of a complex social milieu, in which men and women work as equals, on a defense that functions by stereotyping people and narrowing their range of experience.

Ostensibly organizations support management training so that their managers can become more effective as supervisors, planners, and decision makers. Yet learning about management can itself promote significant anxiety. Behind the problems of management there frequently lie difficult interpersonal problems as managers find it hard to evaluate employees, confront peers, or correct superiors. Paradoxically management training frequently conceals and disguises this interpersonal dimension by offering managers a set of techniques and methods with which they can in fact bypass the interpersonal domain. The trainers promise the managers that they will be in control when they master the methods for evaluating subordinates or negotiating with peers. But this promise of control is nothing but the promise that the manager will not be surprised by anxiety, by feelings of danger and uncertainty. Thus management training functions as a social defense at two distinct levels: It offers defensive techniques, and it functions itself as a mechanism for containing anxiety by in fact denying it.

Training and Learning

A Case of Insubordination

The following description of a management problem was written by the director of a social service agency at a management development seminar I was conducting.

The personnel policies of my agency clearly state that personal days may be used only in the case of family or personal emergency or business. Requests for such days must be made at least one day in advance to me and are subject to my approval. If the request is granted, the staff member is responsible for securing the substitute and advising me of these arrangements.

At an in-service day at the beginning of the year, the entire staff had the opportunity to receive an interpretation of this particular policy and the personnel policies in general.

As she was leaving for the day late one afternoon, a staff member approached me to request a personal day for the following day to celebrate her birthday at a luncheon with friends. I asked her to clarify for me her understanding of the personnel policy as it related to this matter. She stated she was uncertain, so I opened the Manual. Together we read the statement: "Personal days should be used only for personal and/or family business or emergency."

I recalled our in-service discussion and prodded the memory of the staff person to do likewise. "Yes," she said, "I do remember that these days are for business or emergency use." After a brief discussion I asked if she wanted to consider other arrangements we might make (a day off without pay, leaving an hour early). Since she had no remaining vacation days, the use of one was not an option. "No, I withdraw my request" was her response.

Throughout the conversation I wanted to help the staff member realize that her request was inappropriate in the light of our policies. I wanted her to withdraw her request; I did not want to have to deny it. I also wanted to suggest alternatives, so her plans could be kept.

When the staff member left my office, I was under the impression that she would rearrange her plans and work her regular shift the following day. There did not seem to be any hard feelings about needing to do this.

The following day the staff member did not arrive for work, did not secure a substitute, and did not contact me. When I reached her at home by telephone to express my concern, she related that she did not agree with the policy and had decided to take a "personal day" anyway.

This case highlights the difficulties managers frequently face in supervising subordinates. The director is clearly uncomfortable with the subordinate. She strikes a passive stance throughout the encounter. She wants to say no but cannot. Instead, by leading the subordinate through a set of Socratic questions and answers, she tries to get her to withdraw the request. The director refers to the personnel manual, asks the subordinate to interpret it, recalls the in-service training day, and proposes other methods for taking the day off, but she never says no.

The strategy fails. Indeed, it seems on first reading that the director's indirection and passivity has produced insubordination. The subordinate senses the director's ambivalence and uncertainty and consequently decides for herself. Isn't this a case of a "weak" manager who cannot take authority?

Using Role Plays

I have used this case a number of times as a stimulus for role plays during management training sessions. I ask participants to volunteer to play the director and the subordinate. After the participants complete a role play, I discuss it with the group as a whole. Typically, members will propose alternative ways of acting, and I in turn will ask them to enact their suggestions in a role play. Thus in any given training session the group can produce a number of versions of the basic dilemma. The role play functions as a projective test for managers. Their responses, like the case itself, provide valid data about the dilemmas of managing others.

Certain patterns and themes have emerged from these role plays. People who volunteer to play the manager typically start by denying the subordinate's request for a personal day. They refer both to the rules and to difficulties of staffing the service when someone so unexpectedly takes a day off. But those who volunteer to play the subordinate pose new and unexpected problems for the manager in the role play. They argue that they have made arrangements for a backup, that such arrangements have worked before, and that the birthday party is important to them. These arguments stymie the role-playing manager, who typically refers back to the rules, emphasizing that birthdays simply do not come under the category of personal business. The role-playing subordinate may then make a plea based on the excellent quality of her past work and her proven dedication to the agency. She has given much to the agency and has done more than the minimum. Why can't the director show some flexibility?

The director is now in a dilemma: If she continues to say no, she appears uncaring and inflexible. The role-playing director generally chooses among four options. First, she may become even tougher by appealing to the sanctity of the rules, the board that stands behind them, and the authority vested in them. She acts to represent the rules in the encounter and takes on their presumed authority. The rules now appear as ironclad, despite the fact that they appear only in a manual rather than in a contract or charter.

Second, the director appeals to the rules but distances herself from them. She tells the subordinate that she didn't make the rules, that perhaps they are inflexible, but that they must be obeyed. Sometimes role-playing managers carry this strategy further by psychologically siding with the subordinate, noting that "I don't like these rules or the bureaucracy they represent," implying that, "If it were up to me, you could take off."

Third, the manager might ask the subordinate to step into her shoes, to consider the difficulties she would face as a result of this request. "What will happen if I make an exception in your case? How will I handle similar requests in the future? What if everybody else could reinterpret the meaning of personal business for their own purposes?"

Fourth and most infrequent, the role-playing manager, after some fruitless discussion, says, "Take a personal day and don't tell me what you used it for." This strategy has been chosen twice; on one occasion the manager seemed relaxed in saying it, and on the other she was angry, muttering under her breath, "This will cost you some." In almost all cases the role-playing manager feels frustrated and seems stuck.

Abdicating the Managerial Role
What is going on here? At first it looks as though the manager faces a problem of insubordination. The staff member asks that a rule be violated and, when her request is denied, she takes off anyway. She is violating the manager's authority. But is she? Indeed, when we review the actual case and the strategies the role players choose, it is clear that the manager has violated *her own* authority, her role. In the actual case she manages by indirection, never taking a position in the encounter. In the role play she appeals to the fantasy of ironclad

rules or cynically sides with the subordinate ("I don't like this any more than you do") or appears as a victim about to be overwhelmed by requests for more exceptions. In each case the manager steps out of her role and announces that indeed she has no authority. If these role plays uncover the hidden structure of this case—and I think they do—it is not surprising that the subordinate feels empowered to judge the relevance and fairness of the rules without consulting the manager any further.

Yet it should be remembered that role-playing managers choose these strategies because their first "hang tough and say no" strategy fails as well. When they simply deny the request, the subordinate appeals on the basis of her special contributions to the agency and the special circumstances of the moment. It is this appeal that subverts the first strategy.

This moment highlights the particular dilemmas of managing people. A manager's primary task is in fact to interpret rules and apply them to particular situations, to make exceptions when necessary, and to integrate the nonformal flow of information, people, and resources within the formal system of rules of behavior and principles of work. If rules could be applied without regard to context, managers would have no role. They would be police officers charged with catching rule violators, not managers charged with integrating people and tasks in frequently changing settings. The role-playing managers step out of their roles the moment they reject the task of considering whether and how an exception might be made.

The Role of the Self

But what makes this central and defining task of managing people so difficult? Most fundamental, *the manager must bring her person, her self to her role.* She must invest her role with the dimension of her own affects. Because rules must be interpreted, people must use their feelings to direct them in a particular situation. Feelings frame or color a situation, providing a context for the further interpretation of data. Managers must, as the expression says, "go with their gut."

But doing so frequently is difficult because our own feelings make us anxious. Consider the case again. It is likely that the manager is indirect, cautious, and manipulative because she is in fact feeling exploited, being taken advantage of or played with. The request at one level is superfluous. Why can't the employee simply take the personal day without announcing its purpose? Why is she putting the manager in such a position in the first place? But when we feel resentful, we in turn feel a whole congeries of feelings, such as anger, the wish to strike back, the desire to be cruel, self-pity, and guilt ("What bad deed did I do to trigger this attack on me?"). The manager cannot possibly act unless she sorts out these feelings during the encounter.

But in sorting out our feelings, we experience even greater anxieties. The only person who can help the manager understand her feelings is the subordinate herself, the very person who is the cause of all the manager's trouble. The subordinate has the missing pieces of the puzzle, represented by her feelings, which complement the manager's feelings.

For example, at one point I asked people in the seminar to play out the meeting the next day when the manager confronts the subordinate. In one role play the manager nervously stumbled through an opening remark highlighting the conflicts and confusions she faced in enforcing rules she did not like. The subordinate seemed to understand the manager's predicament. She smiled and noted that she too thought that some personnel rules in the agency were inflexible and should be changed. The subordinate in the role play then accepted the penalty of taking a day without pay. She had been understood.

When I observed the role play, I understood for the first time why the subordinate might have come to the manager in the first place. For reasons unspecified in the case description, the subordinate probably felt that the burden of personnel rules in the agency was excessive, particularly for those who committed unusual energy, time, and thought to their work. Thus the subordinate, far from being a hostile and uncooperative staff member, felt exploited. But lacking the maturity to express this feeling directly, she acted it out by requesting that a birthday party be considered personal business. The manager's feelings of being exploited complemented the employee's feelings. However, the real manager could have grasped this only if she had explored her own feelings with the subordinate in the encounter itself. She might, for example, have said, "You know, I am feeling put upon by you. You are a very good employee. Others in your position might just have taken off without telling me why. Why are you making a case out of this? You've put me in a position where I feel silly. What is going on here?"

This statement might then help the employee understand her own unconscious intentions: She has requested a personal day because she wants to feel acknowledged and recognized for the good work she has done. The manager's questions will satisfy her in two ways. The manager acknowledges her contributions and is honest with her. She is likely then to withdraw her request because she feels connected to the manager. But as this example shows, if the manager is to bring herself to her role, she must reveal her feelings to another, and this is at the root of the anxiety people face in managing others.

To manage others is to assess the particularities, the uniqueness, of a single situation. To do so we must bring ourselves, including our affects, to our roles. It is striking, therefore, that management training is predicated on just the reverse set of assumptions. Trainers offer managers a set of tools and techniques they can use to control encounters. For example, when a manager appraises a subordinate, the encounter is potentially a highly charged one. Yet subordinates report that it is almost always disappointing, flat, and frequently unfair. A performance appraisal technology has emerged to defend the manager against his own affects. The manager is told how to give feedback (say something nice, before saying something negative), is advised to define the goals for the encounter (the subordinate should understand his or her weaknesses), and is introduced to a variety of appraisal forms that help categorize what are really gut responses to the subordinate's performance. The central purpose of this technology is to help the manager retain control over the encounter, so that it contains no surprises.

This model of the appraisal encounter defeats the encounter itself. The performances of subordinate and supervisor are intertwined. The weakness of one may complement the mistakes of the other. (For example, the subordinate never knew he was performing incompetently because the supervisor feared telling him so.) But if the supervisor and the subordinate are to understand their interdependence, they must bring themselves to their roles, revealing themselves to each other, so that their particular experiences can be clarified. ("I was afraid to ask you how I was doing," or "I felt so bad giving you so undefined a task that I never asked how it was going.")

This same anxiety plays a central role in distorting management training. The anxiety that surrounds bringing one's self to a role can invade and overload the management training encounter itself. Whenever I have used the just described role play in a training session, invariably a few people become angry with me. Usually their anger takes a paranoiac turn. They believe that I am withholding the truth from them, that even though I know how to handle the encounter, I will not tell them, that I am deliberately frustrating them and deskilling them. One woman was convinced that throughout the role plays I had deliberately ignored her when she raised her hand for attention, that I called on only a selected few of my favorites to speak (even though I knew hardly anyone in the group before the training). Two other men (on different occasions) angrily insisted that I finally give them the answer of how to deal with the subordinate. They faced just this problem in "real life" and needed to know how to handle it.

I could not convince these people that there were no answers. Rather, the answer lay in the way of getting answers, in the way people use their affects in collaborating at work with others. This "meta-answer" had to be experienced, and frequently only if people felt frustrated in trying to find an answer could they understand the deeper dilemma they faced.

Anger and Projection

Why do people become angry with me when I present this case? What might account for the belief that I am persecuting them? The process of projection plays a critical role here. When people in the role play (and those who watch and identify with the role play) fail to control the encounter with the subordinate, their frustration mounts and their sense of failure grows. But when people feel that they have no control, they in fact feel persecuted. The experience stimulates those superego voices within us, voices we acquire early that take us to task for being worthless and helpless. Insofar as these voices are difficult to bear, people project them out onto others, whom they construe as their true persecutors. Thus the attacks on me were basically projections. People who felt attacked, because they felt helpless and out of control, attacked me in turn.

Another example from management training illustrates the process clearly. I was a trainer at a management seminar sponsored by a state hospital association council. I was lecturing the participants on methods and approaches to "retrenchment" in organizations. The lecture was going well, about a third of the fifteen members of the group were participating actively, and Joan, my sponsor from the association, was pleased. She had to leave after lunch but told me that she wanted to do this program again in another city sometime in the spring.

But the evaluations of the seminar revealed that some participants had hated it. They had come to learn practical techniques for laying people off, and I had cast the training materials too abstractly, focusing on strategic planning and cutback management rather than on layoff policies. My approach and their expectations had not matched.

When Joan called me to discuss the evaluations, she seemed desperate. Would I accept a smaller fee, she asked, because she had to return money to those people who had been so terribly disappointed? At first I felt terrible. How could I have failed so badly that my sponsor wanted her money back? But a few seconds' thought led to feelings of surprise and bewilderment. Joan's request was most puzzling for several reasons. First, some participants had enjoyed the seminar. Second, Joan had enjoyed the morning session, and, third, it was rare for people to ask for their money back.

I asked Joan to look again at the evaluations (I had collected them before sending them on to her); I felt that they were mixed. I remembered that about one-third liked it, one-third did not, and the rest had a mixed experience. She responded that those who liked it "were few and far between." This phrase puzzled me. It exaggerated the general scope or dimension of the event itself, as though hundreds had attended so that the five who had enjoyed it represented a tiny percent of those present. Some aspect of her experience had led her to exaggerate the voices of those who had been disappointed. That is why she herself sounded so desperate. (Later, Joan sent me my full fee without further discussion. I assume because she had reviewed the evaluations and seen that indeed the pattern was a mixed one.)

What was going on? I suspect that those who had been disappointed in my lecture had in fact felt stupid and incompetent while attending it. When I initially planned the lecture, I had imagined that hospital presidents and vice-presidents would be attending—people who would have had a central interest in strategic planning. Instead, there was a sizable number of third-level administrators—people who reported to the personnel director, for example. Typically these people do not engage in strategic planning discussions, and they are not used to developing theories of their situation. Rather, they are in charge of implementing particular procedures.

When they receive training, they expect to be given techniques that they can apply immediately. The participants in my seminar simply could not relate to my material. I did not touch their experience and their sense of vocation. Indeed, as Joan told me, several were asked by their bosses what they had learned, and they "threw up their hands," suggesting that they felt helpless to respond, that their experience made them speechless.

Feelings of helplessness trigger feelings of rage. (This is one of the central experiences of infancy.) I suggest that Joan became the repository for these feelings of helplessness and rage, and a chain of rage and anger was created. It began with the disappointed members who felt incompetent at my lecture, helpless in front of their bosses, and enraged at the hospital association and at Joan. Joan in turn felt helpless and desperate and, to punish me, she asked me for her money back. I then felt bad about my failure and guilty for not having developed a clear understanding of who would be attending my lecture. My failure, I suspect, reflected my own ambivalence about conducting training seminars. Thus a process of projection shifted feelings of helplessness and rage from the seminar participants through Joan onto me.

Two Models of the Training Situation

Adult learners face a complex problem when attending management training sessions. In coming to learn, they experience their ignorance, their lack of skills. If they develop a secure relationship with their teacher or trainer, they may feel protected from the consequences of their own ignorance. The trainer stands between them and the superego voices that admonish them for their stupidity. In short, they regress: They become the trainer's children, and the trainer becomes their parent. An appropriate relationship of dependency emerges between the two. But if for some reason they fail to develop this relationship, they can be overwhelmed by the experience of their own helplessness and consequently turn on the trainer, transforming their self-punishing impulse into attacks on the trainer.

The relationship between the teacher and the adult learner is thus central to the learner's experience. The psychoanalytic concept of the "transitional object" is helpful here. Winnicott argued that an object such as a child's teddy bear helps the child separate from his mother.[2] The object stands both *for* the mother and *between* the child and the mother. The child projects onto the teddy bear the good relationship he has with mother and so feels protected by the teddy bear in his mother's absence. As the child develops, he then takes back or reintrojects those images and good feelings associated with his mother. He no longer places them in the teddy bear but rather contains them wholly in his own mind. The teddy bear thus helps the child make the transition from dependency to independence.

Adult learners I suggest, need a similar transitional object to secure both their dependent state and their potential for learning. If they were totally dependent on the teacher, they would not learn; but if they had no experience of psychological support, they would be overwhelmed. Two relationships between the adult learner and the training situation are possible. First, *techniques themselves can function as transitional objects.* They help adult learners make the transition from feelings of incompetence to feelings of competence. As adult learners feel competent, they depend less on the technique and more on their own situational judgments and intuitions. They personalize their use of the technique. Second, a working alliance between the trainer and the learner can create a *transitional relationship.* Adult learners can depend on the teacher to protect and help them as they develop their competence. When neither of these relationships is present, the projective process takes hold, and feelings of hate and punishment distort if not destroy the potential for learning. Let me briefly explore these two relationships.

Technique As Transitional Object

Figure 6.1 depicts the situation in which technique functions as a transitional object. Technique is operating here as a transitional system between the teacher and the learner on the one side and the learner and the outside world on the other. The learner becomes

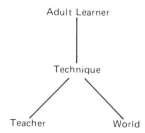

Figure 6.1
Technique functions as a transitional object.

indirectly dependent on the teacher by accepting the authority of the technique that the teacher has mastered and then, by mastering the technique, becomes independent of the teacher. This process actually has four steps. First, the adult learner identifies with the teacher by attributing authority to the technique. Second, the adult learner uses the technique to master a confusing and difficult situation in the world, gaining authority in the world by identifying with the authority of the technique. Third, as the learner becomes more comfortable with the technique and the situations encountered, he uses the technique with increasing flexibility so that his relationship to the world becomes more direct. Fourth, as the technique becomes invisible, as the adult learner internalizes it, he in turn differentiates himself from the teacher.

These relationships will fail, of course, if the technique functions as a fetish. Fetishes are not transitional objects. Like sexual fetishes, they block relationships between people and are used inflexibly. Social-scientific methodologies that are used indiscriminately function as fetishes. For example, social scientists frequently overuse surveys and polls to distance themselves from the complex meanings of particular situations. They eschew interpreting reality because, to do so, they must take the risks of proposing hypotheses and theories that are not clearly evident or retrievable from the data. Thus the technique functions as a fetish in two ways: It distances social scientists from real people and helps them to sustain the fantasy that the technique has the answer. In empowering the technique, the social scientists deauthorize themselves.

The Transitional Relationship and the Working Alliance

When the training is not based on technique, when, for example, the teacher wants to promote the study of self, a much more implosive and complex learning situation emerges. Consider figure 6.2.

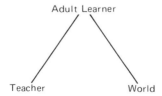

Figure 6.2
Student confronts the teacher and the world directly without the mediation of technique.

Technique drops out, and the adult learner and the teacher depend directly on one another in confronting the world. This implosive arrangement poses a difficult set of problems. For example, when I ask trainees to work through role plays, they must face the particularities of the world without a technique. They feel frustrated, and therefore, as we have seen, they punish me for not protecting them. (Evaluation forms function in part to reduce the overt level of hate by providing a silent mechanism for punishing the trainer.) They can learn and I can facilitate their learning only if I develop a working alliance with them in which I become a complex object for them. They experience me as a source of frustration, but they also experience me as someone who stands to the side of their experience, interpreting it. I am in transition between two frames of reference they use to apprehend me. Similarly, they are in transition between two relationships they have to me. I am their teacher, insofar as they feel dependent on me and look to me for guidance. But I can also become their collaborator as they pass through a stage of frustration and discover their own expertise and capacity to learn. (In psychoanalysis this double relationship is the sine qua non of a positive or therapeutic transference.)

The chemistry of the working alliance depends on two processes. First, I must be able to empathize with their difficulties in learning, and they must experience my empathy. Second, they must identify with my observing and interpreting stance so that they can deploy their own "observing ego." The observing ego helps them to stand to the side of their own helpless feelings and so decreases those feelings of helplessness. This relationship can fail if I fail technically, if I cannot empathize with them and cannot stand to the side of their experience, or if they cannot accept my empathy and discover their own observing ego.

Management Training As a Compromise Formation
Management training thus poses critical emotional dilemmas for those who train and those who are trained. In taking their roles, managers must understand a situation in its particularities. They must make judgments and apply rules where exceptions must be made. To do so, they must bring themselves to their roles and get in touch with their affects. But that, as we have seen, provokes anxiety, and consequently many managers employ techniques, such as per-

formance appraisal methods, to distance themselves from their own feelings and thereby from their subordinates.

The management training encounter reproduces this problem. On the one hand, the trainer and the students may be able to confront one another directly, discovering how and why they have become obstacles to each other within the learning process. If they succeed, the process of learning about managing becomes the model for managing itself. The students do not learn a technique but learn how to use their affects to explore particular situations. Supported by a working alliance with the teacher, they learn how to learn. On the other hand, the trainer and the students can avoid this difficult situation by focusing on techniques that delimit the encounter between the students and the teacher. The technique, in controlling the anxiety of learning, then plays a double role: It functions as a fetish, and it masks the real dilemmas of managing.

Freud described neurotic symptoms as *compromise formations*,[3] which integrate a wish for pleasure with an injunction against the wish. Management training is also a compromise formation. It has emerged as a major activity within companies because senior managers realize that their subordinates must learn to supervise others more effectively. Yet it is paradoxically organized to suppress just this learning. This contradiction is a sign of the anxiety that suffuses both learning and managing.

A Program for Executive Nurses

A Frustrating Encounter

I experienced many of the compromises and dilemmas of the management training setting with a group of executive nurses in a three-week management development program. Not only did I stumble into the problems of the working alliance, but I also learned too late that these problems become immensely more complicated when men and women work together as equals. While thinking that I was challenging the female executive nurses to improve as managers, I actually stimulated the anxiety they feel when working side by side with male managers. I accidently exposed the links between feelings of dependency and sexuality and, by potentiating this volatile combination, I psychologically suffered as well. In its three years of operation, the program was rated highly by the participants, and the chief executive officers of the participating hospitals were satisfied. But my experience suggests that the program's success was purchased at the price of denying the underlying tensions and conflicts that emerge when men and women work together.

The management development program had a prestigious aura about it. It was taking place at an excellent midwestern university that had a well-known public policy and public administration school with strong links to the university's prestigious business school. Its faculty and staff were active in bringing private business techniques to the practice of public administration. Known throughout the region for its innovative management development programs, it had recently completed successful programs for state cabinet officials and hospital administrators. In keeping with the school's prestige, the participants were selected by the chief executive officers of only the largest urban hospitals in the region. The nurses were being groomed for leadership positions at elite health care settings. Although the program for executive nurses fit with its mission, it was the first time that the public administration and business school faculty were teaching an almost all-women group.

The program's content was quite technical. Participants spent the first two weeks studying accounting, computers, budgeting, planning and forecasting, and organizational design. In the last week, however, they studied "human resource" management, reviewing such topics as leadership, labor relations, and managing people. Together with a well-known executive nurse, Ms. Patrick, who was affiliated with the program, I was charged with training the participants in the complexities of managing people. Ms. Patrick and I agreed that I would take the lead role in organizing the day's work. She would participate when she felt she could be most helpful.

My efforts failed dramatically, but the drama of my failure was instructive. At the beginning of the human resource management section of the program, I asked participants to write up a "frustrating encounter" they had had with a subordinate. I asked them to describe the background of the encounter, the encounter itself, and why they felt frustrated with it. I chose the following case, offered by Ms. Jones, one of the participants, for the seminar discussion.

Background

Ms. A was an assistant director who had been with the hospital for eight months. She had been having difficulty gaining acceptance by her subordinates. She was responsible for the Surgical Intensive Care Unit. At the time of the encounter, she was 33 years old. Her previous work history indicated that she had moved frequently. When questioned about this during an interview, she assured the executive nurse, Ms. Jones, that she had had to move because of her husband's positions, then his illness and death. Her references were good.

A number of Ms. A's head nurses and clinical nursing specialists had sought out Ms. Jones, sharing their frustration and lack of trust in Ms. A "because she lies" or "because she distorts things." Ms. Jones had shared these concerns in *general* with Ms. A. Ms. A was bright, clinically competent, and articulate. However, she seemed to have difficulty with taking responsibility for things, finding it easier to blame others. She always had an element of fact in her versions of events, so they seemed believable at first hearing.

Ms. A seemed to have little natural ability to analyze a situation and explore possible alternatives. Rather, she often directed "by the seat of her pants." She had been unable to put systems into place. Instead, since her arrival she had disturbed many of the systems that were already in place. Although she initially came across as self-assured, one soon realized that she was quite insecure, as indicated by her need to attack. She had been known to walk into a unit, observe a nurse in action, and label the whole unit "a cesspool of incompetence." Morale was low in all of her units, her staff was defensive, and she was not seen as an effective leader.

To assist Ms. A in leadership development, many hours of counseling had been provided. She had been encouraged in appropriate ways to establish credibility and had been "walked through" decision-making methodologies.

Ms. Jones had scheduled an appointment to discuss Ms. A's latest problem with a ten-hour shift plan for the Surgical Intensive Care Unit.

The Encounter

Ms. A arrived for her appointment twelve minutes late, out of breath, saying that she had been delayed "by a code blue" (emergency call). Ms. Jones did not believe her because Ms. A was usually late, always with an excuse.

Still out of breath, Ms. A launched into conversation about how "wonderful" it had been since they had had ten-hour shifts. She rambled about using overlap time for "ACLS training." Ms. Jones interrupted and asked her if she had completed her assessment of the ten-hour shift and had a recommendation. "Well, yes, its great, and we want to continue!"

She then asked her how she accounted for the sudden jump in use of pool staff and overtime. Ms. A quickly answered, "The census [the occupancy rate] has been sky high." Ms. Jones informed her that she knew the census had been between 75 and 80 percent and that Ms. A was fully staffed. Ms. A then switched gears and stated that the staff was poorly prepared and that leadership in the unit was weak. Without a pause she changed the conversation to include all the increased acuity in the unit, throwing out lengthy and complicated diagnoses of patients in an attempt to justify the additional staffing needs.

After forty-five minutes the meeting ended because Ms. Jones had another appointment. Ms. A promised that she would systematically review her ten-hour-shift scheduling plan, including all the components discussed. She left the office with the comment, "Oh, yes, my recommendation will be a proposal for five new positions to help get that place straightened out!"

Ms. Jones was frustrated because she realized that (1) she did not have enough information to make a decision about keeping or firing Ms. A; (2) she had been manipulated; (3) she had probably been told partial truths; (4) she was unsure that she had accomplished anything with the encounter; (5) she felt a little stupid because she did not know all the diagnoses Ms. A mentioned; and (6) she was concerned about the potential risks involved in leaving Ms. A in her present position and about what action to take next.

At first glance the case seems fairly straighforward. The executive nurse was having a hard time managing a manipulative nurse who lied, demoralized her staff, and disturbed management and control systems. Why not fire her? Yet the executive nurse was frustrated. She felt stupid because she did not understand all the current diagnostic terms and, despite all that she had said, she felt that she did not "have enough information to make a decision." Was she simply a coward, too afraid to fire her subordinate?

A second reading poses more questions. The executive nurse had been indirect with her subordinate. She had shared her concerns "in general" with Ms. A. Perhaps Ms. A did not know what Ms. Jones was really thinking. Ms. A may have felt that Ms. Jones was feeling hostile but may not have known why. Could this account for her "breathless" behavior, her inability to hear the signals from Ms. Jones? Certain people become hysterical when under attack. The hysterical pose defends them against the inner anxiety they feel when others are attacking them. Perhaps Ms. A had constructed a pose of great busyness (she was late to the meeting because of a "code blue") to assure the indirectly hostile Ms. Jones that she was in fact doing important things.

Moreover, Ms. Jones complained that Ms. A tells only partial truths, but clearly Ms. Jones had told Ms. A only partial truths about her performance. Ms. Jones felt that Ms. A directed "by the seat of her pants" but it seemed as though Ms. Jones was managing Ms. A by the same method. Ms. Jones felt that Ms. A was insecure and therefore she attacked others. But as Ms. Jones noted herself, she too felt insecure in Ms. A's presence (she felt "stupid") and clearly attacked Ms. A throughout the encounter. Ms. Jones complained that Ms. A demoralized her staff. But one suspects that Ms. Jones, by choosing to deal so indirectly with Ms. A, by "assisting her in leadership development" rather than telling her the truth, was demoralizing Ms. A. Perhaps she was giving Ms. A a double message. After all, Ms. A may have experienced the "leadership development" assistance as a sign of Ms. Jones's *confidence* in her! (Ms. Jones was making her into a "leader.") Double-talk is demoralizing. One begins to suspect that Ms. Jones's picture of Ms. A represented Ms. Jones's projection of traits she disliked in herself onto Ms. A. Perhaps that is why she was having so hard a time with Ms. A. Who was manipulating whom?

To be sure, all these suppositions are guesswork, but they highlight the danger of drawing easy conclusions about who is good and who is bad in particular encounters. We too quickly identify the good and the bad characters in order to minimize the anxiety we feel when facing complicated interpersonal encounters. If I am the good person in the encounter and the other person is bad, then our failure to resolve a problem is all the other person's fault. I can project my own superego voices onto the other, punishing him for my failure.

The Failed Role Play
Whether or not my interpretation was correct, I failed dismally to convey any of these complexities in the role-play work itself. I took

the role of Ms. A and invited participants to play the role of Ms. Jones. In the first role play Ms. A was fired; in the second she was suspended; in the third, after being congratulated for her excellent clinical skills, she was told that she "was about to be fired"; in the fourth she was ostensibly treated more gently but was in fact taken through a set of leading questions to determine where she was lying! In each of the role plays, the nurse who played Ms. Jones tried to get Ms. A to admit her guilt. But as the somewhat confused and probably frightened Ms. A, I came up with new facts to explain my behavior. (I was not behaving unrealistically. A subordinate facing a controlling superior feels threatened. The superior appears inscrutable, distant, and uncaring. Consequently the subordinate retreats to her customary defensive posture, recreating those behaviors that have irked and frustrated the superior in the first place. The encounter, ostensibly set up to resolve problems in the relationship between the two, simply reproduces them.) The role-playing Ms. Jones became so frustrated by her inability to control Ms. A's behavior that she fired her in two out of four encounters and suspended her in a third. Thus Ms. Jones failed as well.

Clearly the executive nurses in this training program were going to show that they were tough! They were not out to learn from the frustrating Ms. A. They would simply get rid of her! Indeed, the participant who at first complimented Ms. A for her fine clinical skills later described what "negative vibes" she got from those around her for being so complimentary to Ms. A. Moreover, as the role plays unfolded, people became angry at the "incompetent" nurse who wrote the case. (I had preserved the confidentiality of the case writer. Seminar participants did not know who among them was in fact Ms. Jones.) One participant argued "that it was inexcusable that it had taken eight months for this problem to be resolved." Several others nodded their heads, but none of them came to the defense of Ms. Jones (who later reported to me how hurt she had been by the attack). Yet the other nurses reported feelings of frustration and helplessness when writing up their cases; there was nothing unusual in the story of Ms. A.

I was shocked by these role plays. Blind to the emerging hostility in the room, I assumed that I had simply failed to get my point across. I stopped the role plays and suggested that perhaps people were scapegoating Ms. A. Her clinical competence made her superior anxious and uncertain. Could this be the source of some of the trouble? Is there something about Ms. A's role as the director of a difficult unit that creates such conflicts?

One participant agreed, noting that it was common for executive nurses to have trouble managing the heads of specialty units. Others angrily disagreed, charging that Ms. A was simply manipulative and was clearly lying. "Couldn't this be tested directly?" I asked. "Couldn't Ms. Jones say, 'I don't trust you. I sometimes think you are simply making up excuses'?" I got a resounding and angry no for an answer. It seemed inconceivable to be so direct with a subordinate.

Finally, my silent cotrainer Ms. Patrick stood up and angrily said, "Pragmatism is required. You need all the facts to deal with such a manipulative person as Ms. A." I vividly recall my feelings at that moment. I was angry with her. She seemed strong, centered, and powerful, and she was undermining me. I stepped in and said, "I am going to fight you on this, Ms. Patrick" and proceeded to repeat my claim that the difficulties people have at work are shaped as much by their roles as by their personalities. We can learn from those who create difficulties for us if we can collaborate with them in exploring their role.

But I was out of touch. Several people got up as if to signal for a break. The tension was high. I hastily called a break and retreated to the side to talk with two of my colleagues who were observing the seminar.

"How is it going?" I asked them. Their faces drooped, and it was only then that I began to feel the level of hostility in the room. A senior nurse walked by me and asked angrily, "Are we going to continue with this case?" I asked her what she thought, and she replied that she "had had enough of this one." My colleagues told me that it was not going well, that many people had psychologically dropped out, that some were angry, and that I could not go on. "Some very powerful people in this room are not talking."

When the group reassembled, I said that this seminar was clearly not working and asked what was happening. The hostility seemed to explode. People said they got little from the role plays, which were too naive. They had learned all this already and had done this kind of training themselves. Clearly the role play had provoked the group to be hostile toward me, Ms. Jones, and the hapless Ms. A. Something in the case, in their experience of the role plays, and in their experience of me promoted substantial anxiety. I had failed to form a working alliance with them. They could not tolerate their frustration with me, with Ms. A, or with their own experience.

I beat a retreat, I hoped with dignity. I reiterated my basic philosophy, that one had to take chances in difficult encounters, that one's presuppositions about who was bad and who was good were usually wrong, that to learn you had to take the risks of exposing parts of yourself to apparently troublesome others. I gave an example from my own experience, which seemed to touch them. Afterward several came up to me, ostensibly to discuss some of the points I had raised but actually, I felt, to make sure that I had not been too damaged, that I was psychologically in one piece. I was grateful.

I left the session feeling intensely knocked about. Why had all this happened? Two relationships were key here: the nurses' dependent relationship to the training program and the frequently distorted relationships between men and women at work. Let us examine each one in turn.

A Dependent Relationship

Recall that techniques can function as transitional objects or fetishes. But they may also function as symbols of the trainer's power and competence. They are not neutral. Students experience them as powerful because they belong to the trainer, who breathes life into them. Under these conditions students admire the technique but can never fully own it because they cannot be the trainer. The students become part of an audience watching the trainer's magic. They idealize the trainer; because the trainer appears effective and powerful, they feel small and dependent.

The training program promoted extremely dependent feelings and behaviors among the nurses. Although ostensibly organized to help the nurses develop senior management skills, in fact it made them feel incompetent, greedy, and paradoxically empty. Indeed, these feelings were all interconnected. The more incompetent they felt, the emptier they felt and the greedier they became. Let us examine this network of feelings.

During the first part of the training the participants heard lectures on financial systems, accounting, organizational design, forecasting, operations research—in short, the resolutely technical dimensions of management. Presenters lectured and participants took notes. This format seems innocent enough: The nurses were in school.

Yet as one nurse told me in response to my session, the program trainers had been "spoon-feeding" them for two weeks. The term "spoon-feeding" is suggestive, evoking the picture of a baby who cannot yet feed itself. An accounting professor's experience supports this description of the nurses' experience. At a debriefing session for the whole training program, he described the problems he had had with the group. He was teaching them statistics and had distributed calculators so that they could try out practice problems during the three days he worked with them. But they were quite confused by the calculators and frequently had trouble combining numbers in the right way to carry out complex operations, such as multiplying one set of numbers and then adding the results to another set. He told the story in frustration. How could he teach them accounting and statistics when they were inept at calculator-assisted arithmetic?

As he spoke, I had the image of giggling girls becoming incompetent with machines when faced with a powerful man. Yet he was describing executive-level nurses, many of them vice-presidents who reviewed and controlled the budgets and expenses of large hospital units. How could they be so incompetent when doing calculator arithmetic?

The answer, I suggest, is that *the context made them so.* They felt dependent on the expert teachers and awed by the trappings of the program. The participants knew they were being trained by some of the best and most experienced faculty of the business school. The entire program was designed to make them feel protected and supported, even pampered. The food was excellent, and there was entertainment in the evenings. One nurse quipped, "Even my husband doesn't treat me as well." Consequently, as a group they regressed. They became incompetent in response to the program's format and content.

Yet paradoxically their incompetence seemed to be matched by experiences of emptiness and greed. A colleague of mine gave a three-day lecture on organization design. Some hours later, several participants asked that he meet with them once more. Feeling that he might be able to work with them on even more complex and sophisticated issues, he agreed. He was disappointed. They seemed to want to go over the same material again, to make sure that he had in fact told them all they were supposed to know, to clarify minor points that had little bearing on overall themes. My colleague reported that the participants seemed "greedy" to him. They acted, he said, as though he were withholding materials from them and they had to suck everything out of him.

As the participants' evaluations revealed, they loved the program. Their incompetence did not frustrate them because they could sit in awe of the experts who protected them. They could feel stupid because their teachers were so smart. But their incompetence still came at a cost. They felt that they had to grab all they could get so that they could walk away with at least some of the expertise displayed before them. But greedy people feel empty and angry at those who deny them "food." Thus, insofar as they became dependent on the instructors and on the program, they believed that they had no inner resources. It was as though the ample food and entertainment masked the participants' feelings that they were starving.

A Contrasting Approach

This climate of dependency helps to explain, although it does not excuse, the trouble I had. (After all, I made a great technical error in not anticipating and examining how the program's context might indeed affect my session.) The nurse who spoke of spoon-feeding had added, *"How can you now ask us to show initiative?"* Lacking inner resources, the group could not develop a group process to grasp the more complex learning opportunities embedded in the role plays. But if the group members were to show initiative, the relationships among the nurses had to change as well.

The comments of participants on their evaluation forms are suggestive here. One nurse noted, "The third week [human resources week] was more difficult for people, faculty and students both. I feel we were brought together to work as a group, to interact more. The group process was difficult to deal with." Similarly another participant noted that "the group became uncomfortable because it had to take more risks by becoming involved in active learning."

To show initiative, people in the group had to feel comfortable taking a leadership role, sticking their necks out, pushing the group discussion in one direction or another. This challenge posed new stresses for the group. Recall that my colleague told me, "Some very powerful people aren't talking." Similarly, after the session one participant told me that there was status competition between the chiefs of nursing and other executive-level nurses during the session. Finally, one angry participant wrote in her evaluation that

"Hirschhorn's role playing was an *insult* [her emphasis] to executive level participants. One problem has been the varying level of competency between assistant directors and vice presidents."

In other words, the role plays not only stressed a thin and underdeveloped group process but also heightened the sense of competition between participants in the room. The big shots did not talk, no doubt for fear of failing in front of their subordinates, and the little shots were loath to take risks for fear of being attacked by their superiors.

The fear that competition was dangerous and that people might be hurt if they stuck their necks out promoted paranoialike feelings as well. Again, one nurse's comment on an evaluation is revealing: "L. Hirschhorn had visitors in his session. He did not introduce them. We wondered who they were. We later found out that they were his students." (In fact, they were not my students but my colleagues.) Another noted, "One final word about this session. There were at least three observers not known to the group, nor were they introduced. What was Professor Hirschhorn's intent?" I made an error in not introducing my colleagues, but I suggest that these participants' hostility to them and to me for bringing them was partly due to projection. They felt under scrutiny from their potentially hostile colleagues, and they projected some of these feelings onto my colleagues. I in turn was seen as having potentially dark intentions in bringing them in. In short, to learn through role plays, the participants had to take both initiative and risks. These risks were embedded in the character of their life together as a group. But because they had been spoon-fed for two weeks, they had only a thin group process. They depended on their teacher and on the program to provide them with structure and leadership. Consequently they did not trust one another.

At one level the participants' dependence on experts seemed to contradict the manifest purposes of the program—to transform executive nurses into senior managers. After all, the program treated them like children. Moreover, the program staff suspected that the nurses would forget much of what they had learned. At the debriefing a lead instructor noted that most of the participants would not remember the substantive technical skills they had learned once they returned to work. Indeed, when the seminar staff interviewed hospital presidents about changes they had seen in their executive nurses as a result of the program, many of the presidents thought that the nurses had improved most in human resource management and least in technical areas such as finance!

To be sure, this seeming contradiction between the program's intents and its format appears less significant if we see that the program's basic purpose was not to educate the participants but rather to give them *status* and a new vocational identity, to make them feel that they might some day deal with the "high rollers" of the hospital world (although clearly their bosses had doubts). But we must still explore why the participants complied in their dependency. It came at the cost of feeling incompetent, greedy, and angry. Instructors gain much by being experts and making their students feel stupid. But what do the students gain? The links between dependency and sexuality are critical here.

Sexuality and the Homosocial Culture

One of my colleagues had a telling exchange with a group of executive nurses who attended the same program the following year. (We had talked extensively about my experience, and he had worked to introduce the interpersonal domain earlier into the program schedule.) The group was discussing the problems that female nurses face in becoming executives and working for male bosses. They had to give up the supportive and warm culture of the nursing staff and become tough. My colleague asked why organizations could not be more nurturing in general. A nurse aggressively and angrily replied to my colleague that she was tired of being patronized by men such as he and did not want to be patronized by the "boys" in the hospital. As executive nurses, she said, they had to be able "to play in the locker room as well as the boardroom." Nurses had to be as tough as their male bosses. Another nurse came to the defense of my colleague, noting that nurses nonetheless faced real difficulties in being with the "boys" as opposed to the "girls." Finally one nurse commented on the use of the terms "boy" and "girl" during the conversation itself.

This was a rich interchange, for it highlighted the relationships among dependency, group life, and sexuality in the culture of hospitals. My colleague told me he was shocked by the suddenness of the attack on him by the first participant. Why did she see as patronizing his statement that organizations could be more nurturing?

Her comment on the locker room and the boardroom is suggestive. Locker room talk is both sports talk and dirty talk. Men compete with one another (thus the sports talk), but they control the anxieties associated with competition by downgrading the prize they all want—women. Women become sex objects (thus the dirty talk), and insofar as they are just part bodies and part objects, men feel a certain camaraderie.

On the way from the locker room to the boardroom, however, men soften their dirty talk (and they must do so because the boardroom is a place where minds, not bodies, meet) by *patronizing* women. Women become "girls" who need help, not desirable sex objects. As girls, women are less valuable to men, and so men need not compete for their favors. Therefore they can work effectively together as a team.

The resulting complex of feelings among men shapes what Kanter has called the *homosocial culture*[4] of senior management. To cooperate, men need to control their competitiveness. They do so by devaluing women and elevating the emotional valence of their relationships with one another. I suggest that my colleague's comment evoked the angry participant's feelings about the homosocial culture of senior managers. To be successful, to break up this male conspiracy, women had to enter the locker room themselves. They had to talk dirty and be tough just like the men. Indeed, they had to become men.

Yet, as we have seen, the next participant noted that there is much comfort to be lost in leaving the "girls" for the "boys," and a third pointed to the significance of the terms "boy" and "girl." The women nurses seemed to be caught in the middle of three unsatisfactory alternatives. They could remain comfortable in their own "support" group but consequently act and feel like less-than-sexual "girls"; they could become sex objects for the men (this is the cultural stereotype of nurses); or they could join the locker room, become like men, and so be entitled to enter the boardroom. The first and third options desexualize them, whereas the second makes them into sex objects. The poverty of choice represented by these three options raises the central question, Why can't they be *women*, that is, sexual adults who are subjects, not objects?

Our Roles and Our Sexuality

One participant's comment on the evaluation form from the first training program is revealing here. She noted, "This week [of human resource management lectures, which were generally unsuccessful] has generated a great deal of animosity. My thoughts are that this is primarily related to the shift in the style of presentation and the expectation that there be dialogue and concerted interaction on our part. The control issues really were highlighted among the group. It was very difficult to teach. I don't believe most nurses can learn in experiential settings. Many cannot be introspective and don't want to be taught to be. The physician-nurse relationships are probably key. We are adolescents as a group of professionals." (The participant is giving particular attention to my presentation. Mine was the only one based on "experiential learning.")

This is a rich and evocative statement condensing a series of thoughts. The participant suggests that the group cannot learn in experiential settings because doctors and nurses have adolescentlike relationships. In adolescence boys and girls are uncomfortable with one another, and sex is treated as dirty or impersonal. Indeed, the cultural fantasy of the doctor-nurse relationship is based on the image of doctors patting nurses on their fannies, leering at them, and sleeping with them in spare hospital beds. These are certainly adolescent images. But how does adolescent sex or the feel of adolescent sex limit one's ability to learn from experience?

An episode from another setting is illuminating. I was working for an engineering company on problems and issues in interdepartmental relationships. I wrote a report that was generally well received, and I was asked to discuss it with Ms. Curtis, a manager who played a critical role in shaping the relationships between some of the key design and administrative units. When I entered the room, the report was sitting on her desk. As I sat down opposite her I noticed that it was heavily penciled and annotated; she had clearly given it a careful reading. Indeed, as our conversation developed, it was clear that she believed the report to be useful, to have raised important questions. I was attracted to her. She had, in my eyes, a soft sexuality that was combined with a firmness of self. Her feet were on the ground. As we discussed the report, I became aware of the ways in which I too felt grounded. My attraction to her seemed to be centering me. I could focus clearly on the work we were doing, and our conversation had both a collaborative and charged quality.

She then mentioned that it would be difficult for the engineers to know what I was talking about, and I quite unexpectedly became anxious. Was she telling me that the report was in some way deficient? The anxious feeling did not dissipate, and, as we talked about implementing the report's recommendations, I told her that clearly such people as she would have to play a central role. I had no sooner said this when I became aware of my impulse to gratify her, to flatter her, hoping in this way that she would not reject my report and me. This impulse felt charged with the same sexual feelings that a few minutes earlier had grounded me. Now, however, it seemed to fuel a fleeting fantasy of some liaison between us. This fantasy progressively took me away from work. I began to complain to her about one of her bosses (a violation of my role and the work boundary between us) and failed to note that I was now late for my next interview. I believe that she too experienced the sexual intrusions into our work. My sponsor (in another unit) called to see where I was and why I was late for my next appointment. Ms. Curtis smiled and said, "We were having a party."

This example highlights the power and mobility of sexual feelings at work. First, the sexual feelings actually drew me close to my work by simultaneously grounding me in a bodily feeling and making me aware of the boundary between us. Such boundaries are, of course, the preconditions for work, for they help us understand and enact our roles. The sexual feelings focused me on the work transaction and simultaneously heightened my experience of the work boundary. The resulting charged but collaborative encounter represented the power of *sexual sublimation* at work. Yet, when anxiety got the better of me, when Ms. Curtis's comments evoked some long-standing fears about my ability to talk with engineers, these same sexual feelings led me away from work. I violated role and time boundaries and communicated my wish to party rather than to work.

Sexual feeling and the experience of work are dialectically combined. When one stays centered on one's role, sexual feelings charge the resulting encounter, creating an even more intense experience of focused work. But when anxiety intrudes, the mobility of sexual feelings, their inextricable link to fantasy, amplifies the flight from work. The flight from work in turn amplifies the flight into fantasy, so that one imagines making love to one's co-workers. Thus the value and danger that sexual feelings bring to work are two sides of the same coin. The value is centeredness and thus an even fuller access to one's affects. But if anxiety disrupts the delicate balance between sex and its sublimation, the danger pulls one away from role and into the realm of illicit fantasies or promiscuous wishes.

The Nurses' Program As a Social Defense

This argument suggests that the training program for the nurses functioned as a social defense against feeling like a sexual adult when working or learning, for as we have seen, when people fail to take their roles, such feelings can deepen the anxiety of working itself. But if the experience of one's sexuality is denied, one cannot fully experience one's own affects. One is out of touch and therefore can neither learn nor manage.

The training program thus supported and affirmed hospital culture. As we have seen, nurses can be desexualized girls, depersonalized sex objects, or "hard" men. But they cannot be women. The training program treated them like girls while pretending to make them into hard men. My role play by contrast (although not by design) contradicted rather than affirmed this culture. By stumbling into and through the realistic role plays, I explored the dangers of being a woman, that is, an adult fully in touch with her feelings.

Indeed, my personal experience is revealing here. After my seminar I retreated to my office and recorded the feelings and facts that were running about in my head. I looked at these notes a year later and was struck by the sense of shame they conveyed. The word "narcissism" is repeated frequently. I felt ashamed for having displayed myself in front of the nurses. I felt ashamed for having dominated the role plays (I did not let any participant play the role of Ms. A). I was aware of having showed off to the women colleagues I brought to the seminar and felt ashamed that I failed them.

The intense shame I felt, my feeling that I had behaved in a narcissistic manner, and the attention I semiconsciously gave to my colleagues suggest that I was on sexual display. The core of a narcissistic display lies in the conceit that one's body is beautiful. Similarly, at the core of feeling ashamed is the belief that one's body is ugly and inadequate. As one of the few men in a room of fifty women, as their teacher and leader, I had a chance to excel, to be a hero, to be their man. Having failed, I felt undressed before them, with a shrunken body for show.

The sexual context of my experience can be clarified by asking how other male lecturers managed their relationships to fifty women. My analysis of techniques as fetishes is suggestive here. The male lecturer who stayed within the psychological framework of the training program could show off as well, but he could do so in a contained way by exposing his special "tools," such as his technical formulas and mathematical methods. As I have suggested, the women admired these tools, feeling that they could never use them or have them. The sexual content of this transaction is evident. Men have something that the women cannot have, but they can certainly admire it.

I had no such fetish and took the risk of exposing my real sexuality to them. However, my behavior made them anxious, for it threatened to undermine the defensive structure of the training program itself. Had they joined me, they would have had to examine their own group process, their feelings about competition, their relationships to men in the hospital culture, and, finally, their relationships to their own sexuality, their womanhood. To avoid this, they had to punish me.

The experience of one other male lecturer, Mr. Brown, is suggestive here. He too lectured to the group on the subject of human resources, focusing on such issues as labor relations, discrimination issues, and appraisal systems. These are nontechnical subjects. He infuriated the nurses, however, because they felt that he talked down to them and because several times he called them "girls." He concluded his day's lecture by assuring them that indeed they could become top-notch managers.

As we have seen, other lecturers talked down to the nurses as they taught them, for example, how to use calculators. The critical difference is that Mr. Brown had no fetish, no tool for the nurses to admire. The nurses were therefore more sensitive than usual to being treated as children and dependents. Moreover, to teach the nurses effectively, Mr. Brown had to invest his presentation with his own experience, his manner of making judgments, and his own personality and character. I suggest that doing so made him anxious. He had to expose parts of himself to fifty women. A failure would be humiliating. He contained his anxiety by desexualizing the nurses, by calling them "girls." If they were just girls, then there was less to worry about.

Let us review my argument. To manage others, we must come in touch with our affects, our feelings. They constitute the only sound basis for making decisions when rules and procedures neither describe nor anticipate the range of special situations a manager will face. But when we experience our affects, we too frequently discover the surprises of our denied feelings, our anger as well as our love, and this makes us anxious. We would rather remain in control of our encounters with others so as not to expose ourselves to ourselves or to others.

Management training compromises our ability to learn from our affects. It supports our defenses by promoting our feelings of helplessness. As we have seen, the nurses had a dependent relationship to the seminar. When I proposed that they develop a different relationship to me, they hated me, because the anxiety of getting in touch with affects created feelings that I was persecuting them. (Of course, my own technical errors played a role here as well.)

But the nurses' dilemma highlighted an even more complex dimension to the problem of managing others. The participants' dependency reflected their chosen identity as girls rather than as women. It demonstrated that sexual feeling, as a "metafeeling" for centering us on our other feelings, also poses great dangers. The nurses' use of boy-girl language, their willingness to be dependent, their difficulty in dealing with their own competitiveness, and my persistent feelings of shame afterward signified that the seminar was a defense against sexual feeling as well, against the transformation of girls and boys into women and men.

A Design Choice

This defensive structure of the seminar explains one of its most peculiar features. Toward the end I participated in a design group that was organizing the last two days of the seminar. Hospital presidents (all men) were to attend a "CEOs' (chief executive officers') forum" the last two days of the program. They were the superiors of the nurses attending the seminar and in most cases had personally sponsored their attendance. The program organizers wanted each president and the nurse he had sponsored to get together for some period of time and talk about relevant management issues in their hospital.

There was much anxiety surrounding their visit. The program organizers worried that the presidents would have nothing to say to the nurses, that the presidents would not be interested, and the participants worried that they would not look different in their presidents' eyes. To ease the presidents' entry into the program, the program organizers arranged two events. First, at the CEOs' forum a program leader would quickly review what the nurses had learned (compressing nearly three weeks' work into one hour!). Then groups of three nurses would meet with three CEOs (from hospitals other than their own) to discuss some relevant health care issue. Finally, each nurse would meet with her own CEO in the large auditorium. It was hoped that some of these couples would talk animately to each other and that the resulting noise would stimulate the more reticent CEOs to talk.

The plan sounds strange. How could the CEOs be given a one-hour summary of three weeks of learning? Why did the CEOs have to be stimulated to talk to their executive nurses? Yet creative and experienced program designers concocted this plan.

Defenses of a significant order were playing a critical role. Two processes were key. First, it is clear that, just as the program designers had created a highly dependent participant group, so did they feel dependent on the CEOs. Their anxiety about the CEOs' entry and their fear that the CEOs might not be interested (would they talk to their own subordinates?) reflected their own lack of conviction about the substantive merits of the program itself. If the program were simply window dressing, then the nurses might perform poorly in front of their bosses. The dependency culture robbed both the participants and the program designers of a sense of authenticity and authority. The CEOs were the final judges. Indeed, the presumption that the CEOs could be given a short course, covering in one hour what the nurses took three weeks to study, reflected the organizers' unconscious belief that the program had no content.

Who Competes for Whom?

I suggest that this strange design reflected sexual fantasies. I attended the second of several design sessions. The program chair, Mr. Stein, reported that the participants were nervous. They had asked him who should be the leaders of the group of three nurses meeting with three CEOs. They wanted the seminar staff to pick the leader. Mr. Stein said that the nurses would have to choose their own leaders. I was still feeling raw from my presentation, and Mr. Stein's reply signaled me that the plan was wrong. For reasons unclear to me at the time, the program designers were asking the nurses to mobilize a group process that had been repressed for three weeks. Such requests, I knew, get you into much trouble in dependency cultures, and I argued that the plan for the group of three was all wrong. "They have not been a group up to now, and they are not a real working group back home, so why slap them together now?" My colleagues agreed, one noting that he now realized how artificial the imposed groups of three actually were.

I puzzled over this incident for a long time. The designers' intent seemed punishing and angry; they were about to throw the nurses to the wolves of each other's unconscious anxiety. The results could have been disastrous. Why did they do it? Over time a second question occurred to me: Why was I having such trouble deciphering the meaning of this incident? I wondered if it was threatening for me to understand the event.

Only when I began writing this chapter did the answer become apparent. *This entire design was structured around latent sexual themes.* The program designers had dressed the women up for a liaison with their superior men. Would the "costume" hold? Would the men be interested? If not, these powerful men (CEOs from the "real world") would attack the impotent program designers who were dependent on women performing effectively before other men.

The design of putting three nurses together with three powerful CEOs functioned as a collective fantasy that both expressed and overcame the program designers' feelings of sexual impotence. It expressed men's common sexual fantasy that women should fight among themselves, even destroy each other, for the attention of men. In mapping the structure of this fantasy onto the program design, we were the eunichs serving up the women to powerful men. But in identifying with these powerful men for whom women compete (we would meet them alone first in the CEO forum and talk with them man to man), we could overcome our feelings of impotence.

The Battle of the Sexes
This fantasy performed an even more important function. In the battle of the sexes men can fight each other for women or women can fight each other for men. Typically, at least in modern Western cultures, men fight each other for the prizes of money and sex, whereas the competition among women is suppressed. The richest or strongest man gets the most women and money; women develop a sisterhood of sorts. This system exposes the men to a potentially greater sense of shame because their losses are transparent. Finally, men can partly compensate themselves for this risk by developing their own locker room culture through which they degrade women.

But as we have seen, if women emerge into senior management ranks—and this was the manifest reason for giving them training—

this system for organizing the battle of the sexes is upset. Both the locker room culture and the women's sisterhood are threatened. The participating nurses responded in part by protecting their sisterhood, although at the cost of remaining girls and dependents. The male program designers, who felt threatened by the powerful CEOs, responded by forcing the women to compete for men. In this way, if the nurses failed, it was their fault (they could not organize themselves into groups of three and talk effectively to the CEOs), not the program's. The male program designers could thus be on the good side of the CEOs. In effect, to avoid competing with the CEOs, the program designers asked the nurses to compete with one another. Thus the peculiar design for the CEOs' entry into the program functioned as a defense against the fantasy of men fighting for women by creating a setting in which women would fight for men.

This complex of behaviors highlights what happens to the battle of the sexes when women join men as equals. Men must give up their locker room and women their sisterhood. The competition for sexual prizes intensifies as men and women confront each other as individuals without their respective support groups. The gain, of course, is that people can feel like adults rather than like children. Work can be truly sexualized as people draw on their sense of adulthood to work together. Sexuality replaces sexiness.

But there is much anxiety in giving up the old system. In response to this anxiety, both men and women may in fact *exaggerate* the features of the old system. Men may parade in front of women with their tools, and women may regress to the status of dependents. The old balance is lost.

Finally, it is clear why I had such a hard time understanding the symbolic meanings of this strange program design. I had been injured in my sexual display before women, in my bid for sexual attention. My still raw feelings sensitized me to the dangers of the proposed program design, but its meaning evaded me. I could not understand it because to do so would mean exposing myself to my own sexual failure in front of fifty women. Only in working through my experience by writing this chapter did I become aware of its symbolic contents.

III

*The Breakdown of the Social Defenses
and the Postindustrial Milieu*

7

The Postindustrial Milieu

Let us review the argument of this book thus far. By examining the social defenses, we can see how groups develop and deploy collective mechanisms to contain the anxiety of working. In enacting psychological dramas, they systematically organize their retreat from role, task, and organizational boundaries. This retreat can take groups far from the basic task of the organization. The top executives of ERD (chapter 5) retreated from their leadership role to enact a fantasy of sibling rivalry. Mourning their lost leader and unable to tolerate the anxiety of directing the agency themselves, they undermined one another, prevented Black from psychologically succeeding Harnwell, and created a policy vacuum.

Yet no group is entirely captured by its social defenses. Rather, its collective life is based on a compromise in which people both advance toward and retreat from the work boundary. The resulting set of relationships reflects both the group's task and its desire to contain anxiety. Using the basic assumption as the model of the "flight from work," Bion argued that a collective is simultaneously a work group and a basic assumption group, responding to the demands of the task as well as to the anxiety it generates. For example, the scientists at ERD did complete their work, although in the absence of policy guidance they wasted much time and effort. Similarly, the executive nurses at the training program (chapter 6) did learn about important management practices, such as forecasting cost and revenues and designing information systems.

The emerging postindustrial milieu can undermine such compromises. The social defenses may prove inadequate for containing anxiety, and the group, faced with the prospect of confronting its work, can either move closer to the work boundary and take up its task or move farther away from the boundary and become more irrational. This happens because the culture, politics, and technology of a postindustrial milieu integrate once divided roles, tasks, departments, divisions, and levels so that people and interest groups outside the organization, division, or unit are nonetheless psychologically more present and find it easier to press their claims and demands.[1] The new technologies of automation, communication, and information integrate interdependent units and divisions so that it becomes more difficult for people in one unit to deny the claims, experiences, and requirements of another. People inhabit a more multidimensional terrain where stereotyping and scapegoating become less viable defenses. Just as men and women may experience greater anxiety when losing the protection provided by their stereotyped roles, so can the postindustrial milieu create greater anxiety by complicating and intensifying relationships across role and organizational boundaries. People work in an increasingly imploded organizational environment.

Yet, if people are to accomplish a task or a piece of work, they must ultimately draw boundaries around their roles, departments, or divisions so that they can take specific actions and preclude certain options. Therefore, to be effective, they must take the authority embedded in their roles by maintaining an increasingly *sophisticated* boundary, keeping themselves open to a wide range of claims while ultimately selecting a particular and therefore limited set of actions. Moreover, in a postindustrial milieu boundaries are more permeable and open. They are therefore more likely to change and develop as units and divisions are recombined to take up new tasks or to perform old ones more effectively. More integrated "sociotechnical" systems are more flexible as well. But, in facing the anxiety posed by such work boundaries, groups that are unable to develop sophisticated strategies for maintaining the boundaries may deploy even more powerful social defenses. Ironically, when an increasingly integrated technical and social domain is split apart, the level of psychological injury may grow.

The following examples highlight the psychological impact of the horizontal and vertical integration of units and levels and show the difficulty people face in setting and maintaining boundaries in a postindustrial milieu. Workers and managers in an information systems group, in nuclear power plants, in factories based on self-managing teams, and in a company eager to create a more participative climate all faced the dilemmas of taking roles and setting boundaries that were relatively open and subject to change and negotiation. By examining these four situations, we can understand the challenges posed by a postindustrial milieu to the psychodynamics of taking roles and setting boundaries.

Computers and Integration

The information systems group of a commercial laboratory maintained the computer programs and database that doctors and technicians use to conduct tests and produce laboratory reports. Technicians produced tables and texts for reports from data from laboratory computers that test blood and tissue samples. Yet frequently they made errors that resulted in garbled tables and sentences. Moreover, the head of the company, facing growing competition from many other laboratories, was pressuring the information systems group to create more intricate, varied, and detailed reports for the customers. But as the group worked to introduce new software into the system, the error rate originating in the laboratories grew. Finally, the group tried to impress upon the owner and upon the lab supervisors that small changes in one part of the software often induced changes in other parts. That meant that, if one lab wanted the format for its particular reports changed, other labs might unexpectedly be affected because they used the shared computer system.

The information systems group tried to gain greater control over its own work by instituting strict procedures for helping the lab technicians. For example, they would conduct informal classes on using the system, they would permit only one of their group to answer queries on any particular day, and they tried to limit the labs' requests for new reporting capabilities. Yet the information systems group had a difficult time controlling its boundary. Lab supervisors and technicians felt that they owned the computer system, that they should be given instant access to its capabilities, that their problems should be solved immediately, and that their proliferating requirements for greater detail and precision should be met quickly. When I consulted for the information systems group, I came to realize that the lab technicians experienced the computer system in a distorted way. They did not appreciate how their work related to that of other users. The computer's flexibility was disguising the growing interdependence among the different laboratories. The pressure on the information systems group was produced by the technicians' failure to understand the nature of divisional boundaries in a computerized environment.

The conflict between the labs and the information systems group was resulting in deteriorating relationships between the group's manager and her deputy. The deputy tried to respond to all the labs' requests, even though it meant that she frequently had to work late into the night. Lab supervisors began to see her as the "good" computer expert and viewed the director, who tried to limit the lab supervisors' demands, as the "bad" computer expert. The supervisors stopped asking the director for support, instead going directly to her deputy. Consequently the director felt undercut and undermined, and the deputy felt that the director was not doing her job. Because the information systems group could not control its boundary, could not discipline and organize the ways in which the labs used its services, the director felt personally discounted and ignored.

While working directly with the director and the deputy on their respective roles and on the boundary between them, I also recommended that the information systems group develop liaison personnel within the laboratories to protect the group from excessive and inappropriate demands. In other words, the information systems group could control its own boundary only by extending its presence and asserting its claims *within* the boundary of the labs. Paradoxically, to control its boundary, it had to help create and sustain roles that bridged the labs and the computer group. I was not confident that the computer group could succeed. The complexities of organization integration in a computerized environment could prove too stressful. The different divisions had to integrate and coordinate their work more intensively and still maintain their separate identities. If they failed to do that, the information systems group would prove unable to manage its boundary, and the deputy would continue to undermine the director by responding to too many requests. If the group could not manage a sophisticated boundary, interpersonal relations within the information systems group would continue to deteriorate.

Quality and Safety in the New Technologies
The problem of integration, of building systems that enable people to play roles while not creating rigid boundaries, also emerges when

production managers no longer focus on the one-dimensional goals of more volume or less cost but try to incorporate such goals as quality and safety. Tensions between supervisors and quality control inspectors are legion, just as the sales force and plant managers are constantly wrangling over the timely delivery of promised goods. These conflicts become taxing as the failure to coordinate units with different goals imposes greater costs. For example, many companies facing intense competition in developing new products and wishing to accelerate the process of product development find it difficult to bring engineers, researchers, marketing specialists, and production engineers together in effective teams in which members can pursue their own specialized goals while acknowledging one another's needs and interests.

This problem of integration has become particularly important in plants with continuous process technologies. In modern chemical, steel, and nuclear power plants it is difficult to pursue the goals of safety, quality, and production separately. In an old steel or machining plant, for example, people can separate their pursuit of production and safety goals by maintaining high levels of inventory. If one part of the plant must be shut down to repair a dangerous machine or furnace, workers in other departments can draw on the inventory of semifinished parts to sustain production. The inventory buffers departments from one another and enables the plant as a whole to uncouple safety from production goals.

Nuclear Power

But in continuous process plants the different steps in the production process are tightly coupled. Without inventory dividing them, departments—people—must coordinate their work with one another more effectively. Nuclear power plants, which produce energy from heated steam in a continuous process, pose just such problems of coordination. Safety professionals and line personnel must cooperate to protect workers, the company, and of course the public; yet as was briefly discussed in the introduction, safety workers and line operators are frequently in conflict.

I studied this problem for an architecture and engineering company that built plants. I concluded that safety professionals and plant personnel would not cooperate precisely and paradoxically because nuclear power plants are dangerous.[2] Instead of realistically confronting the dangers they faced, plant personnel preferred in-

stead to blame safety inspectors, whom they described as "nitpicking," "meddlesome," and ignorant of the engineering and hardware
of a nuclear reactor. In the minds of many plant personnel, safety
inspectors were just paper pushers, doing useless audits on past
activities to see if bureaucratic procedures had been violated. Referring to safety personnel, one vice-president in a utility said, "Real
men don't eat quiche," suggesting that there was something soft and
weak about safety inspection work.

I believe that this attitude, although irrational, emerged from a
process of projection. Workers and managers at plant construction
sites or at operating plants felt anxious, lest critical errors be made.
But instead of tolerating this anxiety, managers and workers tried to
deny it by blaming the messengers, the safety inspectors, for the bad
news. Moreover, by showing little respect for the safety inspectors,
they could ignore the significance of their work and findings. They
split off their realistic fear for the work they were doing and projected it onto the safety department, making it difficult for the two
groups to cooperate. The pressure and exacting demands of the primary task—running a continuous plant safely—paradoxically split
apart the two groups that needed to cooperate. Line personnel could
not expand the psychological boundaries of their role to pay attention to safety.

The Systems View

Anxiety may also block workers from developing a comprehensive
understanding of the machinery they control. In monitoring
automatic systems, workers must take a broad view because they
intervene only when feedback controls fail. These failures create
unexpected interactions between parts of the machine system that
can be controlled only if the operators understand the system as a
whole. Yet studies of industrial accidents suggest that workers frequently ignore warning signs to contain the anxiety they feel in
facing a dangerous situation.[3]

For example, the accident at the Three Mile Island nuclear reactor
happened when a leaky valve, thought to be closed, dumped water
from the reactor onto the containment floor, dangerously reducing
water levels that protected the fissionable material.[4] The operators,
misled by faulty indicators into thinking that the valve was shut
tight, nonetheless ignored other warning signs, such as water spill-
ing through a drain tank onto the floor itself, and concluded that

water pressure in the reactor was too high. They then shut off emergency water to the reactor that was replacing the lost water!

The presidential commission studying the accident found that a temperature gauge had correctly indicated that hot water was leaking from the system. But the workers ignored the gauge, some arguing that the gauge had read high in the past because of normal leaks and others suggesting that a nonrecurring leak into the drain tank had created a temporary hot spot there. All signals must be interpreted, but the workers' actions suggest that they did not wish to add to their stress by considering puzzling and potentially contradictory information. By sticking to their initial belief that the reactor had too much rather than too little water, they could control their own anxiety in light of the dangerous situation they faced.

The leaky valve created a new pathway of interaction among the reactor, the valve, and the emergency cooling water, a pathway that operators could not understand for several hours. To diagnose the situation correctly, they could not think simplistically, looking only at immediate relationships between parts of the system. They had to think holistically and tolerate the anxiety of learning. Because they failed to do so, they could not quickly bring the reactor under control.

Team Systems

Because of its dangers, a nuclear power plant can create a high degree of anxiety, even when it is appropriately designed and managed. But the problems of integrating safety and production and thinking holistically highlight the general challenge of an integrated or "imploded" organizational environment. Typically people can limit their anxiety by focusing their attention and effort on a narrow scope of problems, hoping that the division of labor authorizes other people to worry about the rest of the organization. But as continuous process technology integrates the once divided functions of production, quality, inventory control, maintenance, and safety, people have to consider more issues, claims, and other actors in accomplishing their own work and do so while maintaining the integrity of their own roles. This double task of focusing on one's immediate setting while psychologically taking in the work of others stimulates anxiety and flight in its own right.

This problem has emerged most clearly in the functioning of plant teams. In automated plants mistakes in the warehouse, in maintenance, on the line, and in the labs are no longer buffered by time and space from one another. In describing a continuous process steel mill, one worker noted that the mill "requires far more coordination and teamwork than number four [the old mill]. This is because if a man makes only a little mistake by not being on his toes and watching what is going on, the whole mill has to stop."[5] The production workers must be able to perform minor maintenance work, and the quality control worker must understand why, for example, certain feedstocks may yield low-quality products.

To manage such tightly coupled production systems effectively, managers frequently introduce team systems to help workers improve their coordination with one another. Once introduced, such team settings highlight the dysfunctional impact of the supervisor's role. In old factories tightly supervised workers doing narrow jobs interpreted their official job duties as the maximum amount of effort and discretion they were required to exercise. Because written job descriptions cannot exhaustively describe the many varied activities workers should perform to accomplish their tasks, supervisors were left to fill in the inevitable cracks in the production process, becoming, as one plant manager noted, "parts chasers" solving simple logistical and mechanical problems.

Because their initiative was neither recognized nor rewarded, workers were unwilling to coordinate their work with one another. The position of the supervisor as the production coordinator was therefore reinforced, proving to managers that supervisors are essential because workers are simply uncooperative. Thus, when managers introduce teamwork to improve coordination, they find that the supervisor is redundant and the team can and should be self-managing.

But this means that team members must expand their psychological awareness of one another, performing their own roles while paying greater attention to the performance and activities of team members. When the line workers observe team members who are late, intoxicated, or technically incompetent, they can no longer wait for the supervisor to step in and discipline them. Instead, members must manage such problems and their consequences themselves. They widen their perceptual field by becoming attuned to a larger number of issues and problems, and they deepen this field by attending to the more implicit and less visible features of their working relationships. When I interviewed a shop steward who had joined a work team in a phone-operator services office, she told me, "Before as a union steward I had to pay attention to only a few issues and the normal run of grievances. Now as a member of this team it seems that I have to pay attention to every single worker's experience."

Many teams succeed in taking up this complex work of self-management; but as my own past work shows, self-management can fail because team members, fearing the consequences of interpersonal conflict, cut off their awareness of other team members by limiting or denying their relationship to team issues. For example, a team in an automated soft goods factory was dominated by a highly competent technician who said nothing at team meetings and by a talkative senior member who, in the words of the team facilitator, "was an authoritarian sort but was playing the role of the non-authoritarian." The talkative member, anxious in the freedom of the work setting, made use of his right to be open by constantly expressing anxiety. "He was communicating his anxieties to the group about the fact that it was a team."[6]

Together, the aloof technician and the anxious senior member stalemated the team process. As the facilitator reported, the team meetings were unproductive and the team's production goals were not being met. "Yet," as the facilitator noted, "when I spoke to individual team members, I was met with a smoke screen. They gave me the silent treatment. They wouldn't tell me what was going on." The facilitator concluded that these two members had blocked the group process, that no coalition of team members could emerge to take authority for the team's functioning. "The team couldn't confront them, couldn't make them work for the team instead of against them. People started feeling incompetent. They didn't trust themselves or each other. That's why the team couldn't meet its goals."

Unable to take authority for the team's functioning and feeling incompetent to cope with its problems, team members alienated themselves from the team process. By giving the facilitator the silent treatment, they not only kept him out but also denied their own relationship to the team problem. Indeed, by making the facilitator incompetent, they could project their own sense of incompetence onto him. And in failing to function as a team, they could then blame the facilitator who could not help.

Delegation and Management

Plant managers face similar problems in such settings. By taking up roles that are no longer protected by many layers of supervision and the formal accoutrements of social status (for example, separate parking lots and dining facilities), they are more exposed to shop floor workers. One consultant working closely with such a plant manager noted that "leaders in a flat organization can be 'seen' very clearly. What they do [or don't do] speaks more loudly than anything they say. . . . With the 'traditional' protection of positional power and functional identity basically absent, a manager's personal impact becomes a more critical variable influencing performance."[7]

Because teams are relatively self-regulating, managers exercise their authority in difficult or nonroutine situations and thus face the difficult problem of discovering how and why they wish to take their role. Freed from bureaucratic, procedural, and recurring duties, managers find that, instead of their roles defining their actions, their actions define their roles.

In surveying a set of such plants, I found that, when faced with such ambiguity and uncertainty, managers frequently abdicated, hoping that the culture of self-management freed them from making the difficult and risky decision of intervening in a poorly functioning team.[8] In a machining plant one supervisor told me that the plant management "consistently underestimated workers' need for both technical and social leadership" and failed to introduce skills training and adequate work procedures to help workers cope with an unfamiliar technology. The supervisor suggested that management "gave the teams all the difficult problems to solve, like discipline, but not the skills and assistance. An employee would be late, workers would complain, and we told them to deal with it themselves. Team members would come back and report that the late employee said, 'Screw you,' but we would say, 'You work on it.' "

The supervisor described the first plant manager (later replaced by one who brought more structure to the plant) as "oscillating between being participative and being a little Caesar." Such inconsistency suggests that the manager could not find the boundary of his role nor define the scope of his delegation so that both the team and he could act consistently. Both the team and he lacked the psychological sense of a boundary that shaped the relationship between them.

To take a role in such a plant effectively, plant managers must also extend and deepen their perceptual field. They must think more broadly, assessing the meaning of a particular decision and often taking the risk of appearing overly aggressive and untrustworthy when exercising managerial authority. For example, in one team-based chemical plant, workers who were facing severe technical problems in running the plant were nonetheless irate when plant managers introduced a new layer of supervision to bring the plant into a technically steady state.[9] As one worker described it, "There we were in the middle of the winter, up to our knees in the [chemical] junk, because we didn't know how to manage the technology. Plant management panicked. They were watching the bottom line fall away from them and they appointed temporary assistant coordinators to each of the autonomous teams." But she then added that the "teams stabilized when the assistant positions were filled. Before that, when an informal leader would emerge, he was cut off at the head. . . . The assistant coordinator had a unifying affect."

In effect, the plant manager had to risk violating the plant's emerging culture of participation because he believed that the plant's technical viability was threatened. Such decisions, lacking the definitive groundwork of a rule or a precedent, are always risky and subject to much criticism because by definition they represent departures from the status quo. Although the workers were irate at losing some degree of control, they also welcomed the introduced stability and structure. As the internal consultant to the plant noted, "The workers felt isolated and needed support. . . . The teams needed more boundaries between themselves and the rest of the organization."

Thus, just as workers in team-based plants face the complicated problem of taking actions and assuming authority when faced with problems that cannot be solved by simply following rules or orders from above, managers also find that they must take the risks of setting a boundary and defining their authority in response to new or unique situations. To do this, they must bring more of their personal feelings to their role. For example, they face the complicated psychological problem of experiencing and mobilizing aggressive feelings to establish their authority while not scapegoating another person simply to contain the anxiety of acting aggressively. In the machining factory the plant manager who acted like a little Caesar probably rationalized his extreme aggression by assuming that the plant teams were simply incompetent. Unable to acknowledge his contribution to the team's dilemmas, he devalued them in his own mind, thus justifying his aggression against them while failing to contain and modulate his aggressive feelings. Because he was operating in too narrow a psychological field, he was unable to consider the experience of the workers from their point of view.

Social Defenses and Their Loss

The postindustrial milieu can undermine a social defense. For example, in traditional plants relationships between managers and workers are often unconsciously organized to reflect the psychodynamics of parent-child relationships. Although they have narrow jobs that frequently make them feel like children, workers may feel partly compensated by the freedom they have to ignore the broader strategic and technical dilemmas facing the plant. Similarly, although managers bear the burden of worrying about the plant's functioning, they may feel partly compensated by their ability to make decisions without consulting workers. But because the two parties do not trust one another, these arrangements create chronic anxiety and tension. Managers are afraid that workers are loafing, and workers resent being bossed and watched.

Such anxieties can nonetheless be contained when they are organized through the unconsciously experienced parent-child dynamic. Managers, viewing the workers as irresponsible children, feel assured that, by exercising discipline while showing affection, they can control the workers. Workers, feeling irresponsible but also dependent, do not violate basic rules and injunctions, such as sleeping on the job or stealing materials. The resulting relationships are far from stable because, as in actual parent-child relationships, the child tests the parent's limits and the parent is angered by the child's indifference. Living within this covert coalition, people reduce their conscious and unconscious attention to the work itself and focus instead on the vicissitudes of the resulting dependency relationship between managers and workers. The social system as a whole turns in on itself, and the plant's efficiency falls. But, however unstable this covert coalition, it helps workers and managers transform the primary anxiety of working at a role boundary into the now reduced anxiety of coping with a familiar family dynamic.

To be sure, a social defense does not appropriate all of people's attention and energy. People do their work and meet their deadlines, but they do so inefficiently and by hurting and discounting one another. *The postindustrial milieu upsets the balance* between work- and non-work-related behaviors. For example, as we saw in the case of team-based factories, plant managers, no longer protected by routine duties and an extra layer of supervision, take their roles and set a boundary only when the technical system's integrity or viability is at risk. Their authority rests entirely on their technical and organizational competence. By contrast, managers in traditional plants derive their authority from the role they play in the unconscious scripts created by paternalistic cultures. But like all roles that emerge from a basic assumption process, their authority is automatically conferred without work and collaboration, without approaching a boundary.

When challenged to collaborate with the teams in nontraditional plants, such managers experience their aggressive and trusting feelings more directly; and to appropriately take their authority, they need to modulate and integrate them. If they fail to do so, they may simply abdicate their authority or assert it too aggressively. The resulting role relationships may prove too unstable and unpredictable, and, to cope, managers and workers may create defenses more rigid than the social defenses of a paternalistic culture.

For example, I once interviewed a coordinator in a self-managing chemical plant and was struck by the obsessive and intellectualized way in which he spoke about his role and described his theory of supervision. I had a hard time understanding him. Later, I talked with a human resource manager at the company's headquarters; he too expressed his discomfort with the factory. Unable to put his finger on the problem, he felt that in contrast to his expectations the workers and managers at the plant seemed joyless and tense. I had no further interviews with plant personnel but suspect that, to cope with the anxieties of collaborating, managers and workers were treading carefully. Afraid of stepping on anyone's toes, plant personnel were ritualizing the process of self-management itself, hoping that new, more complicated rules would paradoxically tell people how to behave in nonroutine situations. In losing some of the psychological comfort provided by social defenses as well as the pleasures provided by familiar though unconscious dramas but afraid to use feelings and judgments more intensely when setting boundaries, plant personnel had created a constricted and joyless climate in which obsessive rumination drove out thinking and feeling.

Political Implosion: The Regional Phone Company

I came to understand some of the cultural implications of working in imploded settings when consulting for the training department of AB Inc., a regional phone company. As in a classic bureaucracy, decision making at AB Inc. was monopolized by managers at the top while rumors substituted for the flow of information about company priorities and directions. But as the company faced increasing competition from other communication carriers, equipment vendors, and new wiring and installation companies, AB Inc. had to develop more sophisticated marketing, pricing, and service strategies to secure its market. The senior managers came to believe that its vast corps of line workers, office workers, sales force, and lower-level managers could exercise a great deal of influence on how the public perceived the company, the quality of its service, and its commitment to meeting emerging new telecommunications needs. Ironically, as one senior manager noted, because computerized phones and switches were much more reliable and could often be repaired from a central location, line installers, repairers, the sales force, and operators interacted less frequently with customers. This meant that any single interaction was more important than ever if the company was to create a good impression in the local business and residential market. The senior managers concluded that workers had to understand the company's strategic options and dilemmas as well as the value of its products and services. They could no longer regard a worker, a clerk, or a salesperson as simply a pair of hands; they had to see that worker as a person who contributed to the company's development by understanding the company's opportunities and problems.

To develop employee understanding, senior managers had to change the purpose and structure of the training programs they once supported. In the past the company had used these programs, delivered to 20,000 blue- and white-collar workers, to tell employees about the latest rate case that it was bringing before the public utility commission. Because the trainers hoped to use employees as propaganda troops who could justify the company's request for higher phone rates to customers, friends, and relatives, they had designed the program narrowly, emphasizing prescribed purposes and specific facts. To deal with the new situation, however, they needed to design a more open-ended program that raised awareness rather than simply told the facts and that enabled the employees to rethink more openly and generally their relationships to their jobs. How did they add value to the company? Did they have the right mix of skills? And in the case of blue-collar workers, did they and could they identify with the company's strategic dilemmas and still maintain their loyalty to their union and their blue-collar status? In short, the senior managers had to create a more sophisticated boundary between themselves and the company's employees in which the workers would be allowed to take some part in developing the company's strategic relationship to its environment. By asking the employees to think, reflect, and talk back rather than simply listen, senior managers were opening themselves up to influence from below. They were creating a more open and potentially less divided culture.

In the abstract these may seem like small steps to take, but as I soon learned, they were difficult ones for managers in a bureaucratic setting. By working with the training department, I helped them to reorient their approach to training to a small degree. I used the concept of the adult learner to help them think of their employees as active learners who acquire insights, not as passive trainees who receive doses of information. By working with me, the trainers developed a few modules for a day of training that were more participative and open-ended in character, enabling employees to take part in shaping the development of the training session. Similarly, I helped them to restructure the trainer's manual so that it was less prescriptive (previous texts were written as scripts replete with instructions about when to point to a diagram, when to pause, and so on) and gave the trainer more latitude in shaping a particular module.

But it was clear that the trainers and their managers experienced much anxiety in opening up their training program to influence from the participants. Two design discussions were revealing. First, the managers and the trainers worried about not having a final message to give the employees. "Be nice" or "Be friendly to customers" was neither specific enough nor accurate. For example, to compete successfully, the company was providing less service to residential customers than before. What then were the new marching orders? They thought of placing a videotape on community relations at the end of the training day as a potential vehicle for a "rallying cry," but was the message then that employees should volunteer for community activity to help the company? That didn't sit well. I argued that no marching order was required, that the purpose of the program was to raise awareness, not to shape a particular behavior. They agreed, but they were clearly uncomfortable.

Second, in designing an opening module for the program, I proposed that participants in any particular training session talk about how employees in general felt about the company. Just as customers might have good and bad things to say about the company, I argued, so might employees. Recognizing the potential for involving the participants with this question, the managers nonetheless responded ambivalently, worrying that, if the program were opened up to gripes and complaints, the training session would deteriorate. Still fixed on a "pep rally" concept of training, they could not imagine how a program could be successful and give space for the expression of negative as well as positive feelings.

I assumed initially that they were doubtful and anxious simply because, as staff personnel at headquarters, they knew that their senior managers, concerned with control, might not easily create channels of influence and feedback from lower-level managers and workers. But by experiencing their response to a pilot session of the training program, I saw that their resistance was rooted not simply in the politics of control but in a company culture that inhibited learning and openness in general.

The pilot session, conducted two weeks before the final training materials were to be prepared for trainers throughout the company, was successful except for one segment, which was flat and unengaging. Such snafus are typical in pilot sessions, and I saw no immediate need to be concerned, but the responses of the design team (consisting of four people) and of the trainer were dramatic. They were extremely upset, and the trainer, seemingly distraught, lost his role and his relationship to the participants. He stopped projecting his voice, he seemed passive, and he stumbled through the next segment. Predictably the participants themselves stopped paying close attention. By the end of the day the design team seemed gripped by a crisis, and to my astonishment I felt as if I were watching the sudden collapse of the work group. To cope with their obvious stress, they hurriedly imagined reasons and remedies. One person thought that the pilot program participants, white-collar employees at the headquarters building, were simply not smart enough to understand the material. Another, invoking the training approaches of the past, argued that the participants needed to be told what the objectives of the training were, what they were expected to *do* when they left. A third, feeling that the trainer had failed the group and suggesting that trainers throughout the company could not be trusted, argued that the program had to be made "trainer proof." In short, the team was looking for a scapegoat, someone to punish and blame for a seemingly catastrophic error. I recall going to sleep that night filled with their sense of horror.

But the horror was of their own making. A failed segment had tripped a self-exciting process that left the team incompetent and irrational. In working through my own sense of crisis, I realized that I had just experienced the company's culture from the inside. *People in this company could not tolerate learning.* They did not know how to cope with an unfolding process that contained surprises. When I examined my learnings from this event, I understood more deeply the ambivalence and doubts the design team felt when first shaping the training program. If senior managers were to open channels of influence and communication in the company, they would have to create an open-ended process. This process could produce significant gains only if all participants acknowledged their new dependence on actors and stakeholders beyond their control. To do so, they had to develop a learning relationship to their setting, acknowledging that they would periodically stumble and that the gains from collaboration often come at the cost of false starts, errors, and failures.

Indeed, in assessing my consulting relationship to the training team, I felt that they had little feeling for the collaborative process. The director of the team, Miller, was confused by her experience of me. She valued my thoughtfulness, but she was puzzled by my insistence that I work with the team rather than develop a training design and specific group exercises alone. "Maybe we are not used to the way you work," she noted, "but we expect consultants to come in here with a proposal which we then vote up or down." I remember being puzzled by the concept of such a vote. It was their training program, after all, and their needs and values had to shape its design and delivery. How could I second-guess them? Wouldn't we work best by working together? Moreover, the notion that I would work alone, without systematic feedback from the team, and then be judged seemed more terrifying than the difficulty of working and stumbling along with them.

Assuming that her relationship to me was shaped in part by the general culture of relationships at AB Inc., I interpreted her confusion and my own feelings as signs that employees feared muddling through a problem together. Failures and errors were private affairs, and people were expected to produce completely finished plans, designs, ideas for final review alone. Yet ironically, just as I was terrified at the prospect of a vote on my work, the employees, by refusing to collaborate, submitted to the ultimately more frightening role of being judged and evaluated after having worked without support or sustained feedback. Like the victim of a Kafka-esque drama, people were isolated when solving problems and were then judged according to unclear and indefinite criteria.

My work with AB Inc. highlights the cultural and psychological obstacles to living in an imploded setting. When managers acknowledge the claims of new stakeholders and engage in a political dialogue with them, they are creating an open-ended or developmental process. In such settings boundaries separating roles, units, and levels are not fixed forever by bureaucratic rules. Subject to negotiation and defined through actions, they develop and change over time. Boundaries in an industrial milieu primarily protect the work group while enabling it to construct social defenses against anxiety. Boundaries in a postindustrial world, although they protect the work group, also challenge its defenses by introducing outside perspectives and interests. Although potentially disruptive, such outside interests can strengthen the group by connecting it to new resources. The senior managers at AB Inc. were risking their monopolistic control of decision making, but the reward was a potential increase in their effectiveness through collaboration with their subordinates. The sophisticated boundary introduces a developmental gradient into group life.

The rational clash of interests may impede the development of an open-system politics based on developmental boundaries, but there are cultural and psychological inhibitions as well, as was illustrated by the irrational responses of the design team to failure, their initial ambivalence to creating a more open-ended training program, their lack of feeling for collaboration, and the difficulty they faced in using me effectively. People find it difficult to cope with the anxiety of creating and changing boundaries in developmental settings.

To be sure, the politics of interest-group conflict can impede communication. But at AB Inc. I believe that what Bion called the politics of relatedness, the politics shaped by people's fear of being exposed, shamed, and ridiculed in a group, actually undermined senior management's interests. After all, the senior managers rationally recognized that they had to educate the company's workers and managers, raise their consciousness, and treat them less as propaganda troops and more as participants who added value to the firm's development. But despite their rational understanding of the problem, their anxiety stymied them.

In sum, the postindustrial technology and culture brings together tasks, roles, levels, and divisions that were once separate. Indeed here is the hopeful, positive side of the postindustrial economy: The division of labor is reversed. People work increasingly at the boundaries between jobs, departments, and divisions and can develop a more holistic understanding of the value of their efforts. But to sustain this more holistic perspective, managers and workers face the sophisticated problem of setting permeable and changing boundaries so that the needs and claims of outsiders can be fully understood without overwhelming the ability of insiders to accomplish their tasks. If they fail to do so, they may paradoxically create even more rigid boundaries to contain the anxiety of living in an imploded world. By creating a social world that goes against the grain of the task, such boundaries may lead to more extreme scapegoating, discounting, and psychological injuries.

In the next two chapters I examine the impact of the postindustrial milieu in greater detail. Chapter 8, in which I examine bureaucracy as a social defense, explores the case of a bank that tried to transcend its bureaucratic traditions but paradoxically created a more punishing culture instead. In chapter 9 I study the cases of a maximum security prison and NASA, the space agency responsible for the shuttle program, and demonstrate what happens when institutions are exposed to complex environments and are unable to create and sustain sophisticated organizational boundaries.

8

The Bureaucratic Culture and Its Limits: The Breakdown of a Social Defense

Bureaucracy as a Social Defense

The social defense protects people from anxiety by depersonalizing their relationships to their roles and purposes. All organizations create particular social defenses that fit with their specific tasks, their particular history, and the personalities of their leaders. However, the bureaucratic process as a common feature of modern life creates the most pervasive and powerful form of social defense. Consequently it has been the subject of extensive study and critique. Critics of the bureaucratic process charge that, although it is efficient, it nonetheless alienates people by separating them from an organization's goals and purposes. As modern life's "iron cage" it sacrifices our emotional life and our need for values to the requirements of instrumental reason. Other critics have argued that in bureaucracies senior managers monopolize the policymaking process by dividing up the work between those who think and those who do. This division of labor creates a technically efficient work flow. But in the absence of broad participation, critics suggest, senior managers pursue narrow and often dysfunctional goals and act irrationally, despite the technical apparatus at their disposal. In Mannheim's terms the organization, although technically rational, lacks substantive rationality.[1]

The bureaucracy typifies much of modern life. According to its critics, the victory of instrumental reason, based in the canons of scientific thought, has brought both great gains and much alienation. In developing and managing our technologies, individual workers become lost in a complicated and opaque division of labor and can no longer have a moral relationship to work. It is no wonder that critics of modern life have found a sympathetic home in either Marx's critique of capitalism or Weber's critique of bureaucracy. The future of bureaucracy as a social form, its capacity to help us organize our technical resources despite the costs it imposes, may hold the key to the future of modern development.

But the problem is more complex than the now familiar classical critique suggests. By examining bureaucracy as a psychodynamic process, we see that the work is technically irrational rather than technically efficient, that as a social defense bureaucratic procedures detach people from purposes because they are actually erected to contain anxiety, not to divide the thinkers from the doers, and, most important, that workers and managers may well collude to erect such defenses.

The Psychodynamics of Bureaucracy

Let us return to the example of the concurrence chain discussed in chapter 4. The system of multiple signatures on a memo estranges individuals from decision making by ensuring that no one feels at risk when signing. If everyone signs the memo, then no one can be held accountable for the decision; anyone who opposes the decision can veto it by simply not signing, without having to voice an opinion. By helping people to contain the anxiety they feel when making decisions, the concurrence chain also complicates the decision process itself by making it costly to produce a single decision. The organization is thus technically inefficient, with people accepting their estrangement in order to contain their anxiety.

In the bureaucratic process procedures that typically do not help people accomplish goals are developed and enforced simply to separate individuals from the purpose of their activities. For example, as I argued in the nursing case of chapter 6, managers who are required to fill out appraisal forms when they evaluate their employees use these forms to avoid thinking about their subordinates. They mechanically check off ratings in different categories without doing the difficult work of evaluating their employees by comparing them against their potential, their peers, and their responsibilities. Eager to avoid the anxiety of telling workers they have performed poorly, managers produce inadequate evaluations, thus limiting their ability to allocate work among their subordinates efficiently. Complaints about paperwork and meaningless procedures in bureaucratic settings belie people's willingness to collude in their own alienation.

In bureaucratic settings social relationships at work are often quite pleasant precisely because work relationships are depersonalized. In one utility with which I worked, higher-level managers did not delegate authority to those below. They held subordinates responsible for correctly executing procedures ("In processing a work order, fill out the following forms"), rather than producing results ("Income net of work order expenses for your unit should be X dollars"), and checked their actions by reviewing numerous reports. The subordinates, who did not feel accountable for results, experienced little anxiety and therefore liked their superiors and peers. They felt good about the people around them. They called the company a "family," precisely because the actual work was depersonalized. Because they stood outside a chain of delegation, the subordinates never had to face the risks—nor could they experience the pleasure—that comes with proving that they can be trusted to manage the company's resources for particular ends.

By substituting procedures and paper controls for delegation and trust, bureaucracies depersonalize the work relationship and personalize the nonwork ties. By sanctioning what Bion calls the flight from work, the bureaucratic process can persist despite its inefficiency.

The Bank

I experienced the complexities of the bureaucratic process while consulting for a bank as it tried to overcome its bureaucratic past. A regional bank with some sixty branches in its distribution network faced an irrevocably new and turbulent marketplace. The post-industrial economy was reshaping the banking marketplace just as telecommunications, deregulation, and a multinational market had forever changed the financial landscape. Insurance companies were starting to compete with banks, interstate banking was permitted, and larger banks, eager to secure a national market, were buying up smaller ones. The familiar boundaries and historical divisions between financial service companies were breaking down. Computerized databases made it easy for money market funds to offer check-writing privileges, automatic teller machines reduced people's dependence on branch banking, and computer-to-phone hookups meant that insurance companies might offer insurance and banking products through a vending machine located at a place of work. No longer able to monopolize local financial services, banks had to take a more active role in their relationships to customers by increasing the number of personnel who could sell loans; the banks also had to increase their market research, develop new financial accounts and instruments, and give branch managers greater discretion and responsibility to market the bank's services in a particular trade area. But, to delegate more authority to lower-level employees successfully and to increase their ability to plan strategies, banks throughout the economy not only had to develop new methods for organizing and managing work but also had to overcome their bureaucratic practices.

The bank, long a fixture in the regional economy, had weathered past financial crises because its old-time commercial and household customers remained loyal. The regional economy was strong, senior managers reasoned, so the bank could best survive if the loyal customers continued to identify with the bank as their own businesses and incomes grew. Consequently, to protect the bank's market share of deposits and loans and to strengthen its hold on the region, the senior managers decided to secure its market by offering customized services, products, and loans to its customers. Tellers and clerks in the branch would probe customers to learn about their financial situation and potential needs, and the bank would develop a range of products and loans to fit customers' varying needs. Similarly, branch managers would develop close ties to the merchants of their trade area. Using marketing and demographic data, they would develop a deeper understanding of the area's development, its needs, and its prospects. Bank personnel would no longer take the role of functionaries, filling out forms and executing procedures. They were now part of the bank's sales force and marketing program. Psychologically they had to leave their familiar roles and enter into the customers' world. Once protected from the boundary with the marketplace by a bureaucratic process, bank employees now had to approach the boundary.

Realizing that bank personnel were sensibly anxious about these changes, the senior managers offered clerks, tellers, and branch managers courses to help them develop new skills. The clerks and tellers took courses on how to sell to customers, on the bank's diverse product offerings, and on the rudiments of customer financial behavior over the family life cycle. The branch managers, who never before made commercial loans, took courses on lending, credit, and selling techniques.

Six months after the senior managers began to implement this strategy, a vice-president hired me to assess whether or not they were succeeding. On interviewing the key officers of the bank, I saw that the senior managers were not naive. They realized that they were hoping to change not only jobs and skills but also the bank's underlying bureaucratic culture. As they described it, clerks, tellers, branch managers, and higher-level executives had lived in a procedural world in which everyone focused on following rules rather than on obtaining results. In their words the bank had to go "from an operations to a sales culture," from one in which people followed rules to one in which they took initiative.

My own interviews with branch managers, clerks, and tellers confirmed senior management's assumptions. Bank personnel had lived in a classic bureaucratic culture. The scope of work for most managers was narrow, and most employees thought little about the bank's wider strategic dilemmas. Branch managers and their superiors (called zone managers) were not accountable for results, for contributing directly to the bank's profits. Rather, they had only to prevent procedural mistakes, ensuring that the rules for making loans, opening accounts, and moving cash were strictly followed. Indeed, many workers complained that, despite the talk of change, they were still obliged to process paperwork that had never helped and still did not help them to do their jobs.

My interviews suggested that the bank's bureaucratic culture functioned as a social defense to contain the anxiety of feeling responsible for customers' money. As many people told me, workers at all levels, particularly in the old days, engaged in the organized ritual of processing forms and producing reports that were never read or analyzed. Like the concurrence chain discussed earlier, this paper system was inefficient and overdeveloped, providing data and materials that managers did not use. It simulated a system for communication and control but often blocked both. Because they lacked a sense of priorities, managers did not know which reports were more important to write or read. This lack of control, despite the facade of control, was one reason why the bank had once before succumbed to high-flying lenders in the downtown office who made irresponsible loans that ultimately cost the bank much money. The same ritual of communication and control that enabled some managers to estrange themselves from the activities of taking and giving money allowed others to behave in a grandiose manner. The managers developed contempt for the bureaucracy, imagining that *all* controls were petty and foolish when compared to the "genius" of a downtown lender, the high roller in an international game.

Nonetheless this bureaucratic system, despite its irrationality, worked well enough so long as the bank had a secure oligopolistic market, protected by regulations that forbade price competition, interstate banking, and entry by other financial institutions. However, the system became burdensome as the bank entered a deregulated world in which insurance companies, brokerage houses, and banks from other states began offering a wide range of financial services. By redefining the work of the lower-level workers, senior managers hoped to transform the bank's culture so that people would take genuine initiative and feel responsible for results.

The Punishing Culture

Not surprisingly, the hoped-for transformation came slowly. More surprising, far from creating an entrepreneurial culture in which employees identified with the bank's new mission and took initiative, senior managers were creating a more punishing and vindictive environment. Paradoxically, in trying to overcome the social defenses of a bureaucratic world, senior managers were actually creating a more psychologically violent culture.

Lower-level workers complained particularly about a new measurement system that senior managers had introduced. To track the selling effort and assess the success of the bank's training efforts, senior managers required clerks and tellers to fill out a tracking form each time they sold one or more services to a customer. By noting what the customer had initially requested, the senior managers were able to assess workers' ability to "cross-sell" the bank's services and loans. If a customer asked only for a checking account but wound up buying a certificate of deposit as well, the worker had successfully cross-sold one additional product. Each month the marketing department produced a cross-sale report that measured the cross-sale productivity of each worker and each branch.

The workers resented the pressures created by this measurement system. They felt that the senior managers had no understanding of branch-level operations, did not know how busy clerks and tellers were, and did not in fact understand what made a branch successful. As many told me, the branch workers had to focus on service as well as on sales. Because the measurement system implicitly neglected service and emphasized sales, senior managers were helping to create an environment that paradoxically discouraged customer loyalty and commitment. As one worker noted, it was as important for the branch to retain an old customer's deposits as it was to get the deposits of a new customer.

This latent conflict between senior managers and workers at the branches undermined the measurement system itself. Some workers noted that, by neglecting to fill out the tracking form when they sold only what the customer requested, they could inflate their reported sales productivity. "Half the time I forget to fill them out," noted one. Another commented, "Last month I didn't fill out the forms. I was too busy to stop to fill them out and we were hollered at to go on to the next customer and do them later. At the end of the day I don't feel like sitting here and filling out forms." Senior managers, detecting the gap between reported and actual sales by using other bank data, responded angrily. One threatened, "I am serious. If in the future we discover that they are withholding forms, then they are stealing." And another noted that top management could make it counterproductive to beat the system. "If they omit reports to raise standards, then they are in trouble because we will use the standards as a floor," he said.

This conflict echoes the classic struggle between workers and managers over a "fair day's work," with managers demanding more production and workers offering less. But although the interplay and clash of rational interests between the two groups did play a role, irrational processes were also important. After all, senior managers, anxious to create a new spirit of commitment among the workers, had only alienated them further. Moreover, unlike the straw bosses of old who could compel employees simply to work faster, the bank managers wanted the workers to work "smarter," with more initiative and understanding. They could not force workers to feel more responsible. Such feelings had to emerge through a complex combination of incentive, negotiation, and daily collaboration. A gap emerged between the senior management's exercise of power and the promotion of its rational interests.

The Problem of Delegation
In reviewing the problem facing the senior managers, I noticed that they had spent much time defining the new jobs and roles of the clerks and tellers and gave less attention to the changes required in

the branch manager and zone manager roles (the zone manager supervised five branches). The branch managers had taken a lending course, but the results of their lending activities were not formally measured. Zone managers, in contrast to the branch managers and the workers, had no new job duties whatsoever. It seemed as if the lower-level workers were expected to take the lead in reshaping the bank's culture.

In a labor-intensive factory, where operators, working hard and fast, produce the goods and profits, it may be rational to focus on the lower-level workers alone. But in banking the branch manager can play a significant role in setting the climate of the branch. Indeed, a statistical study of bank sales data by branch suggested that branch managers could indeed raise the sales productivity of the clerks and tellers by supervising their work, interacting with customers, and establishing sales and service priorities for particular days and weeks. More striking, in comparing sales data by zone, I concluded that zone managers on the average made no difference to sales. That is, despite their high position and official responsibility (they were one level below the vice-presidents of the bank), their impact on sales was negligible. Because zone managers' efforts were redundant and branch managers' efforts were insufficiently reinforced, the complaint of the clerks seemed justified. Managers above them in the chain of command were not reorganizing the resources of the bank and their own time and attention to support the clerks' and tellers' individual efforts. No wonder the workers at the bottom felt burdened.

Like generals who stay home while the troops are in the trenches, the management structure of the bank was "leading from behind." But why? My hypothesis about the bank's bureaucratic culture is suggestive here. In a bureaucratic system middle managers primarily check and monitor the work of those below them without actually developing plans or deploying resources to accomplish long-term goals. The top of the chain of command thinks, the bottom follows orders, and the middle transmits information from the top to the bottom. Senior managers do not delegate authority to managers below them. One zone manager, who should possess significant authority over bank resources, told me that he had to get permission to spend $2,000 on a community relations effort for a branch under his purview. Moreover, another zone manager told me that he did not even want more marketing authority. "Not having a budget for

marketing gives you the opportunity of not knowing what your constraints are," he said. "I can say, 'Let Bob [a senior vice-president] do
it. Let him wrestle with that one.'"

To create initiative throughout the management system, senior
managers would have to authorize zone and branch managers to
make important decisions. By having authority delegated to them,
personnel in the middle layers of the organization would for the first
time become managers rather than messengers. But as we saw in
discussing the boundary between plant managers and self-managing
teams in chapter 7, delegating always creates risks and uncertainties.
The manager not only has to trust subordinates but also has to dis-
tinguish more clearly competent from incompetent ones, learning
to reward the competent workers while depriving the incompetent
ones of merit raises and other organizational resources. In a bureaucratic system managers are protected from anxiety by the layering of
the control that separates them from their employees, by the routine
coordination of predictable activities of units and divisions, and by
the monopoly of major initiatives. Because they are protected from
confronting the interpersonal processes of delegation and evaluation, the senior managers are relieved of enacting and maintaining
the superior-subordinate and role-person boundaries. Both boundaries are automatically maintained by the system of bureaucratic
procedures. If subordinates follow the rules, they automatically meet
their obligations and play their roles. Similarly, because superiors
do not have to face the complicated problem of evaluating someone
they personally like or of trusting someone who though highly competent "feels" different and strange (for example, a minority person),
they do not have to decide where personal sentiments end and role
obligations begin. By deepening the interpersonal process, delegation and evaluation also highlight the importance of the role-person
boundary.

But the social defenses of the bank's bureaucratic system ob-
structed delegation and evaluation. As we have seen, paper communication, written procedures, and management control substituted
for delegation. Senior managers could avoid the anxiety of actually
trusting others to take and give money by treating them as messengers or order takers. This inherited system of social defenses explains a peculiar dynamic of change at the bank. The closer the
employees were to the vice-president level, the less pressure they

faced to change the ways in which they worked. As we have seen, zone managers faced no changes, and the selling performance of branch managers was not directly measured; but the lowest-level workers found their jobs changed and their performance measured. Senior managers were avoiding the anxiety of delegating by not changing their relationships with their immediate subordinates, by not dealing with those they knew on a firsthand basis. By avoiding the interpersonal difficulties that delegation would create, they projected both their hopes and their anxiety onto the lowest-level workers, the people farthest from them personally, who had the least organizational power and were therefore most easily scapegoated. Feeling unfairly burdened—after all, clerks and tellers could not alone change the bank—the low-level workers resisted senior managements' pressure to change. Senior managers in turn were disappointed and angry and threatened to punish the lowest-level workers. Despite their hopes for an entrepreneurial culture, they were creating a punishing one instead. The social defenses of a once-bureaucratic process were breaking down. Anxiety once held in check by the social defenses broke through, leading to more primitive projection and scapegoating. The impersonal world of paper, which alienated everybody, was becoming the intensely personal world of punishment and anger, where particular people and groups were hurt.

Vignettes and Encounters

Several vignettes highlight the problem of delegation in a bureaucratic culture. I attended a meeting of all the branch and zone managers; in the meeting members of the marketing staff presented the recent results of a survey in which researchers posing as customers had observed all the branches of the bank. On entering the large meeting room, I noticed three things: The vice-presidents were absent, the zone managers sat in no special section and were scattered among the branch managers, and the marketing staff specialist could identify no one in the room who seemed to be in charge and who could introduce her. To begin, she called the meeting to order and introduced herself! In short, there was no palpable authority in the room, and a staff person was forced to bring order to the meeting.

This is typical of a bureaucratic culture. Line managers lack authority, and senior managers rely on the staff specialist to monitor performance. The palpable lack of authority is not surprising, except that the purpose of the meeting was novel and fitted with senior management's program of cultural change. For the first time branch managers were getting feedback on a systematic basis about how the branches might look to a customer. Senior managers were including the branch managers in a process of study and review.

This mix of old relationships and new ones created both anxiety and contradiction. The branch managers listened passively to the survey report and had few questions. The most passionate question came from one manager who asked why the researchers who were observing "bad" worker behavior or a "bad branch environment" had not given the results to the managers on the spot. The suggestion sounds plausible enough—it is good to get feedback right away—but on reflection I felt that the branch manager was expressing different thoughts and feelings. First, he felt punished by the feedback from the survey, which portrayed the branches as rather average settings. Second, if he got the feedback right away, he could then punish the bad workers. Third, he was not interested in thinking about the pattern of results across all the branches so that he might learn what makes an effective branch; he simply wanted to know about *his* branch. Like an administrator in a bureaucratic system, he wanted to catch an employee violating a procedure. The manager was preoccupied with being punished and punishing others.

To be sure, it is hard to hear feedback without feeling defensive, and the bank's use of incognito researchers may have seemed sneaky and uncollaborative, although it is a method typically used by retail establishments. More important, the manager's preoccupation with punishment mirrored the lack of authority in the room. People can listen to feedback when they feel authorized and trusted to act, when they feel that, by listening constructively, they will be able to take constructive actions. But as we have seen, the meeting deauthorized them, turning them into a passive audience, obliterating the distinction between roles, and placing staff officers in charge of the line.

The Training Manager

My interactions with Hatfield, the training manager for the bank, highlighted similar themes and issues. Realizing that the marketing department was rapidly introducing new services for customers, such as various checking accounts, leasing programs, IRAs, and CDs, management asked Hatfield to make sure that the clerks and tellers in the branches understood the features and benefits of these services. After discussing various alternatives with his superiors, the training manager decided to require all branch managers to hold regular meetings in their branches on a particular service. In addition, he would train them on how to conduct meetings, describing it as a "training-the-trainers program." In discussing the plan with me, I told him that it would certainly fail. He headed a staff function, and line managers, even those as low as branch managers, would not listen to him. If he proposed such a program, the branch managers and their superiors would only ignore it, leading to greater contempt for both the training department and the sound idea that workers should spend more time studying the features and benefits of the services they were supposed to sell.

Hatfield concurred and later found a way to introduce training programs to the branches while acknowledging the branch manager's line authority. But his original plan struck me as symptomatic. Hatfield was taking the role of a staff specialist in a bureaucratic system despite management's acknowledgment that it had to construct a nonbureaucratic culture. By calling the managers "trainers," he continued to deny this new understanding, because the term "trainer" applies to staff positions, not line ones. In fact, by taking a "command" role—he would instruct the managers on how to behave—he was assuming a line position while implicitly labeling the line managers as staff. In his mind he was reversing the distribution of line and staff roles.

As we have seen, such role reversals signal that anxiety is shaping people's behavior. For example, to deny the anxiety she felt as the lonely leader, Louise, the director of the legal services program discussed in chapter 1, behaved as if she were in a staff relationship to her subordinates.

Hatfield too appeared quite anxious over the few months that I worked with him. Shortly after we spoke about the training program, he told me that he had been instructed to develop a general training program for the branch managers. He came to my office for help and seemed anxious to get ideas from me, but he was particularly passive in the way in which he was listening. He acknowledged my ideas but failed to write anything down. Feeling anxious that nothing was being heard, I hurriedly summarized on a piece of paper what I had said and gave it to him at the end of the meeting. I remember doing this with some urgency, almost shoving the paper in front of his nose, as if this were the only way to secure his attention. He then asked me if *I* would write his training plan! I was shocked. After telling him that I thought it best for him to formulate the plan himself, I realized why he appeared both needy and passive during our conversation. He was hoping all along that I would do it.

In thinking about this encounter, I concluded that I had been inducted into the interpersonal dynamics of the bank's bureaucratic culture. I understood for the first time the sheer frustration senior managers feel when dealing with the psychosocial systems they cannot change. The chain of command at the bank was weak because in dyadic encounters *one person is active and "overfunctioning," whereas the other remains passive and compliant.* Delegation is a two-way street. The senior managers feared giving up authority, and the zone and branch managers feared taking it. Indeed, as we have seen, one zone manager was grateful for not having marketing authority, and at the consumer survey meeting no zone manager took authority for calling the meeting to order. I suspect that the resulting stalemate only further convinced the senior managers that lower-level managers could not be trusted, and the lower-level managers, watching the senior managers retain control, felt justified in not taking more authority. As a result, an individual pushing an idea or program experiences compliance rather than active resistance and leaves the encounter feeling that he or she is completely responsible for implementing the idea. In taking initiative, the individual experiences no collaborative response.

This bank experience gave me greater insight into the punishing culture that seemed to be emerging at the bank despite the senior managers' stated wishes to promote initiative and entrepreneurship among bank employees. As I reflected on my puzzling experience, I realized that I wanted to wring Hatfield's neck, *simply to get his attention.* I believe that this is how the senior managers of the bank felt. They too wanted to wring their subordinates' necks to shake them out of their apparent stupor. This gave me greater insight into the conflict between the senior managers and the workers in the branches. I suspect that some senior managers quickly joined the fight against the lowest-level workers, because here at last was a struggle they could sink their teeth into! Resistance, however unwelcome, was at least explicit and active.

Authority and Groups

A conversation with Sampson, a vice-president who supervised ten zone managers, gave me further insight into the bank's bureaucratic traditions. Sampson complained that, when he met with his managers as a group, he was never satisfied that they were saying what was on their minds. He decided therefore to deemphasize these meetings and talk with his subordinates one by one. In such intimate settings he had found that the managers were more open. I told him that I thought group meetings were important and that, if he wished, I could attend one and perhaps give him some feedback afterward or, if he felt comfortable, make some comments at the meeting itself. He demurred politely, affirmed his commitment to his strategy and moved quickly to another topic. I sensed that he had withdrawn emotionally from me a bit, that he trusted me less, and that I had overstepped a boundary.

What was going on here? The group meetings made him anxious, he felt ineffective, and he hoped instead to short-circuit them by using the more intimate setting of one-on-one talks. I have little doubt that he was less anxious with the talks, but in my experience he and other managers found intimate talks more satisfying because they did not raise the fundamental issues of authority and delegation that haunt all managers in a chain of command. In group meetings people meet one another in their roles. Subordinates are conscious of the distance between themselves and their superiors and are aware of the competition they feel with one another. These primitive feelings of a distant authority and competitive equals express the fundamental difficulties people have in collaborating across role boundaries.

Sampson was right. People were walking on eggs at the group meetings to protect themselves from feeling competitive and confronting their relationship to authority. In fact, by remaining silent at the meetings, Sampson's zone managers were enacting a symbolic revolt against his authority. By depriving him of the information and resources he needed to be their leader, substituting the more primitive drama of the children's revolt against the parent for the drama of sibling competition, the zone managers could collectively experience contempt for Sampson as a way of denying the authority he actually had, if he chose to exercise it.

But people can learn to collaborate only by working through these anxieties—accepting role differences, acknowledging role boundaries, facing the primitive feelings they evoke, and then collaborating despite them. Sampson's intimate talks were thus a social defense against this experience, for they created the fantasy that role differences need not really interfere in the relationships between people at work, that each subordinate has a special relationship to the boss and therefore is protected from defeat by rivals. The boss in turn can deny fundamental role differences from subordinates and special burdens as a leader and treat subordinates as friends. In short, by retreating to intimate talks, Sampson avoided the difficult issues of delegation and authority. But in fact *this is precisely the kind of experience he needed to learn to take his own role in the bank's new entrepreneurial culture.*

Finally, his withdrawal from me signaled that, if I spoke the truth, he would punish me. Sampson knew that the failed group meetings were telling, but he could not face their meaning directly. By suggesting that I help him learn what they meant, I threatened to undermine his defenses, and therefore he punished me. Ironically, although he said he wanted to hear the truth from his subordinates, in fact he did not want to hear it from me. Just as his subordinates had punished him by clamming up at group meetings, so he would punish me by withdrawing.

The Senior Managers and the Punishing Culture

After a year of work with the senior managers, I saw how this punishing culture was beginning to shape relationships at the top of the chain of command as well. The senior officer of the bank, Cook, appointed an executive named Dry as a vice-president in charge of ten zone managers. I interviewed Dry some months after he arrived and was struck by his nervousness, by the air of tension he created as he spoke. He first told me that he was happy to talk with me but that I really needed to understand him, to see what made him tick. After describing his first few months at the bank, he told me that he was going to be tough with his direct reports and that he had already given several zone managers much lower performance appraisal grades than they expected. They were "furious," he said, but he had to show them that he meant business. At the end of the conversation he invited me with some urgency to return to his office soon because I really had to get to know him if I was to work with him.

Several days later I spoke with Cook, who mentioned spontaneously that he was concerned about Dry. He worried that Dry was stirring up his managers too much and said that some had already complained to him. Cook talked about how Dry had "cleaned up the mess" in his previous position. I asked Cook if he had told Dry about his concerns, and he said that he had not. I suggested that perhaps Dry thought it was incumbent on him to clean up the mess at the bank and go after the bad guys again. Cook said nothing.

This conversation helped me to understand Dry's insistence that I come to understand who he was. He felt typecast, and he wanted me to see that he was more complex than he appeared in his role. If I were to work with him, I needed to see the person behind the role as well as understand the role itself. Pulled from a tough guy assignment, he now felt that he had to enact the tough guy role again, he felt this to be burdensome and isolating. I could help end his isolation if I really understood him.

Cook's reluctance to confront Dry and his lack of response to my interpretation suggest that Cook was indeed colluding in setting up Dry as the bad guy while protecting himself from the fray that Dry was surely to create. I do not believe that this was a deliberate and conscious strategy on Cook's part. He seemed genuinely concerned that Dry might be going overboard. Rather, by disowning Dry, he could project onto him his own anger, his own wish to wring the necks of his managers without giving up on the fantasy that he could create an entrepreneurial culture by simply wishing it. Cook and his colleagues seemed unable to find the terrain in which they could demand results from their subordinates and convey that they trusted them. They could not join aggression and delegation together in a moment of genuine collaboration. Instead they split the two apart so that aggression was located in Dry (and in the responses of the lower-level workers) and delegation was contained in the distorted process of pseudocommunication and pseudocompliance that I had experienced in the conversations with Hatfield. Dry, like the lower-level workers, was being used as a scapegoat to cope with the anxiety created by the bank's stalemated situation.

The Problem of Splitting

The managers' experiences at the bank highlight how and why bureaucracies depersonalize relationships. To work without social defenses, managers must delegate work to their subordinates through a complex emotional process. Although they trust them and therefore believe in their capacity to be effective, they must also be prepared to judge them rationally, suspending the common feelings of loyalty and sympathy that emerge when one person gains another's trust. They must enact and manage a much more complicated role-person boundary.

It is commonly understood that good managers are good delegators, but management theorists underestimate the complexity of the emotional work required to delegate authority to a subordinate. When entrusting important parts of their world to others, managers take substantial risks. They can give parts of their world to subordinates for safekeeping only by identifying with those subordinates.

Object-relations theory helps us to understand how such identification emerges. Managers trust subordinates *by projecting their own image of the good into them.* To be sure, they imagine that the subordinates are trustworthy by rationally assessing them. But to *feel* trusting, they must also irrationally see the reflected images of their own good internal objects in their experience of the subordinates. *They imagine that the subordinates are like the good parts of themselves.* (That is why narcissistic leaders cannot judge the character of their subordinates. They are compelled to see only the inflated or grandiose images of themselves in their "trusted" subordinates.)

But to manage subordinates in nonbureaucratic settings, managers must also hold the subordinates accountable for results, rewarding them when they succeed and punishing them when they fail. Rationally they must detach themselves from their subordinates and judge their performance coolly, but irrationally they must see the reflected images of their own bad objects in their experience of their subordinates. To detach themselves and coolly judge their subordinates, they must devalue them, imagining that they are bad and therefore can be persecutingly judged.

This affective relationship works when managers can integrate their good and bad images of their subordinates in whole images, thus sustaining realistic but emotional ties to them. But as Klein argues, people find it hard to sustain such whole images of others and themselves, for the wholeness itself creates anxiety.[2] People become anxious and uncertain, afraid that in facing the bad parts of those they love they will lose touch with the good parts. The bad will contaminate the good, giving rise to a persecuting world. This is why, for example, lovers frequently idealize one another, why popular culture creates movie star idols, and why people need enemies to create and sustain their heroes. Like taboos and superstitions, these idealizations protect us from our own "demons," from the bad objects of our internal world that make living painful. Arguing that adults can sustain whole images of others only through developmental conflicts that begin in childhood and that are faced afresh throughout the adult life cycle, Klein and her students place this capacity for wholeness at the center of a fully healthy and ultimately moral conception of adult life.

This Kleinian perspective deepens our understanding of the fundamentally defensive role of the bureaucratic process. When work makes us anxious, we are responding not simply to the objective risks we face but to the way in which we introject or internalize these risks. Feelings of anxiety signify that these objective risks have stimulated the bad objects within us. Because we feel persecuted rather than challenged by these risks, we feel compelled to protect our good objects. By idealizing some parts of our world, such as our leader or our own competence, while denigrating others, such as our competitors or workers from the "other" division, we can protect our sense of self-worth in an otherwise threatening setting. Organizations facing complicated and risky tasks are thus threatened with splits, divisiveness, and infighting. In the absence of a mature management cadre and a culture that supports self-reflection, the bureaucratic process contains the impacts of these splits by depersonalizing the management process, ensuring that people need not feel at risk, that managers need not trust, and that procedures will contain aggression. Although irrational on its own terms, the bureaucratic process protects the organization from the more severe consequences of its members' own immaturity.

This psychosocial process clarifies the dynamics of development at the bank. Faced with new market conditions that forced the bank to manage the boundary with its customers more actively, the bank could no longer afford to sustain its bureaucratic process. The dysfunctions it imposed became costly. But to develop a nonbureaucratic process based on a culture of delegation and accountability, managers had to sustain whole images of their subordinates, and this process made them anxious. Unable to contain their anxiety, they split their images of good and bad, projecting the good into their close subordinates, who were not accountable for results, and projecting the bad into their distant subordinates, the workers who became accountable for all progress in the bank.

Feelings of anxiety at the bank were thus nourished from two complementary sources. Nonbureaucratic processes forced subordinates to face the risks of work and challenged managers to develop and sustain whole and often anxiety-laden images of their subordinates. This is why the bank, in trying to transcend its bureaucratic past, could paradoxically create a punishing and vindictive culture. In trying to overcome its social defenses, it actually became more irrational.

Summary

The bank managers lived in a bureaucratic culture in which the rituals of communication substituted for genuine collaboration. By studying how its senior managers tried to create a nonbureaucratic culture, we can understand the psychosocial currents that shape bureaucratic processes. There is little delegation, rituals of communication substitute for collaboration, subordinates are passive and compliant, staff personnel frequently control the line organization, and, by splitting apart the good and bad images they have of their subordinates, managers lose the ability to combine trust and aggression when delegating to them. Although ultimately inefficient and irrational, the resulting organization nonetheless helps people to contain the anxiety of working. In trying to overcome their bureaucratic past, the senior managers came face to face with this underlying anxiety. And because they were unable to contain their anxiety through delegation, new staff-line relationships, and subordinates willing to take authority, they projected their resulting anger and frustration onto the lowest-level workers. Ironically anxiety that was once repressed returned to create a more punishing and psychologically dangerous setting.

The bank's experience highlights the limits and potential dangers of managers' attempts to design or "engineer" company cultures.[3] Companies burdened with a bureaucratic past face the problem of creating a psychosocial climate in which trust and aggression are deployed in a modulated fashion. People will feel motivated to work because they are able to collaborate more effectively with one another. Just as I felt closer to Jim (the client in the architecture and engineering company discussed in chapter 3) by taking my role and sublimating my aggression, we can grow to appreciate and value our co-workers when we sublimate aggression and modulate trust in a nonbureaucratic culture. By successfully working together, we feel closer and, in feeling closer, we are motivated to work together.

But in light of the anxiety this climate may create, many companies hope to motivate workers by idealizing the company instead. Employees will be motivated to take risks, manager's hope, because the image of the company will function as their inner ideal. Just as the members of a faceless crowd may feel linked to one another because they love the same idealized leader, employees who relate poorly to one another will nonetheless feel connected to one another because they are members of the same ideal company. This new culture will enable employees to short-circuit the difficult process of facing each other directly, of learning to use and to sublimate more fully their feelings when working with others by substituting a shared ideal for specific working relationships.[4]

Such a manufactured culture is dangerous because it solves the problem of a depersonalized work system by developing and sustaining a psychological culture of splitting. If the company is the new psychological ideal, what Freud called the ego-ideal, then noncompany people or employees who deviate from its norms are correspondingly bad and dangerous. Such a totalitarian culture supports idealizations by ultimately hurting deviants or outsiders, leading managers, for example, to punish dissenters and disloyalists or to commit corporate crimes to protect the company. Thus, in going beyond bureaucracy, we face a branch point. We can create settings in which people can sustain the anxiety of seeing one another as both good and bad, or we can create settings in which people work together because they idealize the company and devalue outsiders.

9

Open Systems and Growing Irrationality

Boundaries in a Postindustrial Milieu

To function in a postindustrial milieu, an organization must reconfigure its relationship to its wider environment and its internal structure. Indeed, these two developments are connected. As we saw in chapter 8, to develop new links with its customers, the bank had to develop new links between managers and their subordinates. Similarly, the managers at AB Inc., the regional phone company discussed in chapter 7, tried to reconfigure their relationships to lower-level employees because employees had to develop more sophisticated relationships to customers.

In a postindustrial milieu managers and workers face the sophisticated problem of creating permeable boundaries so that the needs and claims of people outside the organization can be understood, acknowledged, and influenced without overwhelming the ability of people within the organization to accomplish their tasks. For example, as we saw in chapter 1, the director of a legal services organization, Louise, had to acknowledge the power and influence of conservative forces in the county to protect the organization's ability to function. In pursuing a program of both co-optation and anticipation, she developed work report forms and new management controls to protect the program against possible charges of corruption, wasteful use of resources, or violation of the rules and regulations of its charter. Unwilling to acknowledge political reality, Louise's subordinates interpreted these steps as a sign of Louise's personal ambitions and need for control rather than as her attempt to protect the program through a sophisticated strategy of anticipating how the organization might be attacked.

Can managers and workers enact and maintain sophisticated

boundaries? Can they face the challenge of being open to their world while protecting the cohesion of their primary working relationships and the fundamental mission of their organization? As we saw in the case of AB Inc., cultural and psychological obstacles may stymie them. Taxed and stressed by the demands of multiple and often contradictory claims and unable to create a learning culture within the company and a developmental relationship to their setting, organization leaders may be tempted to either turn inward, creating a more closed and ultimately destructive organization, or simply abdicate, leaving people without the protection of effective role, unit, and organizational boundaries. If organizations become too closed or too open, the always uneasy compromise between fantasy and reality breaks down, and work life grows more irrational.

For example, two years after my work with Louise and her staff, I learned that lawyers in the program, although facing increasing political hostility, were unionizing and attacking Louise for her arbitrary leadership. Many of the managers with whom Louise worked petitioned to join the bargaining unit, arguing that they too were oppressed. Louise and her associates in the executive office argued that as managers they could not be members of a union local. I heard of this from afar, but the story confirmed my worst fears about the program's psychosocial structure. Although the program faced significant structural and strategic problems and Louise could certainly have improved her performance, a union that isolated her and located the management function entirely within the executive office could only undermine the program as a whole. Unable to acknowledge and confront the hostile setting they faced, the lawyers substituted a drama of conflict within the organization for the conflict of interests outside of it.

To maintain a sophisticated boundary in a postindustrial milieu, managers must develop and maintain organizational systems that are neither too open nor too closed to their environment. If they fail to do so, they may create an organizational crisis and break down. Two dramatic examples of irrationality and breakdown, the case of a maximum security prison and the crash of the space shuttle *Challenger*, briefly explored in the introduction, highlight the complementary dynamics of excessively closed and open systems. By examining these two extreme cases, we obtain deeper insights into the normal crises facing many organizations as they navigate the postindustrial transition.

The Prison

Prison X is a maximum security prison in a rural area of a large state. Until the 1950s such prisons were run as personal strongholds ruled by politically powerful wardens with strong ties to particular state legislators. Prisoners were compliant, and the trusted ones worked in prison offices implementing administrative procedures. The guards, uneducated and poorly paid, frequently lived on or near the prison grounds. The warden was their protector, their guardian, giving them steady work and subsidizing their housing and food. The prison was a closed system.[1]

In the 1960s the political and social environment shaping prison life changed. Influenced by examples of political militancy outside prison walls, prisoners became less compliant. Liberal groups used the courts to force prison reform, and governors gave greater authority to commissioners of corrections, who began modernizing prison management and the guard force. Prison X, designed to house the toughest of the new noncompliant inmates, was a violent institution. Inmates verbally abused guards and threw feces at them. The guards, unable to assert their authority, used mace and clubs indiscriminately to force inmates to obey orders. In 1981 a group of prisoners took over a cell block, raped a guard, and set fire to prison facilities; they were subdued only after an eighteen-hour confrontation. As one guard told me, going to work every day "was like going to war." Because it housed difficult prisoners, Prison X could not be a tranquil institution, but outside monitors agreed that the prison administration had lost control. Guards and inmates were acting out, creating an escalating cycle of violence. Ultimately the prison was brought under control when a new state director for corrections and a new warden replaced key members of the dominant coalition that ruled the prison. When my team and I worked with the new director in a seminar on corrections management, we were asked to examine how and why the prison had become so violent and how the story of its transformation might help other wardens contain and reorganize violent prison settings.

The Closed System

Prison X was a "closed" institution, operating in a political environment that could no longer support the independent warden who once ruled the prison like a personal fief. But despite this disjunction between the prison and its setting, a coalition of old-line lieutenants and the chief of security, invisible to the public, ruled the prison as though the politics of prisons and corrections had not been changed. The warden, officially accountable to the public for the operation of the prison, lacked power inside the prison walls. Instead, the security chief, who ostensibly reported to the warden, was protected and supported by the state's assistant director for corrections, who had greatly influenced the prison's design. The warden, trained in modern corrections philosophy, was unable to confront the combined authority of the security chief and the assistant director. Resigned to his defeat and eager to boost the morale of the guards who felt abused by the prisoners and the courts, he played the figurehead role, making daily tours of the cell blocks so that the guards could see him. Official authority did not match real authority; as one corrections official in the state office told me, "A lot of power people and cliques were running the institution. The program treatment supervisor was writing responses to the American Civil Liberties Union consent decree, an employee relations representative determined hiring and firing, an operations officer read inmate grievances and wrote answers over the warden's signature."

This secret coalition was based in the history of prison governance. The security chief and the assistant director represented the old power elite in the state. Hoping to retain personal control over large state prisons, they worked to shield them from public view and the claims of outside interest groups. The guards, who felt powerless, welcomed this arrangement by identifying with hidden powers who controlled the weapons and pulled the strings. This identification made them feel less at risk in a violent setting that threatened them physically and undermined their legitimacy as presumably professional guards.

Yet, as the guards themselves understood, the gap between official and secret authority created chaos in their own lives. As one guard noted, "The staff didn't even know which way they were going as far as being depended upon to do a job. You could just wind up getting dismissed, you know what I am saying? It goes back to the phrase, 'It's not what you know, it's who you know.' " Because they did not understand their responsibilities, they could not take the authority of the guard role. One guard, reflecting on the guards' failure to stop two takeovers by prisoners, noted, "You were not expected to decipher what was going on. If you had firsthand knowledge and would pass it up, it was like pouring water on a duck's back. You'll go back and tell the supervisor and the supervisor will pass it up through the chain of command. Nothing ever happened until the actual incident took place." Lacking a sense of their own authority and feeling uncertain about who was really in charge, the guards behaved passively. "We felt that the inmates were so locked up, that our buildings were so secure, people became confident that nobody could ever get out of the buildings. I think we got very comfortable."

To contain the anxiety they felt, to feel comfortable, the guards identified with the secret coalition even though its leaders helped create a violent and unstable prison. Hoping to feel comfortable, they actually became more vulnerable. The social defenses of the prison system were failing, leading to psychological and physical violence. In the old setting of a prison fief, the covert coalition between the warden and the guards was based on the model of the paternalistic father who protected his uneducated children and gave them steady work and food. Indeed, because wardens frequently used trusted inmates as workers, the guards and inmates were like siblings joined in their common relationship to the powerful warden. The anxiety of taking the guard role was minimized because the warden transformed inmates into prison employees.

Of course, the new political milieu challenged this arrangement. Prisons became open systems as outside interest groups and stakeholders influenced prison governance. Paternalism as a social defense against the anxiety of working in prisons failed. But, in failing, it was transformed into a more violent defense. The paternalistic coalition did not simply disappear. Rather, it took on a more destructive and malevolent form. The security chief and his lieutenants, not representing official authority as the old-line warden once did, banded together to defy authority and the courts and the law. The paternalistic milieu, sustained by the "father" warden, became a sibling horde to attack the "father." This explains the paradox of the guards' identification with the secret coalition, despite its failings and limits. Feeling abused by the outside world, they identified with the symbol of a secret group that used force to usurp power. By identifying with the secret coalition, the guards felt contempt for the warden who functioned only as a figurehead. By psychologically scapegoating the warden, they could deny their own vulnerability and secretly laugh at official authority. Indeed, in a poignant interview the warden told me that, when he was finally fired, few guards or lieutenants came to his defense even though he had worked to boost their morale.

The psychodynamics of this secret coalition explains one of the more peculiar features of the increasingly violent prison. As a result of the suit brought by the American Civil Liberties Union, the court ordered the state corrections department to end guard violence against inmates, but the warden and guards did not comply. Thus, by disregarding inmate rights and ignoring court orders, the guards paradoxically behaved as though they were outlaws. This is why the guards could not cool down violence as professionals might. But the guards became outlaws not because they were innately violent or simply ignorent but because they had identified with a secret coalition that stood outside the lawful chain of command. Paternalism as a social defense gave way to the sibling horde as the prison itself was exposed to a more open, demanding, and exacting environment. The prison became more psychologically and physically violent.

This example highlights the complexities of operating in an imploded setting. The leaders of both Prison X and the state corrections department were unwilling and unable to manage a sophisticated boundary through which new stakeholders, such as prison rights groups, the ACLU, and a more demanding prison population, were acknowledged while carrying out the primary task of running a secure and safe prison. The warden and the state director abdicated, enabling the assistant director and the security chief to create a closed and ultimately violent prison system. Unable to contain prisoner violence with guard violence, the covert coalition of the assistant director and the security chief was ultimately replaced.

NASA and Leader Abdication

Prisons may seem to be extreme institutions. They are tucked away in rural areas, often deprived of funding and support and prone to violence and instability. But consider the case of NASA, a mainstream institution supported by the public with access to the most talented engineers, scientists, and managers. NASA's failure to prevent the catastrophic launch of the space shuttle *Challenger* highlights the dilemmas of leader abdication, which creates an excessively open and a closed system at the same time.

The shuttle exploded when extreme compression and temperature eroded a primary seal connecting the two parts of the booster rocket.

As the presidential commission noted, NASA faced unusual political and technical pressures. "From the inception of the shuttle, NASA had been advertising a vehicle that would make space operations routine and commercial. The greater the annual number of flights, the greater the degree of routinization and economy, so heavy emphasis was placed upon schedule. However, the attempt to build up to 24 missions a year brought a number of difficulties, among them compression of training schedules, the lack of spare parts, and the focusing of resources on near-term problems."[2]

Faced with budget cuts and a climate of fiscal austerity, NASA hoped to prove that the shuttle was commercially viable, that it could create a source of steady revenue to support its own activities. Such a strategy contradicted reality, for the shuttle launching system was still in its development phase and numerous technical problems still plagued the engineers and managers.

The commission also noted without further analysis that the accident happened because third-level personnel at the Marshall Space Center, particularly Larry Mulloy and Stanley Reinartz, were isolated from the rest of the NASA decision-making chain. At the commission hearing the chief of the Marshall Space Center, William Lucas, testified that in the early morning hours before the launch he had no idea that both NASA engineers and engineers for the company that produced the rocket, Morton-Thiokol, were still worried about the seal. "Had I had the advantage at the time of the testimony that I have heard this week," he noted, "I would have had a different attitude entirely."[3]

Personnel at Marshall Space Center, one of the three centers that cooperates in launching a rocket, approved a shuttle launch by reversing the traditional and mandated practice of safety first. A Morton-Thiokol engineer noted that this seemed to happen without conscious forethought, without awareness. In describing the deliberations on the night before the launch, when he himself worried about launching the shuttle in the cold, he noted, "We had dealt with Marshall for a long time and have always been in the position of defending our position to make sure that we were ready to fly and I guess I didn't realize until after the meeting and after several days that we had absolutely changed our position from what we had been before. [Now] we had to prove to them that we weren't ready. We were trying to find some way to prove to them that it wouldn't work."[4]

In the typical relationship between leaders and technical personnel, the leaders, not the staff, worry about integrating the technical capacities of the organization with its goals and policies. Responsible technical personnel highlight the constraints that leader face. But as the Morton-Thiokol engineer noted, this relationship was turned upside down. Mulloy and Reinartz were acting as if they were the leaders, taking as their constraint the policy contradiction faced by NASA as a whole. They, rather than their superiors, represented the need to launch and therefore reversed the way they typically considered technical judgments. Mulloy and Reinartz were acting as the leaders of NASA. This explains in part why they did not give their superior, Lucas, the critical information. There was no need to let Lucas know because they were psychologically the ersatz heads of NASA.

But how did this happen? In part, Mulloy, his colleagues, and the engineers at Morton-Thiokol grew accustomed to the seal problem. It had plagued them since at least December 1982, and its chronicity enabled them to discount its significance. But on the night before the launch, even Allan McDonald, Morton-Thiokol's chief of engineering, who earlier had cooperated with NASA in discounting the seal problem, opposed the launch.

The presidential commission argues that the decision to launch was due to a "tendency to management isolation" at Marshall so that they "failed to provide full and timely information bearing on the safety of the flight."[5] Indeed, NASA engineers and managers created a closed social system unresponsive to information and warnings from outsiders or disaffected insiders. As one reporter noted, NASA "is like a close-knit family. Problems stay within; whistleblowers are few." Engineers concerned with the problems of the shuttle "would never go outside the family."[6] NASA has centers in Alabama, Florida, and Texas and, as the commission noted, "project managers for the various elements of the shuttle program felt more accountable to their center management, than to the shuttle program organization."[7] No longer feeling accountable to either a wider public or their own superiors, space center personnel, like the personnel of Prison X, created a closed world.

But isolation works two ways. The evidence that we currently have, although not yet conclusive, suggests that the excessively rigid boundaries of the space centers were matched by the excessively open boundaries of NASA as a whole. By viewing the accident as primarily a managerial problem, the president's commission failed to examine the dynamics of leadership at NASA. Newspaper reports at the time of the accident suggest that NASA's leadership was in chaos. At the time of the launch James Beggs, NASA's chief administrator, was on administrative leave. Although he was under indictment for defrauding the government while an executive at General Dynamics, he nonetheless tried to manage the agency from afar. He undermined the authority of the acting director, William Graham, by maintaining strong links to other managers in the agency, and after the crash he vociferously opposed Graham's appointment as the new permanent director. NASA, as one journalist reported, was "split by the strained relations between Mr. Beggs and Dr. Graham."[8]

Indeed, newspaper reports several months after the accident showed that NASA had not had its "two top positions filled for more than a few weeks since 1984"[9] and that NASA leaders at the agency's headquarters "rarely communicated with each other."[10] Moreover, because of leadership turnover, top administrators concerned with the seal problem as early as 1984 did not monitor agency activity to ensure that the problem was immediately addressed. James Abrahamson, associate administrator in charge of space flight, and Hans Mark, the agency's deputy administrator, ordered a review of the seal in March 1984 "after alarming evidence of a near failure in the tenth shuttle flight the previous month."[11] Yet a meeting scheduled with NASA engineers for May of that year was canceled because Abrahamson left the agency to head Reagan's "star wars" organization and because Mark was in Texas "agreeing to take up his new post"[12] as chancellor of the University of Texas. "It's a classic example of having something fall between the cracks," Mark noted. "I should have insisted on holding the review anyway." To justify his decision to cancel the meeting even though he stayed with the agency until September, he noted, "I was essentially a lame duck."[13] In other words, as one reporter noted, even though "the impression given by the final report of a presidential investigating commission was that NASA headquarters did not have sufficiently detailed evidence of trouble with the rocket to act on the problem until the summer of 1985,"[14] later evidence points to significant leadership abdication and irresponsibility beginning in 1984, almost a full two years before the fatal launch.

It remains puzzling that, despite their impending departures, Abrahamson and Mark did not feel fully authorized or responsible for following through on so critical a problem as the seal. When leaders have had secure and productive relationships with their own subordinates and superiors, they are concerned with their legacies and feel responsible for the future of the organization as a whole. Mark and Abrahamson's flight from the seal problem suggests that their relationship to NASA and its mission was already stressed and disorganized. Indeed, "one commission document quotes from an Oct. 26, 1982 NASA memorandum, labeled 'in strict confidence' where Dr. Mark complained that his personal notes to Mr. Beggs had not been acknowledged or answered," although as one reporter added, "There appeared to be no evidence that Mr. Beggs, the administrator, was ever told of the O-ring concerns."[15]

The dynamics of leadership at NASA culminating in Beggs's failed tenure has yet to be fully reported. Beggs's stressed relationships to both Graham and Marks suggest that he had trouble authorizing a deputy and perhaps a leadership cadre to manage as complex a project as the shuttle. But this is all speculation. Nevertheless, our understanding of general organizational dynamics suggests that, when leadership is fractured, an organization loses its direction and is unable to negotiate a coherent mandate from those who support it, fund it, or give it legitimacy. Instead, it becomes the repository for the contradictory claims and ambitions of both insiders and outsiders.

Indeed, after the crash many analysts felt that NASA had failed because it had faced and been unable to cope with the Reagan administration's contradictory climate of insisting on fiscal austerity, fantasizing about American technological superiority, and supposing that "government" is bad and therefore should not be supported. By turning an experimental shuttle into a "space truck," NASA symbolized America's pragmatism as well as its technological sophistication, and by training a team of astronauts composed of Asians, blacks, whites, men, and women, NASA represented America's dream of becoming a truly pluralistic society.[16] Yet NASA had to function as the repository of such dreams while facing severe fiscal pressure and feeling compelled to become like a business to finance its operations. Unable to resolve these contradictory pressures, NASA may have succumbed to the illusions created by its own public relations programs, permitting a schoolteacher to ride the shuttle as if it were as safe as a bus ride. (Other government agencies, facing similar pressure, did not succumb so readily. Bell's role at the Department of Education during Reagan's first term exemplifies a leader who could protect the agency's mission while acknowledging the changed political and fiscal climate it faced. NASA's failure is striking when contrasted to the success of a relatively weak agency.)

This is one reason why NASA lost its coherence. As leadership first failed to protect NASA from contradictory demands and then ultimately fractured, the separate space centers began to act as autonomous agencies of government.

When leaders abdicate, lower-level managers are forced to resolve policy issues that should be set by the top. They are unable to focus on technical issues alone, and indeed their technical judgments can be distorted by the confused policy environment in which they work. For example, as we saw at ERD (chapter 5), the lowest-level scientists and technicians could not complete their analytic work because a fractured leadership system provided no policy guidance. Lacking policy criteria to guide their design choices, lower-level managers typically face two opposing choices: They can burrow even more deeply into their technical work, becoming unable to complete their projects, or they can presume to fill the leadership vacuum, perhaps giving play to their fantasy that *they* can run the organization even if their leaders cannot. Typically, because lower-level managers lack the authority and relationships they need to balance priorities, they make bad political and technical judgments. (Indeed, Mulloy seemed to have stepped into just such a role.) In both cases leadership's failure to set policy and priorities leads to bad technical judgments. In effect, NASA as a whole was too open a system, just as the separate space centers within it were too closed. Its disorganized leadership was unable to provide the protection its professionals needed to pursue their technical work without succumbing to commercial pressures.

As we have seen, organizations with poorly drawn boundaries create much anxiety and may provoke defensive responses. Although we have no access to Mulloy's inner thoughts and feelings, his willingness to discount the astronauts and psychologically step into the leadership role suggests that he deployed what Klein calls the manic defenses to deny his own vulnerability, discomfort, and anxiety. He acted as though he were invulnerable so that he could deny his extreme dependence on technical events far beyond his control. The hypothesis that he deployed such a defense is supported by two facts. First, as we saw in the introduction, Mulloy and his associates violated the elementary rules of probability by assuming that past successes reduced the chance of future failures even though the seal problem had not been addressed. They acted as if they were not subject to the elementary laws of physics and probability. Second, at the commission hearing Mulloy showed little regret for his decision. Remarkably he continued to defend his decision to launch, suggesting that, if he were faced with the same facts again, he would do the same. In analyzing his own decision, he noted, "There was no violation of Launch Commit Criteria. There was no waiver required in my judgment at that time, *and still today*" (my emphasis).[17] He was unable to acknowledge his culpability. Indeed, several weeks after the crash, despite mounting evidence that implicated the seal, Mulloy and his comanagers continued to look for other possible causes of the accident while defending their decision to launch.

In confronting the harm we cause others and feeling contrite, we are psychologically asking them to forgive us, thereby acknowledging our dependence on them. By undoing our manic defense, we suffer for the first time. That Mulloy seemed invulnerable to feelings of guilt and unable to suffer suggests that he felt invulnerable when making his fateful decision as well. To compensate for the lack of leadership, Mulloy created an illusory world in which he did not need it. As a consequence, he and his associates created a closed psychological system and thus felt inappropriately self-sufficient and self-assured.

To be sure, Mulloy was not alone. NASA's public relations campaign encouraged grandiosity. To protect its funding base, NASA's leadership encouraged Congress and the public to believe that the shuttle was about to go commercial, that it was safe enough for schoolteachers to fly on. The shuttle became part of America's fantasy that its unbeatable technology would take it effortlessly to the new frontier. This cultural grandiosity made it easier for NASA managers and engineers throughout the agency to exaggerate the typical "can-do" culture of an engineering organization so that talk of failure and vulnerability was suppressed. Indeed, the commission first learned that engineers had been worried about the seal for several years only after reading the memo of a staff official in NASA's budget office who had been charged with estimating program costs for the coming years. Unable to get the attention of their line managers, discontented engineers had complained to this nontechnical staff officer in the hopes of finally being heard.

The Failure of the Social Defenses

Different as they are, Prison X and NASA exhibited the same dangerous responses to the postindustrial milieu. Exposed to multiple and often contradictory claims, prison leaders turned inward to deny the outside world while the director for corrections did not exercise his authority; Marshall space managers turned inward to create an illusion of their invulnerability while NASA leaders abdicated, leaving the task of denial to subordinates who lacked power, authority, and competence. Functioning social defenses strike a compromise between people's need to avoid anxiety and the organization's need to do work. The organization succeeds but at the cost of psychologically injuring its members. Such injuries, however hurtful, can nonetheless be tolerated. Thus at NASA engineers and managers used the typical bureaucratic process of multiple check to help individuals fee less anxious when making technical decisions. In earlier days this produced approximate caution, although, as in all bureaucracies, professionals periodically felt that their individual engineering judgments were not respected or trusted. Similarly, at the old-style prison, guards contained the anxiety they felt by relying on their paternalistic warden to protect them even though they felt consequently weak and dependent.

But as the organization's environment grows more demanding, as it enters a postindustrial milieu of the "open system" and a multidimensional ecology of active participants and stakeholders, the common social defenses fail, leading to more psychologically and physically violent and primitive forms of defense. Thus at Prison X the old-style paternalistic culture gave way to the sibling horde bent on destroying authority, whereas at NASA the bureaucratic decision process gave way to the manic defense and agency grandiosity. In weakening their psychological ties to reality even further, the people in each setting created increasingly illusory worlds.

Finally, in each case the organization became more irrational as people tried to undermine official authority. At Prison X the security chief, linked to the assistant commissioner, undermined the warden; at NASA Mulloy undermined Lucas by not passing information upward, and Beggs, although officially on administrative leave, undermined the acting director, Graham, by maintaining his links to other lower-level employees. Secret or unofficial coalitions, which typically link lower-level personnel to higher ones by skipping levels, provide the political template for irrational behavior and private fantasy. When official authority is effective, it helps all role holders feel authorized to work. People who are supported by official authority are able to tolerate the anxiety of working because they have been publicly delegated to accomplish a task. When official authority appears vulnerable or fraudulent, people no longer feel delegated or authorized, and because they feel increasingly anxious, they construct an illusory reality that cannot threaten them. But because reality in the form of technical constraints or recalcitrant clients always intrudes, these illusions are threatened. As reality's claims grow stronger and as illusions are reinforced, a vicious cycle soon takes hold until the organization and its members declare war against the real world. The organization becomes destructive and violent, substituting psychological and physical violence for the once chronic injuries of working.

Summary

The postindustrial milieu integrates people, tasks, units, and divisions, creating more tightly coupled systems of production, consumption, and distribution. Organizations operate in increasingly open environments as the number of claimants on their resources grows. Integration sorely tests the social defenses by forcing people to confront the "world of the other," whether customers, other divisions, consumer groups, new interest groups, or the team member at the next work station. The world of work implodes.

In such a milieu, to create sophisticated boundaries that are optimally open, we have to think systemically while emotionally acknowledging our dependency on a world we cannot control. By contrast, in the industrial milieu the division of labor protects us by integrating our efforts behind our backs. People manage their interdependencies in two ways: Rules of interaction are encoded through formal and explicit procedures, as in a bureaucracy, or they evolve incrementally and slowly, much as a culture might. In the second way a person learns a role not by imagining it but by responding incrementally to the actions and expectations of others. Under these conditions a person learning by induction can perform effectively in a role without actually understanding its relationship to the total role system. An "invisible hand," composed of others' roles and expectations, shapes the role-appropriate behavior.

For example, the scheduler in a job shop can effectively coordinate the flow of materials and tools to produce machine parts over the course of a day. But as studies show, the scheduler rarely has either an explicit or an implicit understanding of the system of constraints and resources that shape production. He has no model in his mind of how the job shop is organized.[18] Rather, all other role holders—machinists, stockroom assistants, helpers, and supervisors—pressure him to act and decide while they adjust to his decision and actions. This aggregate sum of adjustments and pressures creates a reasonably stable system of material flow. The scheduler therefore feels effective. He has taken his role, even though he cannot grasp the total social field in which he operates.

These methods for managing interdependencies are becoming inappropriate. People face increasingly novel and comprehensive situations. The nuclear power operator must solve an unexpected problem; the plant manager must decide when to assert her authority on the shop floor; the information system specialist must coordinate the efforts of different divisions, just as new software and hardware change the configuration of uses and modifies the computer system itself. To operate effectively, people must be better able to grasp the social field in which they are operating and to negotiate within it. The scheduler in the job shop would fail if new materials, machines, or methods of operation were suddenly introduced, because the normal practices, expectations, and rules of thumb would prove inappropriate. He could succeed only if he could for the first time develop a comprehensive theory of how machines, materials, and work methods interact to produce a balanced flow of stocks and final parts.

To be sure, experience counts. People can still develop shortcuts and rules of thumb that help them work in the absence of a clear understanding of their situation. Similarly, people can make decisions without full knowledge, hoping that other people's reactions will help them to understand their situation. But the capacity to visualize the social field, to imagine it in one's mind, is becoming increasingly important. As work is reintegrated, we are forced to face our growing interdependence directly. We need a new sensibility that helps us to expand and deepen our awareness. How can we develop it?

To answer this question, we must complement the study of single work groups with a broader understanding of how our culture and our political economy shape work roles and work life. The social defenses of single organizations may no longer suffice to contain anxiety. In a postindustrial work world people must develop the capacity to imagine the wider social field that gives meaning to their roles. They can try to do this in two ways: They can do the work of imagining from the inside out, starting with their own experiences and building up to the broader picture of their setting, or they can do this from the outside in, starting with an understanding of the broadest features of the work world, of the values, goals, and purposes of the society in which they live and work. I suggest that these two approaches complement one another. To work from the inside out, to build on their own experience, people need to understand the wider purposes and values of the society in which they live. They must imagine their own personal experience by framing it culturally and historically. In short, we need a coherent culture of work as well as appropriate organizations, roles, and work relationships to frame the emerging complexities of our work experience.

We cannot predict all the features of a coherent postindustrial work culture, but surely at its base it must produce a coherent set of values, a social consensus about what goods and services are important and why. The culture must help us to see how the work we do contributes to life. But here we encounter the familiar postmodern theme that Freud examined in his pessimistic *Civilization and Its Discontents*.[19] We may wish for a culture that is life defining and life affirming, but destructive forces are growing. We may wish for a culture that helps people assess the value their role creates, but surely many people experience this culture as destroying values. Our near-affluence makes our unhappiness mystifying. Although the imploded reality of a postindustrial world can kill astronauts and injure prisoners, its primary injuries are social-psychological in nature. To contain the anxiety of working, we create new scapegoats so that, just as the raw challenges of physical life fade, the level of intergroup rivalry grows. Yet, because these rivalries are not embedded in "necessary" conflict (such as boss versus worker), the resulting intra- and intergroup conflicts have a seemingly irrational and ahistorical character.

Are there reparative forces—the "erotic" forces, as Freud called them—that might be emerging to overcome these experiences of destruction? Are we simply to develop new social defenses at an even broader cultural level, or can we go beyond them, beyond our chronic anxieties, to a new dimension of collaboration? How can we produce more civilization and less discontent?

IV

Beyond the Social Defenses

10

Work and Reparation

Let us review the argument of the book thus far. As we have seen, groups deploy social defenses to contain the anxiety of working but, in facing postindustrial settings, they find it increasingly difficult to maintain group cohesion while remaining open to influence and information from outside the group. Burdened by the demands of outside stakeholders, claimants, and other groups who work with them, they may create a closed-system culture in which outsiders are scapegoated and devalued. However, because the settings in which they operate have in fact become more turbulent, less predictable, and shaped by a growing number of competitors and claimants, the groups become more irrational and risk their own and others' destruction as they ignore their outer world. How can groups overcome the anxiety of working within an open system and transform a more complicated outer world into a setting replete with opportunities for collaboration?

Let us take up the story of Prison X, as it turned the corner in its institutional crisis. As we saw in chapter 9, prison officials, housing tough prisoners in a maximum security setting, had been unable to limit the violence between inmates and guards. In an aborted takeover attempt guards had indiscriminantly clubbed and maced inmates, and inmates had raped a guard. A new warden, appointed by the new director for corrections, brought order to the prison by training the guards and restructuring the management system. Most important, he introduced a "unit management" system, in which a team consisting of a lieutenant, a sergeant, and a counselor managed a prison building. The team had full authority over critical policies in their building and could decide within limits how much recreation prisoners got, how frequently they could use the telephone, and how to handle inmate complaints and requests. As a result of these changes, inmate and staff grievances fell dramatically.

The guards and the counselors were particularly pleased with the ways in which they had a better appreciation for each other's work. One counselor noted that "the counselor is part of a situation where she is more involved in security, as opposed to treatment. So it's a beautiful plan now that one can see where the other one's shoes have been, rather than just standing on the outside looking in and being judgmental without having had experience."

This is a rich statement. It combines the experience of knowing another's work with the experience of judging it. The counselor suggests that when you do not understand someone else's work, you tend to judge it. At one level this idea fits with the commonsensical notion that it is easy to judge someone when you are not in his or her shoes. But the comment evokes another relationship between understanding and judging: When we do not understand another person who shapes our work and our reality, we are judgmental; we find fault. It is not simply that it is easy to judge, but rather that we are *likely* to judge. Our ignorance makes us anxious; we feel punished by our inability to comprehend and, to contain these feelings, we judge the other as the source of our ignorance. Because the other person is not us or is different from us and yet affects us, we blame that person. We split off the punishing voice within us and project it onto the dangerous other. The counselor's belief that the new prison situation was "beautiful" probably reflected her relief that she no longer felt ignorant and punished. She was at ease.

The links connecting ignorance, splitting, and projection go to the heart of the postindustrial dilemma. As we have seen, people must find ways to imagine the reality of other people's roles. They must learn how others see their combined situation, and they must imagine in their minds a total system of relationships that creates a collective reality. Yet, to do so, they must overcome their tendencies to short-circuit the process of learning by splitting and projection. As they enact and maintain more sophisticated boundaries, they must become comfortable with feelings of dependency and vulnerability in order to give space to the process of learning.

One can hardly be optimistic here. Throughout the case studies in this book we have seen how people must cope with their ambivalent relationship to their own dependency needs. On the one hand they

fear independence; they fear being at the boundary, being accountable, being vulnerable, and being a risk taker. On the other hand,
they hate dependency, and they hate the learner role. When they feel
dependent, they reproduce in their minds their fundamental experiences of childhood—their dependence on but frequent rage at the
all-protecting but all-denying parent. Over the course of development this conflict is internalized in the form of the punishing but
guiding superego, the internal fantasy objects that represent our parental and cultural authority. This superego can both punish and
guide us.

But as we have seen, people frequently cannot contain this ambivalent relationship to their superego. They cannot simultaneously be
punished and guided by this introjected authority figure. Under conditions of stress they tend to split their unconscious experience of
this fantasized authority figure, projecting the hated part onto other
people and retaining the good, idealized part for themselves. In this
way they feel less bad and guilty.

This is where social arrangements and group processes become
critical. Other people, other groups, can become the repository for
the hated authority, for the sense of persecution. A group that feels at
risk may erect and support a charismatic leader in whom they invest
all their hopes and on whom they vitally depend. To protect their
now idealized leader from their own hatred for authority, they must
project their hatred onto others; thus they mobilize the leader in a
fight against the "bad people" outside the group. This is a fundamentally social arrangement and is the genesis of evil.

Looked at from this point of view, evil as a human problem is
produced by innate human tendency but is *reproduced* by social
arrangements. The tendency toward evil is situated in two critical
conditions of human life: the capacity to fantasize and the dependency of childhood. The capacity to fantasize emerges from the ability to create symbols and is thus rooted in our innate capacity for
language. The dependency of childhood emerges from the biological
vulnerability of the infant, who loves and hates its parents for giving
it everything it needs and preventing it from getting what it wants
when it wants it. To protect its fantasy of good parents (for this image
also provides the infant with feelings of self-love), the infant must
split apart the image of its parents into good parents and bad ones.
The almost universal feature of fairy tales—their elaboration of plots

based on completely good and completely bad people—is a sign of the role that splitting plays in the child's fantasy life.

How can we overcome this deep-seated tendency to produce evil? As anxiety grows at work, people need to project their sense of persecution onto others. In a manner that echoes Freud's pessimism in *Civilizations and Its Discontents*,[1] we too can only be pessimistic about our capacity to live and work in a postindustrial world. The demands on our imagination, our empathetic capacities, and our ability to learn seem too great. In this chapter and the next I explore this dilemma. First, I examine Klein's theory of reparation, showing how the production of valued goods and services for others provides us with a framework for repairing our relationships. I show that the symbol of the "good" that is inherent in socially valued goods and services can help restructure the symbols of our internal life.

In chapter 11 I compare two factory startups and assess what a single organization can do to promote a reparative culture. I point to three criteria that may enable people to link the work they do to the production of valued goods and services. I return to the role that social and cultural forces play in shaping the reparative process in chapter 12, arguing that industrial civilization makes reparation difficult by conflating the good or the ideal with the symbol of a punishing authority, by substituting guilt for shame, and by confusing limitation with sin. This constellation leads us to emphasize our triumphs over others. I argue, however, that we have reached cultural, technical, and ecological limits in our capacity to sustain the psychodynamics of triumph.

Finally, I describe the need for a new work culture that would support the psychodynamics of reparation. Such a culture would be based on several building blocks: an ethic of adult development, a social system that would offer people "second chances," a work design that would place people more regularly at the boundaries of their organizations, and, most important, a coherent political economy that would help us to develop a consensus about what goods and services we regard as valuable.

Outlining this culture suggests that we must indeed go beyond the social defenses. Single organizations can help people contain and transmute their anxieties. But we also need to develop the cultural space between organizations and institutions if we are to function without undue anxiety.

Reparation

As we have seen, people have a strong tendency to produce evil acts as a way of containing anxiety. Yet, although the propensity to produce evil is innate, there is a corresponding tendency to repair, to make that which has been split or torn apart whole once again. Klein's theory of reparation represents one of her most important contributions to a theory and pragmatics of human development.[2] She argues that, although people certainly split their awareness of good and bad, they also enter a stage or "position," as she calls it, in which they integrate their once split awareness of the world around them. This tendency can be seen as one expression of the mind's growing capacity to integrate sense perceptions and feelings as it matures.

To be sure, if Klein had arbitrarily posited an "integrating" tendency that opposed a "splitting" tendency, her contribution would have been a minor one. What makes her theory important is that she shows that the tendency to integrate the awareness of good and bad is rooted in an emotional constellation. Although we have a tendency or valence to integrate our different perceptions as we mature, integration itself is propelled forward by feelings of *depression*. We enter what Klein calls the depressive position, because we realize that the people whom we have hated are the people who have also contributed to our lives, people whom we have loved as well. The paradigm of this recognition, Klein argues, is the child's realization that the image of its hated mother and the image of its beloved mother—the proverbial bad and good witches of fairy tales—are images of one and the same mother.

This recognition creates feelings of remorse, shame, and guilt. We realize that we have hurt (in our minds as well as in reality) those who have cared for us. Klein suggests that people can navigate the depressive position if they can contain the anxiety that ensues when the images of the good and the bad are integrated, if they can tolerate their feelings of shame. But if the anxiety overwhelms them, they regress to the "paranoid-schizoid" position, the position of fundamental splitting and alienation.

Work and Reparation

People can work through the depressive position by repairing their relationships with others. They do this, I suggest, by creating and giving something good to those whom they have hurt, *by doing work.* This process of depression and reparation takes place both in relation to real others and through symbolic acts. In the latter instance the gifts we create and the receivers we seek out are symbols of acts we have committed and people we have hurt in the past. In short, to repair the damage we have done, in splitting apart our feelings of love and hate, we must *work*, we must create something of value for others.

In describing the work of reparation, Klein refers to the biography of the painter Ruth Kjar.[3] Kjar's career as a painter grew out of a depressive reaction when a picture was removed from her room. The empty space she experienced on the wall "grinned hideously down at her" and seemed to reflect an emptiness and despair in her inner world. To fill this emptiness, she impulsively painted a life-size figure of a naked black woman directly on the wall. Klein relates Kjar's depression to the destruction of her internal image of her mother and shows how the painter recreated her mother in the painting to fill the hostile empty place inside herself. For Klein, creativity finds its source in the anxieties of the depressive position and the subsequent reparative urge.

Klein uses the word "position" to emphasize that the depressive experience is not a fixed stage in the life cycle but a recurring experience. As we live and transact with others, we inevitably have good and bad feelings about them. These feelings are in turn suffused with emotional memories of earlier relationships, when our love and hate were less modulated and more intense. Thus we continually face the problem of sustaining a "whole" image of those to whom we are close. If we love and hate them, we may split up and distribute our feelings over others, idealizing some and despising others. Or we may simply flatten our experience of them by denying our dependence on them and making them into nonpersons. If and when we reach the depressive position, we can then contain the anxiety of both loving and hating long enough to begin the work of reparation.

A Personal Example

Let me give a personal example from my consulting practice. My research and consulting center faced the prospect of a substantial deficit, and the senior staff members were under pressure to sell the center's services. But I was having little luck. I had hit a slump and could not connect with clients willing to pay. But one day, quite serendipitously, a government agency facing budget cuts called me. I was an expert in retrenchment. Could I help them plan their cutback so that the resulting organization might fit their long-term strategic needs? I agreed to come and meet them, but despite my apparently good luck, I felt curiously unenthusiastic. This particular regional agency was part of a larger national system and, if I did a good job, I might be hired by counterpart agencies in other parts of the country. But I wasn't excited.

On the morning of the appointment I left home slightly depressed. I entered the agency offices feeling passive and low key. The director, Tom, and his staff began to tell their story. I had little to say. I asked some questions but found that I could not intellectually engage with them. Instead, I seemed to strike a quasi-therapeutic pose, asking supportive and clarifying questions but risking little of myself. After forty minutes, the director turned to me and said that this kind of talk was "therapeutical" but asked what I could do for them. I rose only slightly to the challenge, asked more directed questions, and suggested what staffing work they needed to do before they met again. A staff assistant then turned to me and asked, "Well, what is the next step? Would you write a proposal to us?" I felt irritated. I told them that they surely knew what to do and how I would work with them and that we should simply get on with the work. The director looked puzzled and said, "You mean the next meeting would be the beginning of the contract?" I said yes. We shook hands, and the director said he would see how he could work out the purchase agreement process and promised to call. I left feeling as ambivalent as when I entered.

I realized only later how uncollaborative I had been in that office. I had not really engaged in a conversation with them and had refused to make the expected and customary effort of writing a proposal. I was implicitly communicating that I cared little for their problem and had neither the time nor the patience to put down on paper how I would work with them. I was devaluing their reality. Because I was a national expert on retrenchment, they must have felt devalued and belittled. I felt ashamed.

My speculation about their feelings was later confirmed when a contact at the office told me informally (and with much disappointment) that Tom was now thinking that I cost too much. She was puzzled, for he had never mentioned money before. My interpretation of Tom's behavior was that, because I had devalued his concerns, he devalued his own reality. If his problem was so unimportant, then it certainly was not worth spending money on. He had "taken in" or introjected my devaluation of him.

When I reflected on my behavior, I realized that I had used this occasion to project both my depression and my anger over my sales situation. But what were my anger and depression really about? As I thought about it and talked with a colleague, it became apparent that I felt abandoned. My sales failure had left me feeling alone. Yet in reality I was far from alone. My colleagues were most supportive and appreciative of my past contributions to the center, and they were certainly willing to give me the time and resources I needed to find new clients. Clearly my feelings of abandonment were triggered by my current dilemma, but they were nourished by earlier memories of feeling vulnerable and alone. Being out there and alone during a sales effort heightened my feelings of dependency and vulnerability. I was feeling punished.

I had thus used my first real connection with a potential client to dispose of these punishing feelings. I split these feelings off from my awareness and projected them onto my prospective client. The director was now the unimportant one. I would abandon him, rather than let him abandon me. I devalued his reality. I had produced a small piece of evil.

But the splitting was not complete. I remained ambivalent and felt shame. After understanding what I had done, I was determined to make it up to Tom, both to reestablish my connection to him and of course to state my strong interests in working with him. (I knew clearly that I did want the work.) I decided to call, to ask if he felt that I had been "off" that day, to affirm that I had felt off target, and to tell him that a short proposal was on its way. There was some risk in the call—not the risk of losing money but the risk of being out of line, of revealing a part of myself and feeling rejected in turn.

I made the call. Tom denied that I had seemed off, but his affect felt strong to me. He said that I was simply too expensive. I suggested that perhaps he could use me less intensively. I could help his staff establish the agenda for the preplanning process and then review their work at the end. I would not work with them in the middle phase. He thought that was an excellent idea. I had a contract.

Some days later, a staff person at the office told me that Tom seemed to have appreciated my call. "It reminded him of how much he in fact had liked you." My experience suggested a different interpretation. Because I had reappraised my relationship to Tom, he in turn could value his own situation more. He was no longer the object of my punishing projections. After the phone call I came out of my general depression, even though my sales prospects overall had not as yet changed.

The Reparative Process

I believe that this small incident highlights the key elements of the reparative process. First, I was feeling dependent and vulnerable, and I projected my sense of persecution onto the first potential client I connected with, even though he was actually offering me business. As my first object of projection, Tom afforded me relief. Evil begins in relationships; it has its roots in intimate settings.

Second, after I psychologically belittled Tom, I felt the shame that Helen Merrill Lynd emphasizes in her brilliant study *On Shame and the Search for Identity*:[4] shame before myself. I felt stupid and foolish for having been so careless with someone who could actually contribute to my life.

I believe that my shame was rooted in my feeling that I had been petty. I recall that, when Tom's assistant asked if I would write a proposal, I actually felt affronted, as though I were being asked to undertake a demeaning task. But of course the assistant's request was entirely appropriate. My feeling of affront suggests that indeed I was feeling small to begin with, and my petty response functioned as a defense against my feeling inadequate. In this sense I was not unlike the petty bureaucrat who creates laborious ceremonies out of small procedures to elevate the essentially mundane nature of his work. I came into the relationship feeling small and inadequate and protected myself by being affronted and therefore by making Tom feel small, but then, in facing the damage I had done him, I uncovered my own pettiness.

The sense of shame thus appears to have several roots. One is shamed by the damage done to others, particularly when these others have contributed positively to one's life; one is shamed by one's pettiness, and one is shamed by the discovery of one's defensiveness, of the lies one tells to oneself. This analysis suggests Hannah Arendt's argument that evil is born in banality.[5] People are struggling with their inherent sense of smallness, and to protect themselves from being exposed to themselves and others, they become petty, investing the commonplace with their defensive grandiosity.

In a third, key element of the reparative process, my sense of shame led me to repair my relationship to Tom by simply calling him back, but not in order to seek forgiveness. I did not apologize; rather I affirmed that I valued him and his contributions to me. When we act out of guilt, we affirm our insignificance: We cannot transform the feeling that we are unworthy, and we require that others more powerful than we tolerate our inadequacies.[6] In contrast, when we act out of shame, we affirm out value to others by offering something of value to them. I offered Tom the good and valued opinion that came with my status as an expert. I was interested in his problem. In such a situation we do not see the other person as all-powerful, as one who can either punish or forgive, but rather as someone whom we have hurt. We thus overturn our experience of being inadequate by being adequate and important to that person.

Fourth, I experienced the real Tom as someone who could contribute positively to my professional life. In repairing our relationships to others, we overcome our tendencies to split apart our good and bad feelings of others. We stop idealizing others or having contempt for them. We simply affirm their value because of their lively relationship to us. We affirm life in the face of its limits. Tom had become the real representative of imagined figures who had always persecuted me. Yet, as my sense of shame suggests, I could not see the real Tom as entirely evil and bad. My real relationship to him reduced my capacity to split off my feelings of persecution and project them onto him. I saw him as good, even though he had been a source of pain to me as well. Standing between reality and fantasy, between two images of Tom, I struggled to integrate my good and bad feelings for him, with shame signaling the beginning of the struggle.

Fifth, to experience my shame, I had to overcome my anxiety and face my discomfort. I needed a period of "working through." I recall that, after I left Tom, I struggled for some time with the meaning of my experience. I was feeling vaguely bad, out of joint, but I was not sure why. To deny my discomfort, I began to focus on the ending of the episode. Recall that Tom had asked how I could help him; I had replied with rather specific advice. I had outlined what I believed to be the structure of their problem, where they could expect to save money, and how they should organize their planning process. In recalling my experience, I focused excessively on this ending and began to feel pride in the decisive character of my advice. "Didn't I really tell them," I thought, suggesting that in fact I was thinking, "Didn't I really *give it to them!*"

I suggest that these ruminations enabled me to feel triumphant and victorious. I had proven that I was a wonderful consultant. But as Klein suggests, such feelings of triumph are defensive in character, masking feelings of dependency and vulnerability. Indeed, as the word "triumph" suggests, to feel triumphant is to denigrate the other in the relationship, to turn that person into someone who can or should be defeated. My feelings of triumph thus suggest that I could not initially sustain the feeling of shame and acknowledge that I had injured someone who was good. I needed a process of working through. This is the affective basis for the depressive position. It is the moment when we feel depressed because we have injured those whom we also value. The capacity to sustain such feelings of shame and their associated anxiety shapes the capacity to go on to repair one's relationships.

Sixth and finally, by reaching out to Tom, I began to repair my relationships to my internal objects, to the memories of my experiences of others. The experience of shame, as Lynd suggests, is developmental. It involves the whole character, the entire relationship of self to setting, rather than simply one sin, one transgression, one forbidden pleasure. This is why my depression lifted despite the fact that my sales prospects had not significantly changed. Because I related to Tom in the transference, he became a symbol of many past relationships in which I felt abandoned and punished. Thus the reparation of my relationship with him unleashed a developmental process through which my habitual modes of relating, carried by memory, were in some degree restructured.

To recapitulate, the reparative process is shaped by several interdependent moments of experience. First, it emerges when we first become aware that we have hurt someone we value. Facing our pettiness and banality, we are shamed before ourselves. Second, in repairing our relationships to others, we affirm our own value. In contrast to the traditional process of confession and expiation, we do not denigrate ourselves and elevate those from whom we seek forgiveness but affirm both ourselves and the others in our relationships. Third, in repairing our relationships, we overcome our tendency to split off our feelings of badness and project them onto others. Rather, we see others and ourselves as both good and bad, as whole. We do this by standing between reality and fantasy, by simultaneously relating to the other as a transference object and as a real person. Fourth, to experience shame, we must overcome the anxiety of facing our pettiness by working through a set of complex feelings. We enter the depressive position. Fifth, in doing the work of reparation, in offering our efforts to the other, we are no longer grandiose. We affirm our limitations and therefore the inherent value of our life in the face of its limitations. Sixth, by sustaining our feelings of shame in the depressive position, we do not simply relieve our feelings of guilt but restructure our relationships to others. This is why the reparative process is developmental in character.

Work As a Transitional Object

As this discussion suggests, reparation rests on a symbolic process, on the transformation of meanings attached to particular symbols of our inner life. I carried about in my head a symbol of my relationship to others that led me to see Tom as persecutory when in fact he was not. This symbol, which Klein calls a phantasy, represents all the people who I believe have persecuted me. I then saw Tom as *a symbol of this symbol.* He represented the class of persecutory figures who populate my inner world. But in taking in the real Tom, the Tom who was both good and bad, I transformed my relationship to these inner symbols and so, in turn, could experience Tom as whole and myself as whole.

This symbolic underpinning of reparation suggests how work itself can function as a reparative process. Let us look at my relationship to Tom once again. We can say that I used him as a transitional object in transforming my relationship to my own internal symbol system. As I argued in my study of management training in chapter 6, the transitional object functions as a symbol that helps the child move from its mother to the outer world. The child invests a teddy bear, say, with the projected images of its mother. In moving past the mother, the child carries the mother forward by holding onto the transitional object. Yet the object is a transitional one, and the child ultimately gives it up, in the process developing a new relationship to its mother. The child now has a mother whom it seeks for protection and growth in new ways. The transitional object helps the child take a round trip from mother to the world and back; but when the child returns "home," the mother, like the world, has become more complex and varied.

I suggest that the work we do—the services and products we provide and the connections we establish through exchange—can function in this same way. As adults we do not carry teddy bears around with us. Rather, our fundamental tie is to our internal objects, to the fantasies of others that shape how we experience our experience. We are reluctant to leave these internal objects because, as we split off our feelings of badness and project them onto others, we create an inner world of good and ideal objects that give us comfort and security. This conservatism, our inability to relinquish our fantasies, marks the core of our neurotic behavior. Unlike the child who embodies its fantasies in external objects, we have internalized ours, robbing them of their transitional status. That is why as adults we are less flexible, open, and curious than children. Internalizing our fantasies leads to both being out of touch and acting out.

In this context the products of our work can function as transitional objects. In our neurotic state we see others through the prism of our split-off projections, and they appear bad. As we have seen, many work groups function by creating a group culture that enables members to see the outside world as dangerous and bad and the inside world as ideal and good. Yet, insofar as we are open to reality and sensitive to our experience of shame, we also experience the need to repair our relationships to others. Work enables us to do this by allowing us to offer others, who stand on the other side of the organizational boundary, something of value. We invest this product or service with our feelings of goodness and, if it is received by the other, we in turn feel better about our worth and are able to affirm the value of the other. As a consequence of this fruitful exchange, we in turn restructure our internal world of fantasy so that it is less dependent on our prior state of split consciousness, less dependent on the projective process. Just as the transitional object enables the child to take a round trip from mother to the world and back, in the process changing the relationship to each, so can the products of our work, the goods or services we produce, help us take a round trip from our internal fantasies to the client or customer and back. In the process we change our relationship to each.

Yet as my experience with Tom suggests, such a venture is fraught with anxiety. At a critical moment we cross two boundaries: the one between the work organization and its market and the one between fantasy and reality. At that moment we have lost control. Because the customer or client is not simply an extension of our fantasy life, not simply a symbol, he or she may reject our offering. Thus in the bid to affirm our value by offering something of value to others, we open ourselves to the possibility that we will be devalued once again. In my relationship to Tom this critical moment came when I called to ask if I had been off target. He could have responded in ways that would have hurt me. He might, for example, have acted as though my questions were somehow foolish or stupid ("What are you talking about?" or "I can't recall"), as if to suggest that my preoccupation with him was misplaced, that he had no memory of or regard for our relationship. This is the moment of anxiety in the reparative process where we must take a risk and act aggressively, for in facing risk, we acknowledge that others are not necessarily ready to receive us. By choosing to believe that our work is good, we feel for the moment entitled to other people's attention. The products of our work are transitional objects, but only if we invest them with risk and aggression as well as love. This is the core anxiety of working itself.

Beyond Sublimation

This analysis sheds new light on the classical concept of sublimation. Freud suggests that, as we mature, we learn to sublimate our sexual instincts, our desires for pleasure. In so doing, we limit the subversive character of these demands, for they almost always set us apart from group life. The more we pursue our private pleasures, the less we are available for the common tasks of survival and social development. Civilization represses us. Freud notes, for example, that the love between two people precludes the interests of the group.[7] Even today we are wary of loving relationships that do not produce children—a clear societal need. We need to sublimate our search for pleasure, to make it both more abstract and more general, so that our specifically sexual love becomes more generally a love for the group on the one hand and a love for socially useful activities on the other.

Freud's argument continues to vex reformers and revolutionaries who hope that better social arrangements might reduce the tension between social requirements and individual needs. If the two are irrevocably in conflict, if society robs us of bodily pleasure so that the collective can reproduce and survive, then no amount of social change can alter the fundamental frustrations of living with others and therefore our need to find scapegoats to blame for our suffering. Evil is built into social life. Theorists such as Fromm argue that Freud overestimates people's innate wish to hurt others,[8] whereas Marcuse,[9] acknowledging that some level of repression is required for society to function, argues that today we repress our needs for pleasure beyond what is necessary for social cohesion and development.

Object-relations theory offers a different conception of the links between individuals and society. People find concrete bodily pleasure not by withdrawing from social life but by participating in the cultural and symbolic environment it creates. This is possible because cultural symbols can function as transitional objects. When we repair our relationships to others through our work, the others are abstracted others, symbols, as much as they are specific people with specific needs. Because they represent needs that have specific social value, they symbolize our potential capacity to create value for others. Tom represented the chance that I might concretely sell my consulting services to someone who valued them, and he symbolically represented the chance that I might affirm my capacity to create goodness for others. It is the double character of such encounters that enables us to use them as intermediate steps on the way back to our internal fantasies. If we succeed in working through the depressive position, the position of shame, offering something of value across the work boundary, we transform our internal life. This life is in turn represented in symbols. Thus we use one set of symbols, derived from the culture of work, to operate on another.

But paradoxically this operation of symbol on symbol nonetheless reshapes our relationship to our bodies. When the reparative process is successfully negotiated, we feel more whole, less split apart. This feeling helps us to feel more alive. Our bodies as sources of pleasure become available to us because, in integrating the good and the bad, we reduce the power of the persecutory voice within us. This voice, the voice of the superego, devalues our pleasures. Pleasures, after all, make us feel good, and the superego insists that we are bad.

So before reparation we face a dilemma. To feel pleasure, we must project our persecutory voice outward and free ourselves of badness. Somebody else must be bad. To feel pleasure is therefore to cause another pain. Alternatively, insofar as we are ambivalent and resist such chronic splitting, we can protect the pleasures of others by causing ourselves pain. But the self and the other cannot simultaneously find pleasure. As we make the transition through the reparative process, however, we integrate good and bad within us, and we affirm life as something that is valuable in and of itself. This affirmation reduces the power of our persecutory voice, allowing us to feel bodily pleasure while giving bodily pleasure to others. Thus through the reparative process we resexualize our experience. The process of reparation leads us to rethink the relationship between pleasure and civilization that Freud posited. It is through civilization, through the culture of work and exchange, that we finally come into touch with our bodies. Social life is the route to the body.

11

The Reparative Organization

When people are faced with the task and challenge of reparation, they draw on their own particular histories, strengths, and weaknesses, but an organization may facilitate or inhibit the reparative process. If the organization enables its members to understand or relate to the value it creates for customers, the members can link their efforts to the organization's purposes. If the organization inhibits its members from developing these links, the members then focus on the internal dynamics of the organization, forgetting that the organization is ultimately an instrument of its purposes. In the first case the employees, aware of the potential value they can create, psychologically approach the organization's boundary. In the second case, the employees, ignorant of the company's purposes, retreat from the boundary and focus solely on the internal dynamics of corporate life.

Reparation versus Narcissism

Schwartz's concept of organizational narcissism is useful here.[1] In examining the case of the bank in chapter 8, I noted that managers, hoping to motivate their employees, may try to create a corporate culture based on an ideal image of the company. Unable to create a climate in which people can develop deeper and more effective working relationships, managers hope to substitute a shared image of the ideal company in place of such experiences as trust, delegation, and confrontation. Images replace the more difficult process of working through conflicts, misunderstandings, and failures. Such a culture potentiates people's narcissism, that is, their desire to believe that they are wonderful and beautiful. It is a dangerous culture because it suggests that dissenters and outsiders are bad and that insiders and loyalists are good. Not only can such a culture punish those who are different or who think critically but it can also limit the organization's longer-term ability to innovate and adapt.

Narcissists are mesmerized by the illusion of their own beauty and, consequently, see only their reflected images in the environment around them. Blind to the people who shape their world, they value only themselves and gain pleasure only by admiring themselves. By analogy, the narcissistic organization culture is one in which its members believe that the organization is the rationale for its own existence. Rather than focusing on the value it produces for others, managers and employees imagine that the company's presumed beauty justifies its existence and its claim on resources. They lose sight of its broader functions and purposes.

To facilitate the reparative process, an organization must limit its narcissistic tendencies. By creating a climate in which employees view the organization as an instrument for achieving valued ends, the organization helps its employees to focus on creating value for customers and clients, rather than on the internal structure and politics of the organization. Such organizations create developmental cultures because people are free to focus on the work they do, can achieve a greater sense of wholeness, and, as we have seen, can therefore restructure their relationships to their own internal objects. Moreover, because the focus is on the work itself, people are less afraid to scrutinize their working relationships and are therefore less likely to distort them with projections and introjections that limit their capacity to observe and learn.

Two Case Studies

To examine the contrast between reparative and nonreparative organizations, I present two case studies. In the first case the senior managers, by creating a narcissistic subculture, had great trouble introducing a computer-integrated manufacturing technology. In the second case the senior managers created a more developmental culture and were able to design a plant with an advanced technology that achieved its cost and quality goals while building and sustaining a social system that supported self-reflection and learning. By examining the culture of an innovation or an organizational beginning, we can expose and study key cultural assumptions without being burdened by the complicated archaeology of each setting's history. Like the controlled laboratory experiment, the innovation, the attempt at starting something new, highlights the assumptions that senior managers use when designing and maintaining organizations.

Delta Products

Delta Products, a machine and metal parts manufacturer that invested in a computer-integrated manufacturing system, illustrates some of the limits and costs of a narcissistic culture.[2] Led by a chief executive officer who had inherited the company from his father, the senior managers decided that Delta could compete only if it modernized its machining technology by buying computer-controlled machine tools linked by an automated transport system.

Three researchers interviewed the senior managers when this change was first being planned. They were "impressed with the breadth and sophistication of the plant's future culture." Yet, on returning to the plant some sixteen months later, they found chaos and conflict. The automation project was fifteen months behind schedule, the company remained highly dependent on its old machines, even though they were about to be sold, employee turnover was 34 percent, and the company faced critical financial and quality problems.

The workers, who had been promised jobs and influence, felt violated by a planning process that treated them like children. A new package of employee benefits, while presumably based on a concept of "wellness," had taken away as much as it gave. A promised training program to familiarize all workers with computers had resulted in only one introductory class. Discussions with the local junior college for tuition reimbursement to help workers get technical training had led nowhere. Workers who had been assured that they would not lose their jobs because of automation were fired, and machinists who were supposed to become the new cell managers were not provided with management training in such methods as planning and scheduling. Strikingly, of those employees whose jobs were supposed to be protected by automation, 24 percent quit, whereas 28 percent of those who had identified themselves to researchers in a first round of interviews as potential "winners" had quit by the second round.

The skeptic studying this case report might conclude that the senior managers simply designed a public relations campaign to placate anxious workers and contain the predictable consequences of their uneasiness and anger. But the case points to a more complex dynamic. The CEO, the marketing manager, and the chief engineer had constructed a narcissistic image of their new venture. They invested it with images of glory while discounting people's needs and hopes and denying the pain of development. Several features of their effort are suggestive here.

First, to launch their venture, they established a separate company, AM Inc., headquartered twenty miles from the plant. AM Inc.'s mission was not to modernize Delta, although it drew on Delta's resources for its own development, but to function as a management company implementing automation in other companies. Delta was to be their live laboratory, a showcase of AM's competence and success. A marketing brochure touted AM's skills at managing culture change even before the CEO and his colleagues had begun to transform the machining system at Delta.

Although the authors of the study do not examine the motives of the CEO in any great depth, one can reasonably conclude that, by setting up AM Inc., the CEO was treating Delta as an object of his ambitions, a showcase for his special talents. The marketing brochure demonstrates the illusory quality of his effort. The promotion of AM staff as experts at culture change before they showed any evidence of such expertise suggests that the AM staff was interested more in images than in actual results.

Indeed, as the authors point out, the CEO modeled himself after currently popular images of the "excellent manager" who can transcend bureaucracy and get down to the nitty-gritty of a company's life. For example, following the prescription that excellent managers "manage by walking about," the CEO personally handed out all the paychecks to workers on payday. This is harmless enough but, in following other such prescriptions, he failed to match the cultural image of the good and tough manager with his own situation. For example, he rationalized establishing AM Inc. as a separate company because, as the writers of a popular management text point out, innovations start in "skunk works," where daring innovators, living at the fringe of company life, launch new ventures while struggling against the inhibiting forces of mainstream company life. Yet, as CEO with control over all company resources, he hardly stood at its fringes. This suggests that AM Inc. represented his wish to be heroic, enabling him to escape from the nitty-gritty of managing a process of change that in the best of circumstances could only be painful.

Similarly, following the popular image of heroic managers who reorganize the social and economic lives of their workers without causing anyone pain or fundamental disruption, the CEO promised his work force that "no one would lose his or her job due to automation." In truth, only large companies with vast reserves of funds and employment opportunities can make such promises, and the CEO himself soon reneged, firing four women, one of whom had been with the company for fifteen years. As one worker noted, "The four women got fired. . . . They were trying to keep it hushed up. . . . Then we got about three different stories. First of all they were fired, and then they were laid off. . . . Then we were told 'it's none of your business.' . . . But yet we were all supposed to be a team."[3] Juxtaposed against the CEO's dramatic gestures and his image of manager as hero, such broken promises suggest that he genuinely believed that his beautiful factory of the future could bring glory to everyone it touched. Indeed, when interviewed some nine months after the program began, he insisted that "the promise [of no layoffs] . . . was that no one goes to the streets. The concept being just simply that you help people find another job."[4]

Second, unwilling to confront the losses and the gains that basic changes bring, the CEO and his staff at AM Inc. were unwilling or unable to acknowledge the pain and difficulty of the transformation. Instead, they tried to promote a culture in which certain employees were idealized and glorified while others were simply ignored. For example, at an annual progress review meeting, which all Delta Product employees attended, some of the company's "winners" were given testimonials and their photographs appeared on a screen. Predictably, both the honored and the ignored were angry. One worker complained, "What about the rest of us? Don't we count? One of the girls I work with [a winner] said, 'If I had known this is what they were going to do, I'd never have let them do it. Singling out just a few doesn't make for a real team.'" Another "winner" noted, "A lot of people would have wanted their picture on the screen. You're just asking for trouble with all the natural jealousy."[5]

By glorifying certain employees, senior managers were attempting to create a false atmosphere of enthusiasm, like cheerleaders who hope that forced shouting will mask the difficulty that a losing team faces. The authors of the study experienced this cheerleading posture most when attending manager-worker meetings, labeled "let's talk" forums, that were ostensibly designed to create an atmosphere of participation in the change process. The authors write, "Managers spent about twenty minutes describing some of the recent and planned changes in the plant. They would ask for questions and were usually met with bored silence. Occasionally, a single skeptical question would surface or one individual might complain, but we never observed a prolonged discussion involving the entire group." The authors go on to note, "The managerial style during the meetings was aptly labeled by a Delta employee as cheerleading. 'They treat us like little children. Hell, even little kids don't like to be treated like children.' " Indeed, "the chasm between the managers' forced enthusiasm and the skepticism and apathy of the workers," note the authors, "was painful to observe."[6]

The researchers' observations suggest that the emerging narcissistic culture, in which people were either good or bad, winners or losers, was based on the senior managers' denial of their own as well as their employees' pain. Like the whistler in the dark, the cheerleader shouts with forced enthusiasm to avoid the silence, the chasm, the experience of alienation and separation. The workers, too, feeling helpless and ineffective, denied their pain by simply flattening their experience and becoming apathetic. Apparently the only ones able to experience the pain at Delta were the researchers, who observed the gap between the illusion of participation and the reality of estrangement.

Third and finally, the authors of the study noted throughout that the Delta managers consistently overemphasized the technical changes, neglecting the social system of the factory. Acknowledging that managers in factory settings often fail to focus on the social system of roles, relationships, and rewards, they noted that Delta failed to offer managers and workers training in group participation methods, suggesting that the senior managers believed that change in the social system could take care of itself.

But Delta's cultural problems could not have been solved by training alone. As the managers developed a narcissistic relationship to the company, focusing on their ultramodern tools, they not only ignored the workers but also neglected the marketplace, their new relationships to customers and suppliers. Like the narcissist, they emphasized their own inner excellence and neglected their wider setting. They forgot that an organization is ultimately an instrument of its purpose.

Again, their ideas and plans appeared innovative. To emphasize strategic selling and buying, they created a separate "external department," authorized to develop new markets and products, and a new sourcing function, delegated to find new materials for both existing and new products. Yet over the course of fifteen months they paid little attention to these external relationships. The sourcing manager, who was being pulled into internal development tasks, noted, "My time is being dragged off so that I can't even get to sourcing." The external department manager noted that his department was still "an item of controversy" and had developed no new strategic selling program.[7] Indeed, at the end of fifteen months, sourcing, far from developing as a strategic activity, had regressed, buying stock made of low-cost, low-quality materials.

In sum, the CEO was using Delta as an extension of his own narcissistic ambitions. By taking pride in his new tools and his presumed capacity to engineer new cultures, he actually created a culture based on splitting and idealization. In his neglect of the marketplace and of the necessary new relationships with suppliers and customers, the CEO created a transitional culture in which the pain and difficulty of change was denied. He glorified certain workers and neglected others, split off Delta from a new company that would market its presumed capacity to manage technological change, and created a climate of cheerleading rather than a system for problem solving. Drawn to the cultural images of excellent executives who manage by walking about, the CEO seemed unable to understand and experience the actual social process that shaped the workers' experiences.

To be sure, because we lack the data to give a full assessment of how and why the CEO acted as he did, we run the risk of scapegoating him, as if no one else at the company helped to shape or reinforce the narcissistic character of the venture. But whatever its roots, the venture was limited by its narcissistic foundations. Certainly the high rate of worker turnover and the flight of employees who looked like "winners" suggests that most workers experienced the company climate as toxic and dangerous.

Chip Inc.
In contrast, consider the experiences of Chip Inc. a subsidiary of a large and successful computer manufacturing company.[8] The manager and his subordinates were authorized to design and run a new computer module and disk manufacturing plant based on innovative work-design principles. Twenty-six managers and workers, three

company consultants, and three external consultants spent seventeen months designing, developing, establishing, and finally opening and running a modern plant for producing modules and disks. The story of their effort reflects the workers' and the managers' maturity, their acknowledgment of the pain entailed in developing something new, and their awareness that they were ultimately accountable to customers for quality products and dependent on suppliers for quality raw materials. In contrast to Delta's focus on the dazzle of new ideas and management fads, the managers and workers of Chip Inc. focused on the work itself, on the joint system of technology and jobs (called by the participants and others the sociotechnical system) that would ultimately shape the plant's capacity to produce quality components at low cost.

Three issues are salient here. First, from design to start-up the managers and workers acknowledged the necessity of what psychologists call working through a particular problem and the set of social relationships that surround it. Far from denying the difficulty and pain of planning, implementing, and collaborating, workers and managers persisted against problems, despite the difficult feelings their persistence sometimes created, until they found satisfying solutions.

For example, in assessing their experience in modeling the key production process, in which they focused in particular on the errors and failures associated with the flow of materials, a design coordinator stated, "Many subtle and overt group dynamics surface in a newly formed work group that represents all the traditional organizational levels. Group members often found themselves 'violently agreeing' on issues, with the real difference being language or functional perspective. At times it was difficult to ignore traditional roles; head-on confrontation with the plant manager can be a risky business if an adequate amount of trust and self-confidence has not been established." Similarly, in assessing the first phase of the team's design work, one member noted "It's stupid to flounder around, but maybe floundering is a necessary period of adjustment."

Even the plant manager was able to acknowledge his pain. At the end of the first design phase, when the team of workers and managers had sketched the philosophy and organizational components of the new organization, he ended the planning meeting by listing the "highs and lows" he had experienced over the course of the design work. He noted that his highs included the pleasure he took in "changing from operational to visionary and documenting a comprehensive set of visions" that he believed in, realizing that the team had "created a culture and norms" and were already living them while thinking they were "still designing them," and, finally, "seeing how much the so-called direct labor people can participate, contribute, feel ownership, and care." But far from idealizing the experience, he also noted his low points, telling the assembled team that he was "realizing the lack of ownership and leadership around the process" on his part because of his external focus and that he had to face "the first eight months of daily ups and downs around job and plant security and the isolation, rejection, and morale problems these [feelings] created."

Just as the team members acknowledged the difficulty of working together, so did the plant manager acknowledge the fundamental anxieties of building a new organization. In contrast to the CEO of Delta, who promised that no workers would lose their jobs because of automation and then fired many workers, the plant manager at Chip Inc. understood that status anxieties, job fears, and feelings of estrangement accompanied the high points and exhilaration of designing an innovative plant. Indeed, during the seventeen-month design period, the plant manager fired one team member and demoted a team leader, painful acts that were critically scrutinized though ultimately accepted by the workers.

An observer and consultant to the design process who spoke frequently with workers and managers emphasized how pain was an integral part of the design experience and how conscious people were of the difficulties of creating something new and important. "People felt pain from the absence of clarity in key normative areas—decision making, communications, pushback and confrontation, task accomplishment, and relationships. . . . There was also pain in the areas where people felt the behaviors and attitudes being established weren't 'in sync' with what the plant was supposed to be about. The gap between the ideal and the actual caused disillusionment, skepticism about how different the plant was really going to be when all was said and done—and motivated some people to go out and fight all the harder to keep the ideal alive."[9]

Conscious of the "dark side" as well as the exhilaration of designing the plant, team members were less prone to scapegoating one another. After the plant manager removed one member of a design team, the other members wondered "if they could or should have done more to help one of their members. . . . 'How much do we own his failure?' " they asked.

Second, in contrast to the case of Delta, managers and workers at Chip Inc. did not glorify the machines as beautiful or modern tools but focused instead on the *work*, on the combined impact of *tools* and *jobs* that shaped a particular experience of working and a set of interdependent roles. They called this combined sociotechnical system the core of the plant and consistently had to remind themselves that this core, the work itself, would ultimately shape the entire organization design. The design had to be justified by the work.

As they approached key design decisions, a consultant to the design process told them, "Organizing choices should be driven by your need to know the core. The most important work is the core. Work from there out. Everything else is secondary." In other words, the entire system of functions, divisions, departments, and employee status had to be linked to the work itself. The organization was an instrument of the work. As the design team approached the task of laying out the machines, the consultant again argued that all the other issues of design could be understood once the method for combining jobs and machines had been mastered and the group had designed a complete system of work. "It is the work that's going to make this place swing," he noted.

Indeed, the design teams, consisting of managers and workers who would eventually run the plant, spent a great deal of time simply *understanding their technology*. To create a cost-efficient plant, they ιound that they had to reconceptualize the entire production process. They could no longer view the plant as a traditional job shop in which autonomous workers, buffered by inventory and scheduling slips, controlled their own work stations. They had to model the production process as a continuous flow of materials in which actions at one stage, no longer buffered by inventory, time, or a stock of finished goods, affected work at all other stages. To this end the design teams broke the process down into its unit operations, identified the critical errors or "variances" that disrupted the movement of materials from one operation to another, and then specified control tasks that enabled workers to limit or eliminate these variances. After developing this integrated model of the production process, they then worked to develop a role system that enabled workers to experience and grasp the whole operation as well as its constituent parts. By focusing on the work rather than on machines alone or on separate jobs, the design teams created roles that would help workers and managers understand the wider purpose of particular operations.

Third and finally, in establishing the guiding framework and philosophy for the plant design, the plant manager focused on the plant's relationship to its customers and suppliers. The plant manager developed a vision statement for the teams in which he emphasized the characteristics of the plant's products and its responsiveness to changing market demands. He aimed, for example, for a 30 percent reduction in module cost, a 100 percent quality yield, and a significant reduction in the time it took to get new products to market. In others words, the vision statement emphasized that the plant was an instrument of its participants' purposes and that these purposes in turn were linked to the needs of customers and suppliers. Moreover, the plant manager argued that they could achieve these cost and quality goals only by developing regular and consistent relationships with suppliers. To reduce work in process to a minimum, the plant had to be assured that suppliers could ship just the amount of raw materials needed for the plant's unpredictable schedule of production runs. To ensure needed deliveries, suppliers rather than plant personnel would do all the raw material inspection on the basis of clear specifications provided by the plant. In contrast to plants with high stocks of buffer inventory and final products separating the plant from its customers and suppliers and plants with semi-autonomous departments, this plant would be extremely dependent on its suppliers for materials, its customers for feedback, and its members for the accurate and timely coordination of tasks.

The plant was a success. It started up on schedule, the time for production of a standard module fell 40 percent below industry standards, costs fell by 38 percent, work in process was minimized, scrap was at 3 percent of input, vendors inspected all incoming materials, and quality yields were in the high 90s. Yet despite this success managers and workers were sensitive to the pull of grandiosity and narcissism that may infect such a venture. One member of the team assessed the role of visions in shaping the new plant as follows: "We got trapped in wonderfulness. Seeing pitfalls meant you were uncommitted." The plant manager, reflecting on his work to stay connected to the larger company and get support from its central division, acknowledged that the plant's members had been arrogant, as if the plant were the company's only high-performance system. Although the plant's advocates needed to stress its uniqueness in order to win support and funds for an extended start-up period, "the price they paid," in the words of one observer, "was the rigidity around design concepts, and the mistrust of anything traditional." Sold on the basis of its differences, the design process caused people to "overvalue its impact . . . and undervalue their own experience base." As one manager put it, "The longer our list of claims got, the more we turned inward and became dysfunctional."

This struggle to highlight the plant's differences while still finding links to useful company traditions is not surprising, nor is the consequent tension between arrogance and insulation on the one side and openness and humility on the other. What is striking is the team members' capacity to be reflective, to acknowledge that, despite their obvious success, their activities, and their implicit culture, their relationships to one another were both good and bad. As one manager noted, "A high-performance work system has more dramatic high and low mood swings. It's a more vulnerable emotional/social set, because the higher degree of awareness and sharing also means a higher potential for negative energy. The challenge is understanding the balance."

The Reparative Culture

When we compare Delta Products and Chip Inc., three dimensions of a reparative culture stand out. First, managers and employees experience their organization as an instrument for accomplishing valued purposes. The organization's existence is justified only insofar as it accomplishes ends valued by the stakeholders in its wider environment. This can be done by designing the work so that workers understand the whole operation and by developing an organizational mission statement that helps workers and managers link choices they make on the job to the company's valued ends. (For example, "The customer is always right" is the classic mission statement for a sales organization.) Managers and workers have found that the sociotechnical approach to job design used by the team at Chip Inc. helps to link jobs to the organization's purpose. Workers and managers break down a production operation into units that contain relatively whole tasks, such as the production of a complete part or subassembly. By examining one particular unit operation, they assess how it is affected by production errors from prior unit operations and how it in turn affects later units "downstream. ' Jobs are then designed so that workers can correct mistakes when they happen. By focusing both on the unit operations and on the boundaries between them and by controlling errors at the boundaries between operations, workers and managers develop a comprehensive understanding of the system as a whole.

Second, managers and employees are keenly aware of the work itself. As the driving factor in shaping organization design and culture, a combination of technology and jobs, the work system, shapes all other critical dimensions of the organization, from its reward system and role set to its rhythms and norms. Work makes the organization's purpose manifest, representing the organization's value concretely in a particular and continuing flow of products. Organizations with a reparative culture value the quality of the product or service highly and develop norms supporting "pride in work."

Third, the work group develops a relatively nonnarcissistic process in which the good and the bad are acknowledged and psychological splitting is limited. People acknowledge that aggression is necessary, that members' performances must be evaluated, and that certain members may fail to meet the demands of the task. In contrast to fanciful descriptions of modern managers who are urged to be prophets, visionaries, and cultural transformers, managers in reparative settings take actions that pain others while remaining emotionally connected to the resulting suffering. Members face their own experiences of good and bad directly, rather than projecting the sense of badness onto others, and can therefore learn from failures and successes.

Such an organization supports the reparative process for three reasons. First, people understand the purpose of their work and can link the value they create to their wish to restore others symbolically by meeting the real needs of customers and clients. Second, because work and purpose are linked, people experience their ability to create value directly, rather than depending on an organizational ideology to assure them that they are important and good. By assessing their own experiences, they are not dependent on manufactured cultures to discover their purposes. Third, because the organization acknowledges the good and the bad in its process and does not deny the pain and injury of working with others, people feel relatively whole and contain their propensity to scapegoat co-workers or clients.

The Broader Context

As the example of Chip Inc. indicates, people and organizations can develop reparative organizations. But, if the broader cultural, economic and technological milieu is unsupportive, their chances of succeeding are reduced. If the culture inhibits learning, punishes failures, and denies aggression, then people will find it hard to create and maintain nonsplitting cultures. Similarly, if companies do not train workers to manage new sociotechnical systems and do not know how to design postindustrial jobs, then few will use the new technologies to connect the experience of working to the organization's purpose. Instead, the new technologies and the more integrated sociotechnical domain will create more anxiety. Finally, people may find it difficult to value the work they do and understand its purpose if the society as a whole has no coherent sense of what it values. To examine the future of the reparative organization, we must step back and examine its broader cultural and historical context.

12

Steps toward a Developmental Culture

The transition to a postindustrial world creates more psychological violence, but the reparative process offers hope for healing and development. Can reparation outpace the growing violence? As was noted briefly in the introduction, Harry Levinson describes how the devastating hurricane of 1938 had left large parts of New England without electrical power. Public utility employees came from all over the region to help restore service. They worked long hours under dangerous conditions in an unfamiliar territory; yet in six weeks of intensive work there was not one accident. The reason seems clear: The meaning of the work, its value to others, was obvious. Accidents frequently happen when workers anxious about the work fail to pay attention. In trying to contain their anxiety, they daydream or fail to notice warning signs. They withdraw from the boundary of their roles. It appears that the obvious value of the work to others enabled the utility workers to overcome the anxiety of staying at the role boundary, of paying complete and total attention to their risky and difficult task.

Today, however, the meaning of our work is becoming progressively less clear. As we enter the postindustrial society, we lose the cultural framework that enables us to value work in general, that tells us when we are doing "good" or succeeding at work. People feel dislocated from their roles. Pressed against the reality of other people's experiences in an imploded world and anxious about standing at complicated role boundaries, workers may not understand the total social field in which they are embedded and may therefore fail to see how their work produces value for others. As the meaning of work becomes less clear, people find it increasingly difficult to discover reparative opportunities within it. Our capacity to repair our relationships to others thus depends on three forces: our ability to imagine the total social field in which our role and our work are embedded, the clarity of our social purposes and needs, and cultural support for the reparative process itself. How strong are these forces, and what can we expect from them?

A Historical Perspective

A historical perspective is critical here. It is commonplace to argue that industrial civilization provided people with two simple criteria for valuing work: the degree to which the society as a whole made "progress" and the degree to which an individual was upwardly mobile. These two criteria came together in the use of economic growth as a measure: the increase in capital, output, and productivity for the society and the increase in income and status for the individual.

Looked at historically, preindustrial societies had simple economies but complex systems for valuing economic activity. Work was imbued with a multidimensional value system, so that cultural, religious, and historical criteria measured a particular work product. Guilds were not simply trade unions; rather, they were associations for investing work with religious, social, and cultural meanings. In contrast, industrial civilization immensely complicated economic production and exchange, but it simultaneously simplified the valuation of work. The value of a piece of work was its price in the market, the value of an economy was its aggregate wealth. The complexity of exchange, reflected in an increasingly complicated division of labor, was balanced by the simplicity of valuation. This compensatory development helped people to orient themselves to an increasingly diversified and changing social life.

This historical development also had its equivalent psychodynamic implications. It is common to note that industrial culture intensified the experience of personhood. People extricated themselves from broader communal obligations and associations. They wanted more control over whom they married, what work they chose, and how they worshipped. Privacy became important. The rise of Protestant sects, which prefigured the later emergence of bourgeois life in the industrial world, undermined the Church's celebration of celibacy and its suspicion of marriage. The Roman Catholic Church favored the widest understanding of kinship as the basis for human association and suspected that marriage and family ties took people out of the matrix of the Christian community. The new Protestant sects, by contrast, elevated marriage, sexuality, and material life, emphasizing the new autonomous role of the pater-familias in the family domain.

Yet these freedoms were balanced by new "unfreedoms" of a more psychological nature. Social constraint was internalized, and individuals developed a harsher and more demanding internal voice. The superego became superordinate and demanding, replacing social obligations with psychological ones. This new harsh voice was prefigured in the early Protestant sects as the concepts of grace, calling, and election replaced the hope for continuing and sustained forgiveness. Grace meant that only God knew if you were saved; only He could elect you. Your calling in turn was the inner sign of the path you had to take if you had any hope of being saved. Indeed, just as Marx exposed the bourgeois claims about the "free" market by highlighting the backdrop of class power and class relations, so did Freud expose the bourgeois claims of the free individual by highlighting the individual's slavery to inner voices of punishment and compulsion. Thus freedom in the social sphere was balanced by compulsion in the psychological domain. It was this new compulsion that enabled people to make choices and direct their lives in an increasingly complex and changing social world.

The broad sweep and meaning of these changes that organized the transition to an industrial world can be seen in the difference between an introjective and a projective culture. Premodern culture encouraged and sustained projection on a mass scale. Medieval people lived in a world of ghosts, demons, and souls.[1] The living mingled with ghosts of the dead on earth, and souls in purgatory and saints in heaven influenced daily life. In such a world people could easily and safely project their feelings outward, so that ghosts and spirits became the source of unwanted impulses, motives, and actions. The singularly prominent devil represented the cultural screen for projecting out all internal feelings of hatred and despair.[2] The culture could contain projections on a mass scale; indeed, the culture was the sum of these projections. Consequently people did not have to manage these feelings within themselves.

In contrast, an introjective culture, such as our modern culture, does not contain and sustain projections so easily. The person who deploys projections is considered crazy. People manage difficult feelings by drawing on or introjecting the cultural symbols of authority, of the good, the ideal, the right, and the strong. Inner psychological life grows in complexity and richness, whereas culture, the psychosocial space *between* people, is denuded and simplified. Such a cultural process works so long as the resulting feelings of guilt and shame do not overwhelm a person's psychological balance.

In sum, the psychological and sociological life of industrial culture was based on two developments and their compensations: a more varied economic life balanced by a simplified system of evaluation and a freer individual life balanced by the more internalized voice of authority. These two developments were unified in the cultural notion of mobility and progress. The individual heard the inner voice as the compulsion to succeed, to be upwardly mobile, to expand the father's business and capital. The culture as a whole valued profit, growth, and wealth as the primary determinants of value. Thus economic and psychological life were intertwined and consistent.

Limiting Reparation

The industrial culture is psychodynamically unstable because it makes reparation difficult. Recall that, in repairing our relationships to others, we feel shame at our pettiness and affirm life in spite of its inherent limits. But in the psychological makeup of industrial culture, limitation became conflated with sin or badness to a dangerous degree.

Three psychosocial premises in the industrial system of thought play a critical role here. First, the inner injunction, "You must become," was linked to the injunction, "You are bad." Failure to achieve was intimately linked to the experience of sin. Indeed, this was the basis for the original Protestant conception of the relationship of the calling to the potential for grace. Failure at the calling was a sign of one's sinfulness. The image of the ideal was thus surrounded by feelings of *compulsion*, of what McClelland termed the need for achievement.[3] It is this compulsion that gave industrial culture its obsessive, or what Brown called its anal, character.[4] But failure is endemic to much of life. Everyone has limited resources, time, and talents; and accidents and chance disrupt the most carefully developed plans. Industrial culture denied the pressing reality of limits.

Second, this conflation of failure with sin was linked to the Christian assumption that death and disease were produced by sin.

But again death is a natural part of life; it expresses life's limits. These two premises made it difficult for people to face their smallness on the one hand and value their limits on the other.

Finally, guilt and sacrifice sealed this system of thought. When people felt limited and mortal, they did not acknowledge their smallness; rather, they acknowledged their sinfulness. They consequently felt guilt instead of shame. To relieve their guilt for being bad, they sacrificed some part of themselves or another to a more powerful authority (God, the inner parental voice, the nation-state), which in turn would help them become powerful and good. Thus in the industrial culture guilt replaced shame and sinfulness replaced smallness.[5]

In this context of sinfulness and guilt there was a tendency for people to measure their *triumphs*, their victories over sin, chance, and other people. But the feeling of triumph represents what Klein believed to be an extreme reaction to the depressive position.[6] It embodies the fantasy that one is ultimately good because others are bad and terrible. It is the emotional cul-de-sac of splitting. Thus industrial culture inhibited the psychodynamics of reparation. This is the psychodynamic equivalent of what Marx described as the "alienation" of living in a bourgeois society.

The Current Trap

We have reached a cul-de-sac. Over the last sixty years we have grown increasingly skeptical that development brings progress. We have fewer outlets for our triumphs. The prospect of nuclear disaster, the dangers poised by new technologies—both lead us to doubt the viability of a culture once based on such ideas as progress, mobility, science, and rational thinking. Indeed, it is common now for social critics to argue that our success as a civilization is our undoing. We have produced what Bakan called excessively agentic people who are bent on mastering nature as well as other people.[7] Critics suggest that our Faustian compulsion to master has led us to destroy the groundwork for our life. We disrupt the ecological balance, undermine family life, and produce nuclear weapons. The skeptic might look askance at such apocalyptic formulations, but they seem true at the core. Modern life seems precariously balanced. Indeed, cultural developments of the last twenty years (environmentalism, feminism, the global peace movement) represent the hope for a possible corrective to our unbalanced life.

In the United States we are still somewhat innocent. This sad history of the last sixty years is owned more deeply and intensively by Europeans. Yet these same feelings and thoughts have begun to affect us as well. The economic transition to a postindustrial society certainly plays a critical role here. New technologies are reshaping old skills and supervision systems, and new patterns of competition within and between countries are reshaping markets. People are increasingly less sure of what behaviors bring success, what combination of pluck and luck ensures upward mobility.

Psychodynamically the superego voice, the voice of compulsion, is no longer modified by the compelling ego-ideal. It punishes without offering the hope that success will modify one's original failures, one's original sin. The internal balance between the voice that punishes and the voice that promises is upset. Thus people increasingly feel punished. This growing inner burden eventually distorts social life as people project their experiences of self-hate onto others.

The Developmental Culture

Freud was the grand pessimist. He argued that, as civilization becomes more complicated, people increasingly have to renounce their desires, their elemental need and wish for pleasure, to fit into a complicated social order. They repress their wish for pleasure by feeling guilty for desiring it; therefore civilization is stable only if people feel increasingly guilty. Yet, as we have seen, there is a limit to the guilt that people can bear. At some point they project it onto other groups, other "bad" people. Paradoxically the solution to integrating people into society sets the stage for violent struggles between groups. Success in repressing individuals sets the conditions for the society's ultimate decay and self-destruction.

The analysis presented here can hardly be more optimistic than Freud's. The anxiety of the postindustrial world creates increasing psychological violence. But in this view, in contrast to Freud's, the problem does not lie in the unbridgeable gap between the instincts and social life. Rather, it lies in the dialectic between fantasy and culture.

Let us return to the theme of reparation. As we have seen, work can function as a transitional object, enabling people to use the value that is inherent in a product or a service to overcome the splits in their fantasy lives. Such an operation entails risks, however, for people must test their capacity to meet other people's needs in a contingent and unpredictable setting.

I suggest that, when people can do this in a sustained and continuous way, they are participating in a *developmental* culture. To return to the typology, in projective cultures culture contains projections of inner life; in introjective cultures aggression and hatred are internalized. By contrast, in developmental cultures introjection and projection are more complexly combined. People project the experience of the tentative *good* onto the work product and, when it is accepted, that symbol of the good has achieved its potential. It is then reintrojected and metabolized in a way that diminishes the power of the hated object and in turn allows for a unification of good and bad.

Thus, in contrast to the current process of decay, in a developmental culture it is the good object, not the bad object, that is projected. People take the risk of losing that which they treasure in the hope that others will treasure it as well. In this way they strengthen its goodness, because others have also loved it. By participating in the production of goods and services, *they participate in the production of culture.* They use public symbols to repair their relationships to their internal objects, but in the process they invest these symbols with private meanings, affirming their value while perhaps transforming them. In contrast to the dialectic of industrial culture, in which bad objects are projected to exhaust or deplete their real outlets, their projective screens, in a developmental culture good objects potentially enrich and transform their screens.

Yet to describe such a culture is to highlight the obstacles to creating it. Three preconditions stand out. First, such a culture must rest on the bedrock of a sanctioned adult developmental process. The theory of reparation highlights the fact that we cannot transform the world by bringing up children who are free of neuroses. It has been the burden of utopian thinkers since Plato to pin their hopes on early education as the method for transforming social life. But the conditions for sickness are built into infantile dependency and the child's capacity for fantasy. Rather, the theory of reparation suggests that development—repair work, the work of making people whole— need not stop. Reparation, as Klein suggests, takes place in a particular psychodynamic "position," not at a particular stage of life. This position can be attained at any point in the life cycle. Thus failure does not condemn us to sinfulness as it did in the industrial culture. We can recover our wholeness at many points in the life cycle; our failures at one point do not preclude recovery and repair at another. In a developmental culture adults can continue the work of reparation throughout their lives and can do so, in particular, through their work.

Second, jobs themselves should bring people closer to the boundary of the work organization. People should feel accountable for the whole product and more directly aware of the customers' needs. As we have seen throughout this book, standing at the boundary promotes anxiety; yet it is only at the boundary that we have the hope of connecting to the people whose needs we wish to satisfy while understanding the total social field in which we work. To develop a "systems" view, we cannot bury ourselves inside our organizations and departments but must do work at the boundary between systems.

The new technologies of automation and communication offer us much hope here. Automation has displaced workers from the core of the operating system to its periphery, where they engage in boundary management work, understanding the links connecting divisions, units, and departments. The term "service society" itself suggests that as all economic activity, manufacturing included, takes on a service character, people become more aware of the customer's needs and the social life that creates them. As the case of Chip Inc. suggests, we are developing the social technologies to design work systems that connect people to their jobs, enable them to complete whole tasks, and link them to the organization's purposes. The rapid spread of sociotechnical factories, as I have documented elsewhere, is an important and hopeful sign.[8]

But as I have also suggested, reparative organizations can regress when faced with a chaotic environment. Leaders cannot sustain sophisticated organizational boundaries that are open to the environment if these environments are fundamentally disorganized. We cannot construct a developmental culture unless we have broader agreement on the purposes of our economic activity. People must create and offer products and services that match their internalized image of the good. But those real products cannot at the same time be the repository of other people's destructive images. If an industrial chemical, a food additive, or an energy source is believed by many to be a source of death, it cannot at the same time function as a temporary holding environment for the image of the good. Indeed, one way to understand the current social crisis is to say that the stalemated debates over the purposes of our economic system, of our vast productive wealth, deprive us of good enough symbolic images of the good and the useful. Instead, many experience our economic system as death dealing, as committed to the production of weapons and chemical and technical complexes that destroy life.

Are the forces for reparation strong? The transition to a post-industrial society offers hope that we may no longer value triumphs and confuse the small with the sinful. The more realistic discussion of death and dying suggests that we are learning to affirm life as valuable in itself. Similarly, our large and flexible adult education system provides us with the institutional tools we need to promote adult development and learning through the life span. The growth in corporate and continuing education programs suggest that an increasing number of people might find the time, the space, and the resources to develop a systems view of their work and role.

But although some cultural, technological, and institutional changes offer hope, our political economy seems disorganized. By creating severe disruption and dislocation, the transition to a post-industrial economy based on automation and boundary jobs increases anxiety and creates new scapegoats. By transforming our productive apparatus in the framework of a still primitive social security system, the new technologies create victims as well as oportunities. As we have seen, a reparative culture rests on the twin pillars of risk and love. Development through work is impossible unless we expose our competence and judgment to the test of those who buy our goods and services. But today too many people face the risks of social degradation and homelessness and never face the more subtle tests of their competence and value. We need to design a system of social supports that helps shape a forgiving economy, that helps people to recover from failure and gives them second chances.

Most important, we seem unable to create a politics that helps us to clarify the purposes of our immense productive apparatus. What goods and services do we value? How do we evaluate the chemicals, drugs, power systems, medical technology, and leisure services we produce? How do we link what we can produce to the needs of poor people around the world? What institutional and political mechanisms can we invent or improve to address these issues in a sustained way? How can we use the marketplace to help us to allocate resources sensibly, without imagining that it can substitute for the collective dialogue we need to establish our priorities and give collective meaning to our individual efforts?

The clarification of values and purposes at a cultural and political level can help facilitate the process of imagining and learning. A coherent culture and politics at the social level could take the place of the social defenses at an organizational level. Moreover, if we can make this substitution, we can transform defenses into developmental gradients. We can move from mechanisms of group life that contain anxiety to mechanisms of social and cultural life that help us overcome it.

But in the current political milieu this is only a hope, an almost utopian sketch. We need our chemicals, our nuclear plants, and our capacity for genetic engineering. But that is only my opinion. As a society we lack the capacity to construct social purposes, to invest our activity collectively with meaning, so that a culture of good symbols can emerge. Instead, it seems that the current spate of "free market thinking" militates against such discussion while our government commits itself to an extensive military buildup and dedicates itself to discovering communism everywhere.

Summary

In the current transition to a postindustrial society, we risk losing our roles. The social defenses at work, which help to contain the anxiety of working, are breaking down. Consequently we are on the lookout for scapegoats. The single work organization finds it difficult to make itself whole and good in such a context. The problem is cultural and historical.

The social defenses are based on the psychology of projecting the bad object onto others. We injure others so that we can feel safe. The injuries are always present as the hallmark of our alienation. The only questions we face within the industrial society are the extent of these injuries and the stability of the defenses that produce and contain them.

But we are reaching the limits of a culture based on projecting the bad. We need a new cultural system that enables us to contain our anxieties, to manage them without projecting our self-hate. We must replace the social defenses with a new culture of work that supports the reparative process. The anxiety of working must now be managed and organized by a broader system of symbols and meanings that allows us to take risks, permits us to fail, but gives us second chances. We cannot eliminate risk, for that is the core of work. But we can value learning and we can forgive failures. This is the hallmark of a developmental culture.

As we make the transition to a postindustrial society, we must erect a new symbolic framework for our institutions that can contain anxiety as the social defenses once did. The individual will no longer depend on the vicissitudes of a single organization for managing anxieties but on a broader culture of work. This is the sense in which work in a postindustrial society becomes "socialized." It is not, as Marx thought, that property will be owned by the collective. Rather, the individual's psychodynamic relationship to work, in its most intimate details, will be mediated by a cultural process.

But again I sound utopian. Adult development, a service economy, automation, and political processes that help us shape the purposes of our economic life—these are the building blocks of a developmental culture. Social forces that support these developments are beginning to emerge, but they are admittedly weak. In the meantime civilization grows more discontented with itself.

Appendix: Consulting As a Method of Research

Consulting is both a method for collaborating with organizations to help them improve and a method of research for understanding them. I typically follow a three-step process when consulting for an organization. First, I interview organization members whose roles and interests are centrally connected to the presenting problem that leads executives to ask for help. For example, I may interview the partners of a law firm, the program heads of a social service agency, the branch managers of a bank, or team members in a particular work unit. I ask each participant to describe their role, the organization's problem and their relationship to it, and feasible solutions. I do not use formal surveys or work climate instruments to assess the organization's functioning, finding that they frequently function as a social defense by leading me to avoid the anxiety of directly experiencing the client system.

Second, I write what practitioners at the Tavistock Institute call the working note. Based on the data of the interviews and couched in the form of a hypothesis, the note presents a theory of the client's presenting problems. In contrast to some other forms of consulting I do not simply feed back the data of the interviews, saying, for example, that "forty percent of those interviewed said they were satisfied with the work setting." Rather, I construct a model of the client's situation and take the risk of inferring causes from often incomplete interview data. Clients appreciate this approach, even when they disagree with the note's conclusions, because it shows that I will take the risk of appearing wrong or foolish in the interests of helping them understand and resolve their problem. (In chapter 5 I described some of the contents of the note I developed for the executive team of ERD.) The note represents my willingness to collaborate with the organization and not just stand back and observe.

Third, I meet with the participants to discuss the note, review its implications, and develop a general plan for the consultation.

After this opening phase each consulting effort is designed to meet the particular needs of the client I am working with. I might design a retreat with them, do a study of their role system based on a technique known as responsibility charting, or work with different people on problems and issues that are both specific to their roles and linked to the client's general problem. (For example, in my work with the bank described in chapter 8 I worked across five levels over a two-year period.) The scope of my work depends of course on how much money the client wants to spend for my consulting services.

Four Research Methods

There are at least four ways to study work groups: interviews and surveys, field observation of the work setting, participation in the work group, and consulting with members of the work group. Each has its limits and strengths, but scholars and methodologists increasingly agree that quantitative surveys, formal interviews, and research organized by well-defined a priori hypotheses make it difficult for the researcher to understand the *meanings* that workers attribute to particular events, the *feelings* they harbor about their work world, and the *intentions* that shape their relationships to coworkers, bosses, and their own ambitions. In neglecting the subjective or phenomenological dimension of organizational life, such research has produced literature that is "inconclusive, helter-skelter, noncumulative, and inconsistent."[1]

Field work, by contrast, can provide more detailed data on people's motives and feelings. By observing shift workers in an automatic factory, Charles Walker could uncover how they experienced the new technology, how conflicts between the old and the new systems of labor relations emerged, how workers experienced their new work identity, and what sense they made of their new roles.[2]

Participant observation may enable the researcher to develop an even richer understanding of workers' feelings, motives, and purposes, because the researcher-cum-worker can study his or her own feelings as well as talk with co-workers frequently and informally. Freed from the trappings of the research encounter, the participant-observer experiences workers as they really are, not as they pose to the researcher.

Consulting As a Research Tool

Even though the methods of interviewing, observation, and participation are useful, consulting as a research tool has several distinctive strengths that enable the consultant-researcher to understand the feelings and meanings that workers and managers bring to organizational life. Consulting mobilizes the client as a coresearcher, as both the consultant and the client work to make sense of organizational problems.

As a research tool, consulting has several distinctive strengths. Because clients pay consultants, they want to cooperate with them and tell them what most vexes them, what is most on their minds. Surveys, by contrast, are frequently biased by what the researcher believes to be important. Similarly, in studying the normal or routine operations of organizational life, the field researcher may not observe workers when they are actively and purposively trying to make sense of their own experiences. They observe the ritualized adaptations to the contradictions of the workplace but cannot observe the subjective process that shapes these adaptations and makes them either stable or unstable.

Consulting encounters are effective as research tools because they are both real and artificial events. They are artificial because consultants frequently work with clients outside the normal boundaries of organizational life, but they are real because clients bring all their subjectively experienced relationships to the consulting encounter. This has two consequences. First, the clients—in contrast to research subjects—want to make the consultant as effective as possible. They want to bring as much information as they can about the organization to the consultant.

Second, in working to marshal their conscious thoughts, clients also mobilize their unconscious relationship to the problems they face and bring that to the encounter as well. Psychoanalysts argue that this process of transference is the medium for all therapeutic work. Therapists can help patients heal their wounds only because the patients transfer the character of all their troubled relationships onto the analyst. Then by working through their relationship to the analyst, they recapitulate all the conflicts of their past and, it is hoped, resolve them. The therapeutic encounter, like the consulting encounter, is both real and not real.

The interplay of the real and the artificial and the creation of

transference give the consultant a unique source of information. Recall that, when Hatfield, the training director of the bank, came to me
for help, he brought the way he related to other bank managers to his
relationship with me. The feelings of dependency and helplessness
that shaped how he took his role as a bank officer were transferred to
the consultant-client relationship. In responding to his helplessness,
I was inducted into the bank's socioemotional system. By becoming
a repository for Hatfield's feelings of helplessness, I understood in a
way that I had never understood before why the senior managers felt
so frustrated and why they had become so punishing. Before that
moment I was puzzled by their punishing stance and its irrational
consequences. Had I been a field researcher, I might have concluded
that the senior managers said that they wanted employees to take
initiative but ultimately could not give up control. But as a consultant who responded actively and dynamically to Hatfield's helplessness, I experienced "in my bones" how his passivity made me feel
ineffective as well. Just as I felt like wringing Hatfield's neck to get
his attention, I could imagine that the senior managers wanted to
wring their subordinates' necks, to wake them from their apparent
stupor. As an unconscious response to the behavior of their subordinates, their punishing stance now made sense to me, because I too
had felt this way when meeting with Hatfield.

This example also clarifies the epistemological value of a feeling.
In traditional survey research scholars face the problem of integrating findings from different questions into a coherent conception of
how respondents make sense of the situation *as a whole.* Respondents, for example, may note on a survey form that their supervisors
are fair but that their work is too hard. How do these two statements
come together to form a coherent whole? What is the overall attitude
of the respondents to the workplace? Feelings, as Tomkins argues,
are the internal signals one uses to make overall sense of one's situation.[3] A feeling state enables one to develop an overall orientation to
the situation and is thus the experiential basis for the meaning of the
situation. Researchers may puzzle over the intellectual problems of
creating coherence and never solve it to their satisfaction, but people
actively create coherence because they develop intentions and must
ultimately act. *The feeling links meaning and intention.* By knowing
what I feel, I know what the situation means, and then I know, in
light of my intentions, how to act. This is why decision makers are
frequently counseled to get in touch with their feelings and why we

feel most satisfied with a decision when it comes from the "gut" as well as the head. We are listening to our internal signals.

Returning to the bank example, Hatfield undoubtedly had many complicated feelings about the bank but, in asking me for help and then behaving helplessly, he communicated the feeling with which he oriented himself and acted in situations that were important to him: dependence.

Consulting and Relationships

My interaction with Hatfield also highlights another value of the consulting role as a research tool. In an excellent example of participant observation research, recounted in his *Chaos on the Shop Floor*,[4] Tom Juravich, taking the role of a worker, was able to study how a supervisor in a small wire shop could create a chaotic working environment. Yet, although the study is compelling and convincing, the managers of the company are shadowy if not invisible actors throughout Juravich's study, even though they undoubtedly had a great impact on the shop floor itself. Clearly Juravich was restricted by the role he took as a worker, and like many workers in low-level jobs he found it difficult to develop a broader and more developed systems view of his situation. By taking on the world view of the worker, he failed to grasp the world view of the manager and the resulting relationship between the two.

In consulting, by contrast, one invariably attends to a particular relationship in which at least two roles share a boundary and two sides of a problem come into focus. For example, in consulting with Hatfield, I did not, as I might in a participant observation study, enter into Hatfield's world and identify with him. Instead, I was inducted into the world of Hatfield's important "others" so that, by emotionally responding, I learned something about the relationship *between* Hatfield and his superiors. Hatfield, feeling anxious in his meeting with me because he was dealing with a difficult problem, reduced his anxiety by inducting me into the same relationship he used to contain his anxiety in his work role.

Initial encounters with clients are often powerful for this reason. Frequently the client reproduces the core of his or her problem when first negotiating for consulting services. A scientist from a research organization was delegated to ask me to facilitate a retreat for senior scientists. In a brief conversation she told me that the junior and senior scientists in the organization felt undersupported and unappreciated and believed that the controller and president were "nickel and diming" the labs to death. She thought that the retreat would be a difficult one. I asked her about the preparations for the retreat and inquired, as I always do, about provisions for facilities and food. She stated that everyone was being asked to bring a brown bag lunch. Having heard that the major presenting complaint was "nickel and diming," I urged her to tell the president that it would be better to provide lunch for the retreat. After all, I noted, people were going to be asked to do difficult and emotional work; they would appreciate such a symbol of support. She responded with hesitation, feeling that the president might never agree. Puzzled and irritated, I realized that I was experiencing the same feelings that bothered the scientists of the company. As a consultant I knew that retreat participants might be less able to work if the president could not meet such simple dependency needs as food, and as their consultant I would feel less effective. So the president, even before I met him and before I even had a contract, was nickel and diming me to death as well!

To be sure, no single encounter can provide the consultant with all the data necessary to assess a total system of relationships. But the efficiency of the consulting encounter, the fact that it provides data about relationships, about the links among systems, roles, and data, means that the consultant can more quickly assess the total set of meanings that organization members use to interpret their experiences.

To use consulting and field observations as research tools, one must of course interpret events rather than simply count them, and interpretation introduces a radically subjective dimension to the research enterprise. As in the study of historical events, interpretations are bounded by facts but not produced by them. One needs to know who said what to whom and when, but the meaning of the encounter and its relationship to the total system of encounters that describes the client system is always subject to error. In field observation researchers are asked to confront their own biases so that they can suspend them and come to their data and observations open and unprejudiced. It may prove impossible to be completely open and without bias, but this standard for observation serves as a guidepost for assessing one's thoughts, just as the statistical model of the perfectly controlled experiment stands as the paradigm for observation when researching social activities without laboratory controls.

In using consulting as a tool for research, consultants face an even more complex problem. The researchers must face their own often unconscious emotional biases to situations of anxiety. As we have seen throughout this book, I faced settings in which I distorted the meaning of my consulting encounters because it was too difficult for me to face certain truths. For example, I could not tolerate Jane and Henry's helplessness when they came for advice on consulting for the agency for the aging, so I saw them as pathetic and unworthy as a way of containing my own anxiety.

Similarly, if I had been made anxious by my anger at Hatfield's dependency, I might have rushed to overcome my anxiety by denying my anger, perhaps by appearing particularly solicitous and doing Hatfield's work for him. (Recall that I did not write his plan for him, as he had requested.) Had I done so, I would have missed the meaning of the encounter. To use consulting as a research tool means that one must be maximally open to one's own feelings and prejudicial ways of coping with anxiety so that, when stimulated to feel in a particular way, one can use the feeling as data about relationships in the client system.

As analysts have clarified, this imposes a special discipline on the therapist and consultant. In contrast to older theories of "countertransference," object-relations theorists no longer consider that the therapist's sexual, angry, or dependent feelings toward a patient are a sign of weakness or vulnerability.[5] On the contrary, these feelings are critical indicators of the patient's unconscious intentions and wishes. The therapist cannot squelch these feelings or push the patient away from their source because they make the therapist uncomfortable and anxious. Anxiety must function as a signal that calls for more attention, not less, and for greater study, not flight.

There are no special techniques that enable consultants to stay in touch with their own characteristic modes of feeling. In contrast to participant-observers, who might deliberately and consciously make a list of personal biases ("Uneducated people are not articulate" or "Managers cannot relinquish control"), consultants by definition cannot consciously expose an unconscious process. The unconscious is observed only when it acts in the "here and now" of an encounter. At best, consultants must entertain an openness toward its effects; they must not try to prevent their characteristic mode of feelings from erupting but rather try to interpret their feelings by linking them to the encounter at hand. Consultants learn this, however partially, only by coming to accept their defined and therefore limited ways of being in the world.

Notes

Introduction

1. Isabel Menzies, "A Case Study in the Functioning of Social Systems as a Defense against Anxiety," in *Group Relations Reader*, Arthur Coleman and W. Harold Bexton, eds. (Sausalito, Calif.: GREX, 1975), 281–312.

2. For an introduction to this school of thought, see Morris N. Eagle, *Recent Developments in Psychoanalysis* (New York: McGraw Hill, 1984).

3. Menzies, "A Case Study," 284.

4. Jay Galbraith, *Designing Complex Organizations* (Reading, Mass.: Addison-Wesley, 1973); James G. March and Herbert Simon, *Organizations* (New York: Wiley, 1958).

5. Charles Perrow, *The Normal Accident* (New York: Basic Books, 1984).

6. William J. Broad, "Silence about the Shuttle Flaw Attributed to Pitfalls of Pride," *New York Times* (September 30, 1986).

7. Broad, "Silence about the Shuttle Flaw."

8. For a general introduction to the work of Melanie Klein, see Hannah Segal, *Melanie Klein* (New York: Viking Press, 1979), and Hannah Segal, *Introduction to the Work of Melanie Klein* (New York: Basic Books, 1974).

9. William J. Broad, "Silence about the Shuttle Flaw."

10. Harry Levinson, "Reciprocation: The Relationship between Man and the Organization," in *The Irrational Executive*, Manfred Kets deVries, ed. (New York: International Universities Press, 1983), 264–285.

11. Maria Ruckers Ovisignkina, "The Resumption of Interrupted Activities," in *Field Theory as Human Science: Contributions of Lewin's Berlin Group*, Joseph de Rivera, ed. (New York: Garden Press, 1976), 49–111.

12. Fred E. Emery, "Characteristics of Sociotechnical Systems," in *Design of Jobs*, Louis E. Davis and James C. Taylor, eds. (Middlesex: Penguin Books, 1972), 177–198.

13. Melanie Klein and Joan Riviere, *Love, Hate and Reparation* (New York: Norton, 1974).

Chapter 1

1. Hannah Segal, *Introduction to the Work of Melanie Klein* (New York: Basic Books, 1974), ch 7.

2. Kenneth Smith, "Rabbits, Lynxes, and Organizational Transitions," in *Managing Organizational Transitions*, John R. Kimberly and Robert E. Quinn, eds. (Homewood, Ill.: Irwin, 1984), 267–291.

Chapter 2

1. Daniel Katz and Robert Kahn, "Open Systems," in *Readings in Organization Theory: Open System Approaches*, John G. Maurer, ed. (New York: Random House, 1971), 13–29.

2. See Jay Galbraith, *Designing Complex Organizations* (Reading, Mass.: Addison-Wesley, 1973); and James G. March and Herbert Simon, *Organizations* (New York: Wiley, 1958).

3. Eric J. Miller and A. Kenneth Rice, *Systems of Organizations* (London: Tavistock Publications, 1967).

4. See Elliot Jaques, "On the Dynamics of Social Structure," *Human Relations* (1953), 6(1):3–24; and Eric Trist, "The Influence of Wilfred Bion's Ideas on Groups," in *Bion and Group Psychotherapy*, Malcolm Pine, ed. (London: Routledge and Kegan Paul, 1985), 1–46.

Chapter 3

1. Hannah Segal, *Introduction to the Work of Melanie Klein* (New York: Basic Books, 1974), ch. 7.

2. Melaine Klein, "Notes on Some Schizoid Mechanisms," in her *Envy and Gratitude and Other Works, 1946–1963* (New York: Dell, 1975), 1–24.

3. Melanie Klein, "On the Theory of Anxiety and Guilt," in her *Envy and Gratitude and Other Works, 1946–1963* (New York: Dell, 1975), 25–42.

4. Sigmund Freud, "Inhibitions, Symptoms and Anxiety," in *The Standard Edition of the Complete Psychological Works of Sigmund Freud*, James Strachey, ed. (London: Hogarth Press, 1955), vol. 20, 94–96.

5. A. Kenneth Rice, *The Enterprise and Its Environment* (London: Tavistock Publications, 1963).

Chapter 4

1. Wilfred Bion, *Experiences in Groups* (New York: Basic Books, 1959), ch. 5.

Chapter 5

1. Otto Kernberg, *Internal World and External Reality* (New York: Jason Aronson, 1980), chs. 12 and 13.

2. Sigmund Freud, "Totem and Taboo," in *The Standard Edition of the Complete Psychological Works of Sigmund Freud*, James Strachey, ed. (London: Hogarth Press, 1955), vol. 13, 141–146.

3. Joseph Weiss, Harold Sampson, et al., *The Psychoanalytic Process* (New York: Guilford Press, 1986), 101–113.

4. Salvador Minuchin and H. Charles Fishman, *Family Therapy Techniques* (Cambridge, Mass.: Harvard University Press, 1981), 78–97.

5. Sigmund Freud "Group Psychology and the Analysis of the Ego," in *The Standard Edition of the Complete Psychological Works of Sigmund Freud*, James Strachey, ed. (London: Hogarth Press, 1955), vol. 18, 132.

Chapter 6
1. W. Gordon Lawrence examines management training as a process through which the tensions between both the individual and the organization emerge and are contained. While also examining management training as a social defense, this chapter looks at its broader defensive functions: as a defense against the interpersonal dimension of the management process itself. See W. Gordon Lawrence, "Management Development: Some Ideals, Images and Realities," in *Group Relations Reader*, Arthur Colman and Marvin Geller, eds. (Washington, D.C.: Rice Institute, 1985), vol. 2, 231–240.

2. D. W. Winnicott, *Babies and Their Mothers* (New York: Addison-Wesley, 1987), ch. 9.

3. J. Laplanche and J. B. Pontalis, *The Language of Psychoanalysis* (New York: Norton, 1973), 76.

4. Rosabeth Kanter, *Men and Women of the Corporation* (New York: Basic Books, 1977), 63.

Chapter 7
1. Larry Hirschhorn, *Beyond Mechanization* (Cambridge, Mass.: MIT Press, 1984).

2. Hirschhorn, *Beyond Mechanization*, 159–162.

3. Hirschhorn, *Beyond Mechanization*, ch. 8.

4. Hirschhorn, *Beyond Mechanization*, ch. 8.

5. Charles Walker, *Toward the Automatic Factory* (London: Oxford University Press, 1957), 41.

6. Hirschhorn, *Beyond Mechanization*, 134.

7. This is a quote from the internal company report, which has been given only limited circulation and can therefore not be cited. The content of the report, a case study of the design of a factory, is described in chapter 11.

8. Hirschhorn, *Beyond Mechanization*, 130.

9. Hirschhorn, *Beyond Mechanization*, 124–125.

Chapter 8
1. Karl Mannheim, *Ideology and Utopia* (New York: Harcourt Brace, 1936).

2. Melanie Klein, "Our Adult World and Its Roots in Infancy," in her *Envy and Gratitude and Other Works, 1946–1963* (New York: Dell, 1975), 255.

3. For a general critique of corporate culture and its consequences, see Howard Schwartz, "The Psychodynamics of Organizational Totalitarianism," *Journal of General Management* (1987), 13(1):41–54.

4. This distinction is analogous to Freud's distinctions between genuine sublimation, in which the operation of an instinct (that is, the particular ways in which the instinct links thinking and feeling) is transformed, and idealization, in which an abstract ideal, such as "country" or "our leader," is sexualized and is therefore loved as a person loves his or her own body. In the latter case the instinct is deployed in its primitive state; only its aim changed. The abstract ideal supports the person's narcissism.

Chapter 9

1. James B. Jacobs, *Stateville: The Penitentiary in Massachusetts Society* (Chicago, Ill.: University of Chicago Press, 1977).

2. *Report of the Presidential Commission on the Space Shuttle Accident* (Washington D.C.: Government Printing Office, June 6, 1986), 164.

3. *Report of the Presidential Commission*, 101.

4. *Report of the Presidential Commission*, 92.

5. *Report of the Presidential Commission*, 200.

6. William J. Broad, "Silence about Shuttle Flaw Attributed to Pitfalls of Pride," *New York Times* (September 30, 1986).

7. *Report of the Presidential Commission*, 199.

8. Phillip Boffey, "NASA Soon to Get an Outside Chief: Reagan Aides Say," *New York Times* (February 22, 1986).

9. "Restructuring Puts NASA on Way Back but Doubts Persist," *New York Times* (December 29, 1986).

10. "Restructuring Puts NASA on Way Back."

11. "Top NASA Aides Knew of Shuttle Flaw in '84," *New York Times* (December 21, 1986).

12. "Top NASA Aides Knew."

13. "Top NASA Aides Knew."

14. "Top NASA Aides Knew."

15. "Top NASA Aides Knew."

16. Howard Schwartz's article "On the Personal Communications Psychodynamics of Organizational Disaster: The Case of the Space Shuttle Challenger," presented at the International Conference on Industrial Crisis (New York City, October 1986), was important in clarifying some of the issues

addressed in the text, although in contrast to the argument here, Schwartz does not assess the link between organizational leadership and disasters.

17. *Report of the Presidential Commission*, 98.

18. Jay Galbraith, *Designing Complex Organizations* (Reading, Mass.: Addison-Wesley, 1973), 23–24.

19. Sigmund Freud, "Civilization and Its Discontents," in *The Standard Edition of the Complete Psychological Works of Sigmund Freud*, James Strachey, ed. (London: Hogarth Press, 1955), vol. 21, 59–145.

Chapter 10

1. Sigmund Freud, "Civilization and Its Discontents," in *The Standard Edition of the Complete Psychological Works of Sigmund Freud*, James Strachey, ed. (London: Hogarth Press, 1955), vol. 21, 59–145.

2. Melanie Klein and Joan Riviere, *Love, Hate and Reparation* (New York: Norton, 1974); Hugh Griffith Clegg, *The Preparative Motif in Child and Adult Therapy* (New York: Jason Aronson, 1984).

3. Hannah Segal, *Melanie Klein* (New York: Viking Press, 1979), 138–139.

4. Helen Merrell Lynd, *On Shame and the Search for Identity* (London: Routledge and Kegan Paul, 1958).

5. Hannah Arondt, *Eichman in Jerusalem* (Middlesex: Penguin, 1965); and Ernest Becker, *Escape From Evil* (New York: Free Press, 1975), ch. 8.

6. This critique of the limits of guilt as a transforming feeling is based on Norman O. Brown's argument that guilt is intrinsic to society's power struggles. See Norman O. Brown, *Life Against Death: The Psychoanalytic Meaning of History* (Middletown: Wesleyan University Press, 1959), 278–280.

In suggesting that shame rather than guilt plays a critical role in shaping the reparative process, I am amending Klein's own discussion of reparation. She argued that guilt feelings accompany the depressive position and help create the wish to make amends. I believe that, in describing reparation as a developmental experience, she was in fact describing shame rather than guilt, for only shame provides the context for total self-revelation and thus development. I agree here with Lynd, who suggested in contrast to most psychoanalytic theorists that, because guilt is expiated through single acts of contrition, it sustains rather than develops a person's mode of relating to others, thus preserving the person's state of split-consciousness as well. Shame, by highlighting the lies one tells to oneself rather than to others, therefore creates much more anxiety and is potentially a sign of greater development.

Psychoanalytic thinkers from Freud on have for the most part ignored the critical role of shame because they failed to explore the links connecting *sexual pleasure*, the body's experience of its potential *integrity*, and the person's experience of *truth*. Shame and its converse, pride, unite the three. In feeling genuinely proud, people have no need to keep secrets and therefore tell no lies; they willingly reveal their bodies, which they experience as beautiful, and feel entitled to pleasure by virtue of their standing. But, if we follow the spirit of Freud's thinking, we are tempted to isolate a person's experience of truthfulness from sexual experience, relegating truth seeking to a "reaction formation"; for example, the truth seeker is nothing but a paranoid uncovering potential dangers everywhere.

In general, because he preferred to work "in the basement" rather than on the "rooftops" (as he once noted), Freud did not apply psychoanalytic thinking to people's ideal-seeking and value-seeking behaviors, suspecting that they were cover-ups for neurotic conflicts. Thus charitable people were hiding their contempt for the poor; generous people, their innate stinginess, and so on. With her theory of reparation, however, Klein took a critical step forward by linking reparation—the process of giving to others—to a person's attempt to feel more whole in mind and body. But in positing that guilt rather than shame played a critical role in this process, I believe that Klein compromised her advance by linking the desire for wholeness and therefore truthfulness to a person's escape from guilt feelings. She implicitly retained Freud's conception that truth-seeking and ideal-seeking behaviors were simply "reaction formations."

7. Richard Wollheim, *Sigmund Freud* (Cambridge: Cambridge University Press, 1971), 264.

8. Erich Fromm, *Escape from Freedom* (New York: Avon Books, 1969), ch. 1 and the appendix.

9. Herbert Marcuse, *Eros and Civilization* (Boston: Beacon Press, 1955).

Chapter 11

1. In writing this chapter, I have been helped a great deal by the work of Howard Schwartz on organizations and narcissism, see his "Maslow and Hierarchical Enactment of Organizational Reality," *Human Relations* (1983), 36(10):933–956.

2. David Roitman, Jeffrey K. Liker, and Ethel Roskies, "Birthing a Factory of the Future: When Is 'All at Once' Too Much?" ITI Working Paper 86-21 (Ann Arbor, Mich.: Industrial Technology Institute, 1986).

3. Roitman et al., "Birthing a Factory," 22.

4. Roitman et al., "Birthing a Factory," 12.

5. Roitman et al., "Birthing a Factory," 21.

6. Roitman et al., "Birthing a Factory," 24.

7. Roitman et al., "Birthing a Factory," 17.

8. The report of this experience is based on an internal company document that has been given only limited circulation, and I am therefore not free to cite it. I wish, however, to acknowledge the exemplary work of its author, Barbara Perry.

9. Internal company document.

Chapter 12

1. Natalie Davis, "Ghosts, Kin, and Progeny: Some Features of Family Life in Early Modern France," *Daedalus* (Spring 1977), 87–109.

2. David Bakan, *The Duality of Human Existence* (Boston, Mass.: Beacon Press, 1966), ch. 3.

3. David McClelland, *The Achieving Society* (Princeton, N.J.: Van Nostrand, 1961).

4. Norman O. Brown, *Life against Death* (Boston, Mass.: Beacon Press, 1959), pt. 5.

5. For a provocative discussion of the limits of sacrifice, see David Bakan, *Disease Pain and Sacrifice* (Chicago, Ill.: University of Chicago Press, 1968), 116–128.

Lasch, Lewis, Lynd, and Chasseguet-Smirgel all argue that psychoanalytic theory has neglected the distinction between the superego and the ego-ideal and correspondingly overemphasized guilt and neglected shame as central to the regulation of self-esteem. Chasseguet-Smirgel in particular argues that the ego-ideal represents the beneficent object, the good and the beautiful, and that, by identifying with it, we regulate our self-esteem without recourse to the punishing and castrating voice of the superego. (Her argument is of course much more complex; she systematically relates these differences to differences in the father and mother images and to differences between the castration threat and the threat of abandonment.) Lewis, like Lynd, argues that shame regulates the relationship between the self and the ego-ideal. We feel shame when we have failed to live up to our conception of the good and the beautiful; we feel guilty when we have transgressed and violated a particular injunction. In contrast to the bias of earlier psychoanalytic thinkers, such as Piers and Singers, Lewis argues powerfully that shame is not a developmentally more primitive feeling than guilt; it is, as she notes, less subject to control, and it invokes a larger part of the body in its expression (for example, blushing, turning the face downward, making oneself small). Like Lynd, she shows how shame, based on the sense of one's smallness and nakedness, implicates the whole self rather than a particular impulse. I suggest, however, that the psychoanalytic fusion of the superego and the ego-ideal, the tendency on the part of psychoanalysts to neglect the ego-ideal and the psychodynamics of shame, was no accident. It reflected the relative balance of the two in industrial society. See Christopher Lasch, *The Minimal Self* (New York: Norton, 1984); Helen Lewis Block, *Shame and Guilt in Neurosis* (New York: International Universities Press, 1971); and Janine Chasseguet-Smirgel, *The Ego Ideal* (New York: Norton, 1985).

6. Hannah Segal, *Introduction to the Work of Melanie Klein* (New York: Basic Books, 1974), 84.

7. David Bakan, *The Duality of Human Existence*.

8. Larry Hirschhorn, *Beyond Mechanization* (Cambridge: MIT Press, 1984), ch. 11.

Appendix

1. Helen B. Schwartzman, "Research on Work-Group Effectiveness: An Anthropological Critique," in *Designing Effective Workgroups*, by Paul S. Goodman and Associates (San Francisco: Jossey-Bass, 1986), 237–276.

2. Charles Walker, *Toward the Automatic Factory* (New Haven, Conn.: Yale University Press, 1959).

3. Silvan S. Tomkins, *Affect, Imagery and Consciousness* (New York: Springer, 1962), vol. 1, chs. 5–9.

4. Tom Juravich, *Chaos on the Shop Floor* (Philadelphia, Penn.: Temple University Press, 1985).

5. Robert Langs, ed., *Classics in Psychoanalytic Technique* (New York: Jason Aronson, 1981), pt. 2.

Index

Shame
vs. guilt, 210, 235, 255 n6, 257 n5
roots of, 209–211
self-esteem and, 210, 257 n5
Sibling horde, 186
Simon, Herbert, 3, 31–32
Skills, 36–37
Social arrangements, genesis of evil
and, 203–204
Social defense
modes of, 11–12, 57, 68–70 (see
also Basic assumption concept;
Covert coalition; Organizational
ritual)
in nursing, 2
open systems and, 194
psychodynamic processes and,
2–4
as term, 67
Society, pleasure and, 214–216
Space exploration. See NASA
Splitting, 2
bureaucracies and, 177–180
in developmental culture, 229
innovation and, 223
integration and, 205
postindustrial dilemma and,
202–204
production of evil and, 203–204
Sublimation
vs. idealization, 254 n4
reparation and, 214–216
Symbols
reparation and, 212
tendency toward evil and,
203–204
transitional object and, 215
Systems view, nuclear plant personnel and, 148–149

Task, and role, 55–56
Task completion, 8
Tavistock Institute, 32, 243
Team system, 149–155
holistic thinking and, 149–151
plant managers and, 152–154
self-management and, 12, 149–151
supervisors and, 150
Technical change, and social system, 222
Technique
as fetish, 117, 134–135

as transitional object, 116–117,
126
Technology. See Dangerous tech-
nologies; Postindustrial milieu;
Technical change
Thompson, James D., 3, 31–32
Three Mile Island accident, 148–
149
Tomkins, Silvan S., 246
Totem and Taboo (Freud), 104
Transference, 21–24
Transitional object
cultural symbols and, 215
management training and,
115–117
work as, 212–214, 236
Trist, Eric, 32
Triumphant feelings, 22, 211, 235
Truth, sexual experience and, 255
n6–256 n6

Uncertainty
boundaries and, 31–32, 37–38
delegation of authority and,
170–171
economic values and, 11
organizational routines and, 3
stepping out of role and, 47
Unit management system, 201–202

Vulnerability, 22

Welfare department, 40–49
Wholeness
anxiety and, 178–179
reparative process and, 215–216
of work, 8
Winnicott, D. W., 115
Women in management, 138–139.
See also Sexuality
Work
historical perspective on, 232–
243
in industrial culture, 232–234
meaning of, 231
organization design and, 226, 229
psychodynamics of, 10
reparation and, 205–216
as transitional object, 212–214,
236
Workaholic. See Anhedonic culture